Dec. 25 - 1960

mhow / op / 30°°

706486

"Merry Xmas" Aunt Gwen 4/81

and

Uncle Oa

from your Godson

BRIAN Kretsch

Our Lady of Guadalupe
530 Andrew St.

Grade 7 - 8

W9-ABY-599

YALE PUBLICATIONS IN AMERICAN STUDIES, I

David Horne, Editor

Published under the direction of the American Studies Program
and with assistance from the William Robertson Coe Fund

JAMES P. SHANNON

CATHOLIC COLONIZATION

ON THE WESTERN FRONTIER

New Haven: YALE UNIVERSITY PRESS, 1957

London: Oxford University Press

© 1957 by Yale University Press, Inc.
Printed in the United States of America by
Vail-Ballou Press, Inc., Binghamton, N.Y.
All rights reserved. This book may not be
reproduced, in whole or in part, in any form
(except by reviewers for the public press),
without written permission from the publishers.

First published, June, 1957
Second printing, October, 1957

Library of Congress catalog card number: 57-6876

TO

J. G. M.

Land without population is a wilderness, and population without land is a mob. The United States has many social, political and economic questions, some old, some new, to settle in the near future; but none so fundamental as the true relation of the land to the national life. The first act in the progress of any civilization is to provide homes for those who desire to sit under their own vine and fig tree.

James J. Hill, Highways of Progress

Preface

AT THE TIME of the great migrations to the United States during the 19th century people of good will on both sides of the Atlantic, aware that the migrants were undergoing hardship both in transit and after their arrival, were prompted to formulate plans to alleviate their suffering. Among the leaders of these humanitarians were Catholics in England and Ireland and on the Continent who attempted to provide not only transportation but large tracts of land for the establishment of farming communities in America. In this way a considerable number of Catholic colonies were established. Unfortunately, many of them failed to survive.

One of the important reasons for their failure was that closely ruled, paternalistic communities, whether patterned after the 17th-century Jesuit model in Paraguay or the 19th-century Mormon model in Utah, were hardly suited to the twin standards of democracy and individualism which ruled the American West. Disillusioned Catholic leaders soon found that the religious bond was not enough: immigrants could practice their religion just as well in the cities as on farms or in small villages; some prominent churchmen, such as the Archbishop of New York, even went so far as to warn that in moving to western colonies, Catholics ran the risk of losing their faith, since, he assured them, they would have no priests on the frontier to minister to their spiritual needs.

Into this hostile atmosphere in 1876 moved a man with enough idealism to render him impervious to the previous failures and enough realism to enable him to find a way for industrious immigrants to earn a fair living from the hard ground of the West. John Ireland, Coadjutor Bishop of St. Paul, who never tired of reminding urban Catholics that "man made the city but God made the country," successfully established between 1876 and 1881 ten rural villages and farming communities (De Graff, Clontarf, Graceville, Minneota, Ghent, Currie, Avoca, Iona, Fulda, and Adrian) in five counties (Swift, Big Stone, Lyon, Murray, Nobles) of western Minnesota. In most of these colonies the land was furnished by land-grant railroads; in all of them the settlers were Catholics—recruited partly from Ireland, England, Belgium, Germany, and French Canada, partly from the states east of Minnesota. The present study undertakes to analyze the distinctive features of these religious settlements, the history of their founding, their significant role as archetypes in a projected national colonization association, and the reasons for their growth or decline.

During the years that Bishop Ireland was most active, the Church, the state, and the railroads were all equally anxious to secure settlers for the newly opened western lands; and since it was possible for good citizens to be at the same time good Church members and frequent railroad patrons, a common interest shared by these three agencies worked toward the rapid population of Minnesota and often toward jointly sponsored programs of colonization. Ireland was named a land agent by five different railroads, and the layman he selected to direct Catholic settlement was named by the governor to the State Board of Immigration. The distinctive conditions accompanying the settlement of Minnesota offer unusually clear illustrations of the dual role played by the Catholic Church in America as an agency of Americanization and as custodian of the Faith.

Although the original home of many of Ireland's settlers was the eastern seaboard, a good number came from overseas. The cultural variety and religious uniformity that characterized these colonists offer provocative materials to the historian who would concentrate on the culture which immigrants brought to the frontier as well as on the impact of the frontier on the immigrants. There has not been lacking among recent scholarly publications in American history an abundance of material on how the American environment shaped and changed the immigrant, but these studies sometimes seem to assume that immigrants were indistinguishable one from another. Thus the primacy that has often been accorded to the significance of frontier influences in American history has tended to obscure the need for more detailed study of the origin and character of the culture that settlers on the western frontier brought with them. This is in part the meaning behind Marcus Hansen's statement, "It is likely that the Turner hypothesis appeared a generation too early." Historians are in general agreement that it is now time to re-examine the factual basis of our most cherished generalizations on the contributions which immigrants have made to our national life. By its nature this approach implies a sharp focus and intensive rather than extensive study. For these several reasons a detailed look at particular religiously oriented settlements on the frontier should be enlightening.

The original impetus for this study of Bishop Ireland's colonization program came from an essay written by Marcus Hansen shortly before his death.* Before attempting to write anything, however, I sought the opinions of several scholars on the feasibility of the project. For advice and encouragement in that initial stage of research I am especially indebted to Ralph H. Gabriel, Maurice R. Davie, and George W. Pierson of Yale University, to Theodore C. Blegen of the University of Minnesota, and to Grace Lee Nute of the Minnesota Historical Society.

Among the students of American Catholic history the prodigious collections of the American Catholic Historical Society of Philadelphia are only slightly less famous than the genial and helpful custodian of that collection, Father Bartholomew Fair. Without Father Fair's daily assistance during my visits to these archives and his extensive knowledge of these uncatalogued papers, I would probably have found only a fraction of the valuable materials which I gleaned from the records. For similar courtesies and hospitality at the University of Notre Dame I am indebted to Father Thomas T. McAvoy, C.S.C., who has built and organized that university's collection so well that it now ranks as a primary source for anyone studying the Catholic Church in America.

During my several visits to the Mullen Library and the archives of the Catholic University of America, Monsignor John Tracy Ellis and the Reverend Henry J. Browne have been gracious hosts and helpful counselors. I am particularly grateful to Father Browne for his judicious advice and his published articles on the attitude of Archbishop John Hughes toward western colonization. At the Minnesota Historical Society Lois Fawcett and Lucille Kane have on many occasions directed me through extensive manuscript and

* "Immigration as a Field for Historical Research," in *The Immigrant in American History* (Cambridge, Mass., 1948), pp. 191–217.

pamphlet collections. Miss Fawcett has even gone beyond the call of duty by sending last minute telegrams on material necessary for the completion of this study.

The kindness of librarians and archivists in general has long been one of the most commendable features of the American academic tradition. I have discovered that the reception given to visiting scholars by the custodians of railroad land records and archives is no less cordial and helpful. Frank Klein, land and tax commissioner of the Chicago and North Western Railway System; John Roche, general secretary of the Chicago, Milwaukee, St. Paul, and Pacific Railroad; A. G. Dupuis, assistant public relations officer of the same line; and James Maher, retired land commissioner for the Great Northern Railroad, have been most generous in opening their respective archives for study and equally hospitable in their personal reception.

For their patient cooperation in answering many letters and especially for their courtesy in opening to me their respective diocesan archives I am grateful to the chancery staffs of the Archdioceses of Omaha and St. Louis and the dioceses of Winona and Richmond, and in particular manner to the Very Reverend Gerald O'Keefe and Paul Daggett, chancellor and attorney for the Archdiocese of St. Paul, who have been tireless in helping me to find and tabulate pertinent material in the St. Paul chancery archives. Many of my fellow priests in the Archdiocese of St. Paul and the Diocese of Winona—especially the Very Reverend Rudolph Neudecker, and the Reverends John Siebenand, Vincent Hope, Melvin Blais, Richard King, William Gorman, and Earl Byron—have courteously responded to my many letters and requests for records covering the history of their western parishes. The Reverend William Busch and the Reverend Thomas J. Shanahan of the St. Paul Seminary have been similarly helpful in directing me through the collections of the Catholic Historical Society of St. Paul.

The Rt. Reverend Monsignor James H. Moynihan, in whose possession the Archbishop Ireland Papers rested until recently, kindly made these papers available to me and brought to my attention other valuable materials outside this collection. At Yale University the staff of the Sterling Memorial Library have sup-

plied indispensable assistance at every stage in the preparation of
this study.

During the preparation of this work I have made at least two
visits to each of the colonies in Minnesota, Kansas, and Virginia.
On these occasions I have profited greatly by conversations and
interviews with old settlers or present-day residents especially
qualified to discuss local history. For interviews of this type I
am especially indebted to Charles Gorman of Currie, Minnesota;
the late Sister Grace Aurelia, C.S.J., of Graceville, Minnesota; Leo
Hennen, Sr., John Brewers, and Abel Schaefer of Ghent, Minnesota; James Boulton of Minneota, Minnesota; and Daniel Murray Howerton of Red Oak, Virginia.

It is no longer possible to count the ways in which I profited
from the scholarly criticisms and direction of David M. Potter during the months this work was in progress. For his continued interest
in every part of it, for his encouragement of the project from the
beginning, and for the benefit of his critical judgment throughout
the period of composition I am deeply grateful. Without the original endorsement of John Gregory Murray, late Archbishop of
St. Paul, this work would never have been attempted. His interest
in it and his sympathetic assistance at several stages in its preparation are kindnesses which I acknowledge with profound gratitude.
I wish also to express my sincere gratitude to William O. Brady,
Archbishop of St. Paul, for his gracious and generous endorsement
of this work and for his paternal and scholarly interest in its publication.

J.P.S.

College of St. Thomas
St. Paul, Minnesota
November 6, 1956

Contents

Illustrations

Figures 1, 4, 6, and 7, and the threshing scene opposite the title page, have been reproduced by courtesy of the Minnesota Historical Society.

CHAPTER ONE

Railroads Open the West

WHATEVER freight transport there was within Minnesota during the 1850's and 60's was supplied by Red River ox carts. These ponderous two-wheeled vehicles were fashioned entirely of wood, bound with leather, and had no metal parts. The wheels were never lubricated, and travelers report that the shrieking of the wooden axles in a Red River caravan was almost deafening. The bull-whackers were usually half-breeds from Pembina, the northern terminus of the St. Paul–Red River trail, and the 500-mile trip, one way, took at least thirty days. Outbound from St. Paul the carts carried groceries and provisions for trappers and pioneer wheat farmers in the fabulously fertile valley of the Red River of the North; inbound to St. Paul they were laden with buffalo hides, mink, beaver, otter, and muskrat pelts.[1] Usually the trail followed the water level of the Minnesota River from St. Paul, looping south past Mankato, swinging northward around Big Stone and Traverse Lakes, and thence into the valley of the Red River.

Without water, rail, or turnpike transportation within the state these cumbersome trains of carts were the only feasible means of getting the valuable Hudson's Bay furs into American markets. Laborious transport even for this compact cargo, the carts were especially inadequate for moving people, household goods, or grain crops. The settlement of western Minnesota in fact was delayed at least two decades after the Sioux Treaty of 1851 for want of an adequate system of transportation. As late as 1870, twelve years after Minnesota entered the Union and five years after the Civil War, the Red River trail was still the only major trace through the western part of the state. At this date a huge triangle of fertile farmland—bounded roughly by the present-day cities of St. Paul

1. Cf. Frank G. O'Brien, *Minnesota Pioneer Sketches* (Minneapolis, 1904), pp. 305–7. See map below for places mentioned in this chapter.

in Minnesota, Fargo in North Dakota, and Sioux City in Iowa—
remained for the most part unsettled and uncultivated.

In the dead prose of geologists' reports, these lands are classified
as Group 3, in a graduated productivity series ranging from 1 to
14. "They are prevailingly black or brown silt loams, clay loams,
and loams with heavy subsoils. . . . The soils included in this
group, being well-supplied with lime and nitrogen, are capable
of enduring continuous grain growing comparatively well; they are
adapted to alfalfa and sweet clover, crops especially sensitive to
lack of lime in the soil." [2] The average number of days in the crop-
growing season for this latitude is between 130 and 140, which
compares favorably with northern Iowa, the center of the corn
belt, where the growing season is about 150 days.[3] The average
annual precipitation ranges from 24 to 26 inches, a rate "equal to
that in northern Illinois, Indiana, and Ohio. . . . And the slower
rate of evaporation at the latitude of . . . Minnesota makes the
. . . summer rainfall worth as much as a larger amount in states
farther south." [4] Given these statistics, it would be more correct
to consider Minnesota's western triangle the western edge of the
corn belt than the eastern edge of the Dakota plains. In rainfall,
growing season, and productivity, these lands belong to the Mississippi Valley into which they drain.

This is neither the "flat land" of Willa Cather nor yet the "Dakota
Plains" of Hamlin Garland—in fact, the Middle Border country is
one hundred miles farther west than the western boundary of
Minnesota. A more useful literary bearing might be the lands described in Sinclair Lewis' *Main Street*. The fertile farmland supporting Gopher Prairie is that of Stearns County, Minnesota. It is
described by Carol Kennicott, as she sees it for the first time
through the windows of the train that brings her to her new home
in the West:

> Here, she meditated, is the newest empire of the world, the
> Northern Middlewest; a land of dairy herds and exquisite
> lakes. . . . An empire which feeds a quarter of the world—

2. *Land Utilization in Minnesota,* Report of the Governor's Committee on Land
Utilization (Minneapolis, 1934), pp. 39–40.
3. Ibid., p. 45.
4. Ibid., pp. 45–6.

yet its work is merely begun. . . . She saw the prairie flat in giant patches or rolling in long hummocks. The width and bigness of it . . . began to frighten her. . . . Shorn wheat-lands of autumn, a hundred acres to a field, prickly and grey near-by but in the blurred distance like tawny velvet stretched over dipping hillocks. The long rows of wheat shocks marched like soldiers in worn yellow tabards. The newly ploughed fields were black banners fallen on the distant slope. It was a martial immensity, vigorous, a little harsh, unsoftened by kindly gardens.[5]

Even more specifically, this is the sea of grass through which Ole Rolvaag's Per Hansa pushed his plodding ox team in 1873, en route to his homestead in Dakota Territory, just west of the Big Sioux.[6]

In 1870, then, this vast tract still lay open, waiting for settlers; but before the settlers would farm it, they had to have assurance that they could transport their grain to market. It was small consolation to the Red River farmer to have his land yield twenty-five bushels of wheat to the acre if he had no means of getting the bumper crop to a market. In the columns of Horace Greeley's New York *Tribune* one pioneer Minnesota farmer eloquently described the plight of the land-locked settlers in an open letter to President James Buchanan:

We came to this part of the country with the hope that by a few years of labor, economy, prudence, and deprivation, we could pay for enough land to make homes for ourselves, and our families. In this we have been disappointed. Many of us have raised enough produce and stock, which, if they could have been sold . . . at fair prices, would enable us to pay for our lands; but we have no market at home, and no railroads to carry it abroad. If we wish to exchange our produce for necessary articles, we must carry it from five to fifteen miles to find a store, and when there, we must give ten bushels of wheat

5. Sinclair Lewis, *Main Street* (New York, Harcourt, Brace and Co., 1920), pp. 24–5.
6. Ole Rolvaag, *Giants in the Earth* (New York, 1927), p. 5. See also Theodore Jorgenson and Nora O. Solum, *Ole Edvart Rolvaag* (New York, 1939), pp. 328–9.

to buy a pair of boots, and four bushels of corn to buy a yard of coarse woolen cloth.[7]

States farther east had procured market outlets in earlier years by building canals; but it was too late for the western states to think of digging artificial water routes. Rail lines had already crossed the Mississippi, and it was just a matter of waiting for them to reach the grain belt.

A further obstacle to the settlement of Minnesota in the period following the Civil War was the haunting fear in the minds of many prospective settlers that the great Sioux massacre of 1862 might be repeated if more white settlers pushed into the West.[8] In reality there was no longer any possibility of such an uprising, since the Sioux and Winnebago tribes had been banished from Minnesota by an act of Congress on February 16, 1863.[9] But to appreciate the significance of the massacre as a deterrent to western settlement it is sufficient to read the startling summary of it given in an official state history: "The formidable . . . outbreak of the Sioux Indians of Minnesota against the whites in 1862 was the most . . . noteworthy incident of the kind in American history. More white people perished in that savage slaughter than in all the other massacres ever perpetrated on the North American continent." [10]

7. Quoted by Ruby G. Karstad, "The New York Tribune and the Minnesota Frontier," *Minnesota History,* 17 (1936), p. 417.

8. Benson *Times* (July 10, 1876), p. 4.

9. William Watts Folwell, *A History of Minnesota* (4 vols. St. Paul, 1926), 3, 22.

10. Frank R. Holmes, ed., *Minnesota in Three Centuries, 1665–1908* (4 vols. St. Paul, 1908), 3, 269. This standard history of Minnesota maintains that the number of white persons massacred by the Sioux in Minnesota in August and September 1862 exceeds the total of all white persons killed in all previous Indian wars within the United States. Folwell relates (*History of Minnesota,* 2, 391–2) that Thomas Galbraith, Minnesota agent for the Sioux, gave as the official state estimate on white men killed in this uprising 644 civilians and 737 soldiers. Folwell implies that this estimate is too high. Governor Ramsey reported to President Lincoln that more than 500 whites were slain. Lincoln himself later stated that the number was 800. Another historian, Marion P. Satterlee, estimates that a grand total of 477 soldiers and civilians were killed ("Narratives of the Sioux War," *Minnesota Historical Collections,* 15, 1915, 349–70). Using any one of these estimates, the reader can gain some impression of the extent of the massacre if it is recalled that the total number of Minnesota officers and men killed in both the Civil War and Indian Wars of this period was 635. Probably two-thirds of this number were killed in the forty-day Indian fight on the frontier of Minnesota in August and September 1862.

Fig. 1. A Red River ox-cart train driven by half-breed Indians. St. Paul, at Third and Washington Streets, 1857

In spite of such fears, however, new immigrants attracted by the reports of bumper wheat crops in Minnesota continued to trickle into the young state. For the most part, such early arrivals stayed close to the terminals of water transport. In Minnesota this meant St. Paul on the Mississippi, Duluth on Lake Superior, and Pembina on the Red River of the North. When the railroads eventually did come, their first lines were laid out to connect these already established trade centers. The Lake Superior and Mississippi Railroad began carrying wheat from St. Paul to Duluth in August 1870.[11] The next year the St. Paul and Pacific (later to be part of the Great Northern) reached Breckenridge in the Red River Valley,[12] and in the same year the Northern Pacific linked Moorhead on the Red River with Duluth on Lake Superior and gave the wheat farmers their long-awaited direct route to the grain markets of the East.[13] One year later the Winona and St. Peter Railroad (later to be part of the North Western Railway System) reached Dakota Territory and gave the grain belt of southwestern Minnesota its first open line to the Mississippi and the river markets.[14] Overnight the hunting grounds of the Sioux were cut up into booming frontier farming settlements, and the unhappy braves were forced back still farther into the Black Hills of Dakota Territory, with the solemn assurance that these hills were theirs "as long as the grass shall grow or the waters shall run."

The grass continued to grow until August 1873, when a cavalry scout attached to Fort Abraham Lincoln, near Bismarck, Dakota Territory, brought in news that he had found gold traces on the west slope of the Black Hills.[15] The national economy had been badly shaken by the panic of 1873 and the number was legion of those who were ready, on hearing this news, to violate the government treaty with the Sioux in hope of making a strike. A spontaneous rush of gold-seekers formed at once and headed for the Black Hills. Sitting Bull's warriors, ably led by Gall and Crazy

11. Folwell, 3, 48.

12. Harold Fern Peterson, "Railroads and the Settlement of Minnesota, 1860–1880" (unpublished master's thesis, University of Minnesota, 1927; copy in the manuscript division of the Minnesota Historical Society, St. Paul), p. 10.

13. Ibid., p. 15.

14. Folwell, 3, 61.

15. Robert J. Casey and W. A. S. Douglas, *Pioneer Railroad, the Story of the Chicago and North Western System* (New York, 1948), p. 167.

Horse, felt that their treaty rights had been seriously violated by the mining operations begun on their reservation, and at the battle of the Little Big Horn, just across the Hills in Wyoming, Custer and his men were later to experience the full fury of the Indian vengeance. In the meantime hundreds of frontier families loaded their household "plunder" into Conestoga wagons and moved in to claim the rich lands deserted by the harried Sioux and the adventurous gold seekers.

The gold rush also did something to offset the slump in railroad building that had overtaken all the western roads after the failure of Jay Cooke.[16] In the spring of 1876 a Black Hills prospector, John Pearson, announced that he had discovered a new gold lode in Deadwood Gulch; within a week Deadwood was a roaring mining camp of nearly 7,000 inhabitants. The western roads began advertising immediately in all the eastern papers.

Now the western triangle of Minnesota was no longer virgin land. Each day hordes of prospectors took the Winona and St. Peter to Lake Kampeska in Dakota Territory, or the Northern Pacific to Bismarck, en route to the Hills. And with the creation of a new and daring frontier to the West, Minnesota's western lands changed with incredible speed from buffalo grazing sites to tidy farmsteads. The rails had come from the East and the Sioux had departed into the West; the barriers that had held back the tide of settlers fell away. After this it was never difficult to attract new homemakers to the region, and during the decade ending in 1880 the state's population rose from 439,706 to 780,773, an increase of 77.6 per cent.[17] The acreage of farm lands increased 107 per cent and that of improved lands 212 per cent. It should have been obvious to any observer of that day that the cheap lands of the western part of the state would soon be filled. Actually, the frontier was to pass beyond Minnesota even before 1890!

Until the close of the Civil War the Mississippi had been virtually the western boundary of the heavily populated states; now, with the Union Pacific through to the West Coast and parallel lines edging west every day, a second push got under way. Before the advent of the railroad the complete settlement of the West

16. See below, p. 11.
17. Folwell, 3, 138.

would not have been possible. The relative scarcity of watercourses greatly restricted the use of the steamboat for transportation, and the treeless prairies, so well suited to large-scale wheat farming, could never have attracted new settlers until these pioneers, as noted above, were assured a transport system capable of hauling

Fig. 2. Minnesota, 1881
⊙ original colonies of Bishop Ireland

heavy pay loads long distances to markets. In these years American agriculture was shifting from a production standard of self-sufficiency to a commercial economy, and in this shift the role of the railroad was paramount. As Hacker and Kendrick point out, "The story of America since the close of the Civil War is the story of its public lands, its wheat growing country, its immigrant hosts, its industrial cities and, not the least in the array, its mighty railroads." [18]

Very often the directors of the western railroads, not content with merely waiting for the more daring settlers to find the prairies of the West, undertook formal programs of colonization to attract settlers in whole groups or communities. Such artificial stimulation of the westward movement does not quite follow the traditional sequence of trapper-rancher-farmer so often mentioned in our history and literature of the West, but its influence has been nonetheless real.

> The story of the colonization of the West is not altogether the story of fearless men pushing at random into an uncharted country, nor of bands of settlers traveling in covered-wagon trains, desperately withstanding one dire calamity after another. It is also a story of farmers from the older states, crowded into uncomfortable trains, moving, undisturbed by spectacular adventure into the fertile middle-western farm lands, already surveyed and partially settled. It is a story of colonies . . . journeying out to the prairies [of the West], not with wagons and ox-teams, but in the drab passenger coaches of the early western railroads. . . . Directing and encouraging this sort of settlement were the western railroads. Forced, as they were, to adopt definite colonization programs in order to make their existence on a profitable basis possible, they became the most important single factor in the development of the Trans-Mississippi West.[19]

The earliest successful experiment in large-scale colonization on railroad lands was sponsored by the Illinois Central in 1854 when David Neal, chairman of the Land Department for that road, decided that "the natural flow of immigration into Illinois would not settle the Company's lands nor build up the traffic for the road

18. Louis M. Hacker and Benjamin B. Kendrick, *The United States since 1865* (New York, 1949), p. 124.

19. James B. Hedges, "The Colonization Work of the Northern Pacific Railroad," *Mississippi Valley Historical Review*, 13 (1926), 311. Cited below as *MVHR*.

as rapidly as was desired." [20] Convinced that European nations, especially those of the North and West, were the most promising sources of immigrants, Neal sent Oscar Malmborg, a naturalized American born in Sweden, back to Scandinavia to lecture and to publicize the advantages of settling in Illinois.[21] Malmborg's success during his two trips abroad in 1864 and 1871 is evidenced by the vigorous denunciation his work received from Sweden's largest commercial farmers, who feared that emigration would draw off their cheap supply of farm laborers.[22] Malmborg estimated that in the single year 1871 his lectures, visits, and pamphlets convinced 7,000 Scandinavians to leave their homeland for farms in Illinois.[23]

The success of the Illinois Central colonization plan proved the feasibility of railroad colonization and inaugurated the era of railroad-sponsored western colonies. For lack of funds the western states, though convinced of the value of colonization, most often restricted their operations to plans for immigrant aid and information. It remained for the more enterprising railroads, especially those financed by land grants, to underwrite the expensive work of formal colonization.

One of the most successful settlement plans executed in this period was that of the Northern Pacific. In 1870 Jay Cooke and Co. of Philadelphia gained control of this railroad and secured land grants sufficient to extend it from St. Paul to the Pacific Ocean.[24] Acting on the valid precedent established by the Illinois Central, Cooke announced that the Northern Pacific would begin the settlement of its huge land grant at once and would "promote, as far as possible, immigration by colonies." [25] The western railroads needed settlers in a hurry. The western states were equally quick to realize their own stake in filling up the land grants of their respective rail lines. It was Minnesota's junior congressman Ignatius

20. Paul Wallace Gates, *The Illinois Central Railroad and Its Colonization Work* (Cambridge, Mass., 1934), p. 188.
21. Ibid., p. 189.
22. Ibid., pp. 192–3.
23. Ibid., p. 194.
24. Folwell, *3*, 445.
25. Jay Cooke to the president of the Indianapolis Immigration Convention, printed in the Duluth *Minnesotian*, December 31, 1870.

Donnelly—then the youngest member of the House of Representatives—who proposed in 1864 the establishment of a national
bureau of immigration to regulate and direct this incoming flow
of settlers.[26] As early as 1866, in fact, the Northern Pacific had
planned to establish a bureau of immigration, with a full-time
agent to be stationed in Germany,[27] but at this early date the road
was not able to assume the financial burden of creating such a
bureau. Once the resources of Cooke were behind the road, however, lack of capital was no longer a problem and the Northern
Pacific entered the land settlement business on wholesale proportions. In 1872 it established the Northern Pacific Emigration Bureau. George Sheppard, general agent for the Bureau in Europe,
persuaded the directors of the railroad that northwestern Europeans would make the most desirable settlers. He established his
main office in London, with branches in Bristol, Exeter, Hereford,
and Liverpool.[28] Agents were also hired to staff emigration offices
in Scotland, Germany, France, Holland, Norway, and Sweden.[29]
In the spring of 1873 the Northern Pacific opened an emigrant aid
office in New York City, at No. 3 Bowling Street, just outside the
Castle Garden port of entry.[30] The decision to establish this office
came after the railroad officials discovered that competing rail
lines often stole immigrants at the pier in New York and sent them
out to rival colonies in the West.

There had been some discussion among the directors of the
Illinois Central on whether to direct their publicity appeal to
European nations or toward the eastern urban centers of the
United States.[31] In the end a compromise was effected and the
emigration bureau of that railroad carried on a dual program of
foreign and domestic publicity. In this decision the Northern Pacific later followed the lead of the Illinois Central and advertised
its lands extensively in eastern newspapers, chiefly those of New

26. Folwell, 3, 12.
27. Peterson, "Railroads and the Settlement of Minnesota," p. 31.
28. Northern Pacific Archives, General Offices, St. Paul, Minnesota: five
bound volumes of correspondence labeled "Foreign Agents," Vols. 1, 2.
29. Ibid., Vols. 1–5.
30. Peterson, "Railroads and the Settlement of Minnesota," p. 47.
31. Gates, The Illinois Central Railroad, p. 189.

England, at the same time that George Sheppard was directing the campaign abroad.

In spite of occasional bad press notices on the snow and cold of Minnesota winters,[32] the Northern Pacific's program of emigrant encouragement proved a sound investment; it was making satisfactory returns when the panic of 1873 fell upon the nation. On May 1 and June 1 of that year the St. Paul and Pacific, then part of Jay Cooke's Northern Pacific system, defaulted on the payments of interest on four different issues of its bonds.[33] Even the fabulously rich land holdings of the parent company were not sufficient to hold off the creditors. The panic was on; and Jay Cooke and Co. of Philadelphia if not a cause of the crisis was certainly its greatest victim. The foreign emigration offices were closed at once, though not before their publications had been spread across the face of northern Europe. Thanks to these pamphlets and hand-bills, the main line of the Northern Pacific was already the site of several young but successful colonies.[34] The road had learned that it does pay to advertise. The financial crisis was to prevent any further extension of the colonization program for three years, but at the end of this period railroad officials would be eager to listen to Minnesota's Bishop John Ireland when he proposed his plan for bringing Catholic colonies to settle on railroad land.

The success which had been achieved by state and railroad propaganda between the time of Hans Mattson's appointment as the first emigration agent for Minnesota in 1867 and the closing of the Northern Pacific Emigration Bureau in 1874 was reflected in the comment of local newspapers during these years. On June 15, 1869, the editor of the Mankato *Union* remarked: "Thanks to the efforts of Colonel Mattson, our State immigration agent, who has been on a visit of months to his home in Sweden, and to the documents sown broadcast by the wise and liberal provisions of our legislature, the Scandinavian swarms of the North, the hardy Germans of Central Europe, and the sons of the Green Isle,—all

32. Peterson, "Railroads and the Settlement of Minnesota," p. 78.
33. Folwell, 3, 446.
34. Hedges, "The Colonization Work of the Northern Pacific Railroad," pp. 322–31.

are rushing, filled with eagerness and hope, to the free homesteads and healthy climate of Minnesota." [35] In August of the same year a correspondent from Ottertail Lake in Minnesota wrote to the editor of the Boston *Journal:* "We have met today a long train of wagons, filled with emigrants, who have come from Wisconsin, Illinois, Indiana, and some from Ohio, to make their homes in this fertile region." [36] The St. Peter *Tribune* for June 18, 1869, reported that "the ferry across the Minnesota River, at Saint Peter, Minnesota, was crowded from morning till night with immigrants, their household goods, and their fine droves of horses, cows, oxen, and sheep." [37] The possession of such extensive livestock holdings among these people is significant. They were by no means indigent squatters. On one occasion the driver of the stage coach running from Faribault to St. Peter, a distance of forty miles, reported passing over 200 wagons moving west. "The Minnesota Valley," the St. Peter *Tribune* recorded, "has never before witnessed such a tide of immigration. . . . Night after night our commons have become the camping ground for many sturdy pioneers with their families, and our adjacent prairies the pasturage for droves of cattle, horses, and sheep, all bound for the frontier." [38] The same prosperity was noted among the wagon trains passing through the state farther north and was reported in the columns of the Forest City *News:* "Every road leading to the rich and fertile prairies west of the woods is lined with emigrant wagons. Nearly all have fine droves of cattle. It will not be long before every foot of the rich prairie . . . counties will be under cultivation." [39]

Even before the advent of the western railroads the center of America's wheat growing region had been steadily moving west, ever closer to the optimum conditions for wheat raising which were to be found on the western plains, and this advance had been drawing with it a steadily increasing tide of farmers. The vast open stretches beyond the Mississippi offered no obstacles to the large-scale seeders and the wide-swath harvesters recently

35. Mankato *Union*, June 15, 1869, quoted by J. W. McClung, *Minnesota as It Is in 1870* (St. Paul, 1870), p. 286.
36. Quoted by McClung, p. 286.
37. St. Peter *Tribune*, June 18, 1869, quoted by McClung, pp. 287–8.
38. Ibid., p. 288.
39. Ibid.

patented for bonanza farming. Moderate rainfall on this level land protected crops against erosion and assured them sufficient moisture by preventing too rapid drainage. In time the rich prairie soil proved ideal for the cultivation of wheat. Once New York's Genesee Valley had been the center of American wheat production; by 1849 the center had moved to Ohio; by 1865 it had shifted to Wisconsin; and by 1868 it extended to Minnesota and the Dakota Territory. In a report for that year a federal agricultural commission announced, "The cheap, fertile lands of Minnesota and Dakota became the new sphere of operations for the wheat-grower, and the land-grant railroad made his operations possible." [40] Even ten years later the *Northwestern Miller*, a trade publication, could report, "The grand land craze caused by the immense wheat yield in Minnesota . . . does not abate but on the contrary increases daily. Parties went out on Friday [early in November 1877] over the Northern Pacific, the St. Paul and Pacific, and the Sioux City roads to hunt for farms. People appear to be coming here from all parts of the Union to get a slice of Minnesota lands." [41]

Press reports of its good harvests, encouragement from the state office of emigration, and easy credit terms from the land-grant railroads had assured Minnesota more than its share of settlers in a period when Americans generally were finding the western frontier a land of opportunity.

40. See Hacker and Kendrick, *The United States since 1865*, pp. 140–1; and the *Report of the United States Commissioner for Agriculture for 1868*, p. 16, quoted by John G. Thompson, "The Decline of Wheat Growing in Wisconsin," *University of Wisconsin Bulletin*, 5 (1908), 130.

41. *Northwestern Miller*, November 9, 1877, quoted in Thompson, p. 130.

CHAPTER TWO

From Immigrant Aid to Colonization

THE EASE AND RAPIDITY with which Minnesota was settled after
the Civil War bespeak an enlightened policy on immigration at the
same time they belie the significant role played in this great undertaking by three leaders with vision and an ability to cooperate
with one another.

Colonel Hans Mattson, who was appointed the director of immigration for the state in 1867, was the first. He was then at the
peak of his career and enjoyed the complete endorsement of the
legislature in his work of bringing farmers to the newly opened
lands of the upper Mississippi Valley.[1] John Ireland was another
leader. As a young seminarian he had lamented the failure of
many premature proposals for settling Catholic immigrants on
western lands, and when he became Coadjutor Bishop of St.
Paul in 1875 he thereby secured the authority necessary to revive
some of the earlier plans for Catholic colonization.[2] James J. Hill
—whose marvelous plan to build and operate steamboat lines on
the Ganges River had by chance been commuted to the more
modest but still staggering project of stretching a small local rail
line into one that would run from St. Paul to Puget Sound—took
office as general manager of the St. Paul, Minneapolis, and Manitoba Railroad on May 23, 1879, and embarked at once on a vigorous campaign to publicize the opportunities in the West.[3] More
gifted and energetic than most of their contemporaries, Mattson,
Ireland, and Hill realized that their territory, the Upper Midwest and Northwest, called for a new mode of settlement. To wait

1. Hans Mattson, *Reminiscences: the Story of an Emigrant* (St. Paul, 1891), p.
97.
2. James H. Moynihan, *The Life of Archbishop John Ireland* (New York, 1953),
p. 13.
3. Joseph Gilpin Pyle, *The Life of James J. Hill* (2 vols. New York, 1917), *1*,
20, 33, 289.

for the random, piecemeal infiltration of open western lands by individual families would have involved an intolerable delay in exploiting the vast area and resources of that region.

State, Church, and commercial leaders thus agreed on the necessity of wholesale settlement in the West. At this late date, of course, the concept of colonization was by no means novel. As far back as the 17th century, state-assisted colonies had been sent out to claim new lands for the mother country. Within the Church the idea of religious colonies was even more venerable. The original Spanish settlements in Florida and Mexico were considered, at least by the more pious *Conquistadores,* as Christian missions for the evangelization of the pagan Indians of America. Moreover, state officials like Mattson were really following closely a pattern of settlement that had been tried and proved in Wisconsin; [4] and the railroads in Minnesota were using the very formula of colonization that had worked so well for the older Illinois Central.[5]

Within the United States, colonization movements multiplied rapidly after the success of the Mormon foundations in Utah became generally known. After the initial hardships of 1847, the Latter Day Saints, under the iron rule of Brigham Young, had demonstrated that closely-knit communitarian settlements could prosper in the West, even on the inhospitable alkali flats of Salt Lake Valley.[6] Hence when Bishop John Ireland proposed his scheme for Catholic colonies in 1875, he was well aware of the successful Mormon settlements in Utah Territory. His plan, however, was not based on the Mormon model. It was, in fact, a variation on a plan originally suggested for Irish emigrants by Daniel O'Connell in 1841 and proposed again, unsuccessfully, in 1858 in America by Thomas D'Arcy McGee.

In his youth in Ireland McGee had been a loyal disciple of Daniel O'Connell and a firm believer in the "Liberator's" plan for assisted emigration. In the decade following 1823 O'Connell, it

4. Theodore C. Blegen, "The Competition of the Northwestern States for Immigrants," *Wisconsin Magazine of History,* 3 (September 1919), p. 13.

5. Gates, *The Illinois Central Railroad,* p. 194.

6. Alice Felt Tyler, *Freedom's Ferment* (Minneapolis, 1944), pp. 103, 106–7. Levi Edgar Young, *The Founding of Utah* (New York, 1923), pp. 190–1.

will be remembered, had headed a vigorous and articulate "Catholic Association" which had organized the Irish peasantry for the first time and brought effective pressure on the landlords to secure "fixity of tenure" for the landless Irish. O'Connell was then at the height of his popularity. Within a year after its inception his plan for assessing each member of the Association a penny a month was bringing in more than 500 pounds a week.[7] As the success of this land plan increased, however, land available for purchase in Ireland became correspondingly scarcer, at which point he conceived the idea of planting large emigrant colonies on the cheap farmlands of the American West.[8]

Unlike many such proposals emanating from Europe, this settlement plan did not try to regulate completely the lives of the emigrants. It was concerned only with the major problems of land selection, creation of capital, spiritual guidance, and reasonable direction. Under O'Connell's sponsorship, in 1841 the Catholic Emigration Society of Ireland was established in Dublin. Land scouts sent out from this office were to purchase large tracts of land in Ohio, Indiana, Illinois, and Wisconsin, and funds for the purchases were to be supplied by the sale of stock certificates in Ireland and England and on the Continent. In each settlement, agents were to buy tracts of land large enough to afford each settler a farm of eighty acres; and each colony was to consist of at least one hundred families, a group large enough to support its own priest, church, and school. The eighty-acre tracts were to be numbered, and the odd-numbered eighties were to be sold to the first comers at cost, plus 6 per cent interest; the even-numbered eighties were to be held for sale at a later time at as high a price as the market would allow, plus 6 per cent interest, to those later settlers attracted by the success and improvements of the earlier

7. *Dictionary of National Biography*, 41, 381. James A. Reynolds, *The Catholic Emancipation Crisis in Ireland, 1823–1829* (New Haven, 1954), p. 61.

8. The details of this plan are supplied by an undated letter of M. R. Keegan, of Chicago, addressed to Bishop John Ireland. This letter, part of the Ireland Papers in the archives of the St. Paul Seminary, is among the documents relating to John Ireland's work at the national colonization convention held in Chicago, March 17, 1879. The point-for-point correspondence between this plan and that realized by John Ireland's colonies in Minnesota could hardly be a coincidence, although none of Ireland's extant writings credit O'Connell for the details of the plan.

pioneers. The profits from these sales were to be divided equally between the parent Emigrant Society in Dublin and the local colony, and the latter was to use its share to build roads, bridges, schools, and other public buildings.

A village plat was to be set aside for church, school, pastor's residence, teacher's residence, and cemetery. Land, including lots in the town plat, was to be sold only to Catholics, and prospective settlers were to be required to produce testimonial letters from their former pastors confirming their status as devout Catholics. In each settlement a large temporary emigrant house was to be erected for the convenience of the new settlers during the time their homes were under construction. This structure was also to serve as a temporary church for the colonists.

The parent society in Dublin was to hold the land patents in its name as security for the stockholders in the company. Before any lands were purchased, however, the bishop in whose diocese the lands lay was to be consulted, and if he and his council approved of the selection the site was to be purchased. Such lands were then to be placed under the control of the respective American bishops. A local board for managing each colony was to consist of two priests and two laymen appointed by the bishop of the diocese. This board was to take charge of the colony, appoint a business agent, supply settlers with information, receive payment for the land, and transmit this money to the home office in Dublin.

The plan was received enthusiastically in both Ireland and the United States:[9] offers to buy stock in the new company flowed into the Dublin office. The approval of some members of the Irish hierarchy (no small item in view of this group's earlier disapproval of planned emigration) was secured. Several bankers, Sergeant Murphy of Cork, and even some bishops of the Church of Ireland espoused the cause.[10] But in spite of such encouraging prospects

9. New York *Freeman's Journal*, March 27, 1841; April 22, 1843; May 6, 13, 1843; June 21, 1845. Also Richard J. Purcell, "The Irish Emigrant Society of New York," *Studies: an Irish Quarterly Review*, 27 (1938), 592; Henry J. Browne, "Archbishop Hughes and Western Colonization," *Catholic Historical Review*, 36 (1950), 262. The latter article is a comprehensive and penetrating study of the complex motives behind Archbishop Hughes' celebrated opposition to western colonization.

10. Purcell, p. 592.

the plan was dropped abruptly in 1845, with no public explanation offered. The cause for this sudden shift must be sought within
the sphere of Irish politics, for at this time American opinion
was united in support of any scheme for westward expansion,
and Bishop John Hughes, though he had succeeded to the See of
New York, had not yet begun his quarrel with western colonizers.[11]
The demise of the O'Connell plan may have been only one more
element in the general decline of the "Liberator's" fortunes. Death
was to claim him within two years; and even before that event
his political prestige had been considerably diminished by the
rise of the Young Ireland patriots, who fiercely opposed any plan
for assisted emigration.[12] It is clear that O'Connell's contemporaries in Ireland considered his encouragement of emigration
the most objectionable feature in his program. Had he proposed
popular subscriptions or a joint-stock company to settle Irish paupers on Irish farms at this time, there can be no doubt that his
plan would have been accepted. In fact this is precisely what
Michael Davitt and Charles Stewart Parnell later proposed and
achieved in their Irish Land League of 1879.

Between the death of O'Connell and the rise of Davitt and
Parnell three decades intervened; and during this period the
colonization program of Daniel O'Connell was given one more
chance through the efforts of Thomas D'Arcy McGee. Within a
year after the death of O'Connell, McGee's facile tongue and
prolific pen had convinced the police authorities in Ireland that
his continued freedom was a threat to civil order. They were perfectly correct, but before they could arrest him he managed, with
the help of the Bishop of Derry, to disguise himself as a priest
and sail for the freedom of America.[13]

In Philadelphia, New York, and Buffalo, McGee carried on his
journalistic campaign to free Ireland, though during the passage
a sea change had come over him. After O'Connell's death, he had
thrown in his lot with the fiery Young Irelanders, who frowned on
emigration and opposed any scheme of colonization as a means

11. Browne, pp. 262 ff.
12. Elizabeth R. Hooker, *Readjustments of Agricultural Tenure in Ireland*
(Chapel Hill, 1938), pp. 19–20.
13. Alexander Brady, *Thomas D'Arcy McGee* (Toronto, 1925), p. 23.

of curing Ireland's economic ills. According to their plan for a cultural restoration every Irishman was expected to stay in the land of his birth to suffer and work for the awaited renaissance. True to the Irish pattern of assimilation, however, McGee quickly became an American of the Americans, regularly proclaiming to his Irish readers the advantages of settlement in the United States and Canada.[14] His energy was the driving force behind an abortive but historically important colonization meeting, the Irish Immigrant Aid Convention, which met in Dudley Hall, Buffalo, New York, on February 12, 1856.[15]

The startling success of the Know-Nothing candidates at the polls in 1854 and the recent organization of the "Order of the Star-Spangled Banner" had alarmed many Irish and German Catholic immigrants, against whom these secret nativist societies had largely been formed. In this crisis, "The West [loomed] as the Utopia where the foreign masses, despised and reviled with increasing vehemence by the Know-Nothing leaders and their riotous adherents, might . . . achieve their real destiny." [16] By the time McGee summoned his Buffalo Convention in 1856 this tide of nativism was at last beginning to ebb; but it was still strong enough to move many American Catholics, particularly those in the East, to consider the possibility of migrating to western regions less hostile to their religion. The real support for the convention, however, came from the West. Of the ninety-five delegates who assembled in Buffalo, more than two-thirds came from a distance of over five hundred miles.[17] In this, as in all subsequent colonization proposals, support in the West always exceeded that offered in the East.

At the Convention, McGee, who had misinterpreted a financial report which listed Irish immigrant savings on deposit in the

14. Thomas D'Arcy McGee, *A History of the Irish in North America* (Boston, 1855), pp. 187–96.

15. Sister Mary Gilbert Kelly, O.P., *Catholic Immigrant Colonization Projects in the United States, 1815–1860* (New York, 1939), p. 231. The doctoral dissertation on which this is based was directed by Marcus Hansen; it is a compendium of information on Catholic colonies in the United States before the Civil War. The eighth chapter, "The Buffalo Convention," is an excellent summary of the accomplishments of this convention.

16. Ibid., p. 216.

17. Ibid., p. 230.

Emigrant Industrial Savings Bank of New York and thought they totaled an astonishing $48,000,000, "had come to the conclusion that Catholics in the United States and Canada possessed sufficient capital to provide settlements for their own denomination who desired to live on the land." [18] Acting on this information, he upbraided his countrymen for not showing an energy and interest in colonization comparable to that of other national groups. "The German Catholics were going straight to Iowa, Wisconsin, or other Western regions; the Norwegians, Swiss, Scots, Frenchmen and New Englanders all had their townships picked out, bought up and settled under the ordinary exercise of their own judgment. Were the Irish alone to have no plan, no system of united action? Was 1856 to find them as drifting, heedless, headless as before?" [19] He reasoned that if the Irish in America had the funds attributed to them, they had a corresponding obligation to back his joint-stock company. Needless to say, the Irish sensed no such responsibility.

It had been McGee's hope that a second Catholic settlement convention could be summoned in Chicago in the spring of 1857, but long before this date it became clear to him and his followers that their anticipation of popular support for their project had been too sanguine.[20] This plan failed for the same reason countless similar plans failed—lack of financial support. The problem of finance was never to be solved effectively until John Ireland came forward in 1876 with a proposal that Church leaders interested in settling colonists on the land should never buy or gain title to the land but should act only as land agents for the railroads or the government, thereby not only eliminating the need for capital in the hands of the colony leaders but actually providing a means of revenue for the leaders, who could collect the usual real estate agent's fee for their sales.

McGee could not have known that the future development of the western railroads would benefit his plans and make them workable two decades later. Disappointed at the apathy and hos-

18. Ibid., p. 234.
19. Thomas D'Arcy McGee, in *The American Celt*, September 22, 1855, quoted in Kelly, pp. 224–5.
20. Kelly, pp. 261–9.

tility shown to his program, he gave up the American colonization effort and moved to Canada, where he became editor of the
New Era.[21] Although his later efforts in that country were largely
directed toward the establishment of the Dominion, the work for
which his name is chiefly famous today, he remained convinced
of the intrinsic value of colonization in general and of the great
good which his Buffalo Convention had brought about by publicizing the virtues of life in the West.[22]

To say that his plan failed for lack of financial backing is of
course simply another way of saying that it did not receive widespread popular support. And the ultimate reason for its failure
on this level was the fact that it was publicly opposed by John
Hughes, Archbishop of New York. The New York *Freeman's
Journal*, then edited by James A. McMaster, was the official spokesman for the Archbishop in denouncing the "mischievous plan" of
the Buffalo Convention.[23] The reasons which prompted Hughes
to take this stand are summarized in one of his private papers,
discovered after his death.

> It must not be inferred that the writer is opposed to the dif-
> fusion of emigrants into those portions of the country in
> which land may be obtained. . . . But the idea of disturb-
> ing the minds of those who may be already established in
> the East or in the West by a gilded and exaggerated report
> of theoretical blessings, which are in reserve for them, pro-
> vided they can acquire the nominal ownership of 60 or 100
> acres of uncultivated land, not infrequently teeming with
> fever and ague, remote from the school, remote [from] the
> Post Office, remote from the physician, remote from the neigh-
> bors, this idea is dangerous, just so far as any Catholic emi-
> grant is liable to be misled and deceived thereby.[24]

Presuming that Archbishop Hughes was convinced of the
dangers of western settlement and not motivated solely by his

21. Brady, *Thomas D'Arcy McGee*, p. 39.
22. McGee, in *The American Celt*, July 5, August 16, 1856, quoted in Kelly,
p. 264.
23. New York *Freeman's Journal* (March 1, 1856), p. 1.
24. Quoted in Browne, p. 271.

personal antipathy toward McGee, it is extremely difficult to reconcile his stand on the Buffalo Convention with an address which he made a few years later in Cork, Ireland. In July 1862 he visited France, Italy, and England on a diplomatic mission for Secretary Seward to secure the sympathy of these countries on behalf of the Union forces and the Lincoln administration. Possibly such official service in the interest of his adopted country had made him more aware of America's latent opportunities for growth and prosperity. Whatever the reason, his public address to the citizens of Cork in late July 1862 must have been at least puzzling to McGee, and possibly infuriating:

> I know there are in this country what are called plains or prairies, where the cottages of the poor man were, and they are now occupied by the ox and swine. The poor man is not there, but where is he? I can trace him. He is in the west of the United States (cheers), and he is, instead of being the humble cottier afraid of having his cottage taken from him, now the owner of this section of land in America, perhaps of 300 acres or more of what was until lately Government land, and the property of the Government; and even lately he was the proprietor of it under the Government protection, allowed to do what he pleased with it (applause).[25]

No doubt it was small consolation to the priests and laymen who had sponsored the colonization meeting in Buffalo to hear that Archbishop Hughes had now apparently changed his mind, for the damage was done. Word had gone abroad among the Catholic immigrants in the eastern cities that the Archbishop of New York frowned on western colonization.[26] That was enough to slow down the westward movement among Catholics for at least two more decades.

Ten years intervened between the death of John Hughes and the consecration of John Ireland as a bishop in 1875—a decade in which the colonization movement suffered acutely from lack of funds and prestige. In this period Church leaders restricted their

25. Cork, Ireland, *Examiner*, August 1, 1862, quoted in Browne, pp. 282–3.
26. John Lancaster Spalding, *The Religious Mission of the Irish People and Catholic Colonization* (New York, 1880), pp. 147–8.

welfare activity to a variety of small-scale immigrant-aid programs which relied more on expediency and resourcefulness than on any colonial tradition in their efforts to meet the needs of the arriving immigrants.

In contrast John Ireland saw colonization as a long-range plan which promised to solve many problems—nativism, slums, poverty, loss of religion—for the Catholic immigrants who would go West. And with the passing of time various welfare agencies in eastern cities were forced to admit that their limited programs of hand-to-mouth assistance for the immigrants were little more than first-aid at the docks. Among many American leaders a new respect arose for the far-sighted type of social engineering which sought to give settlers independent status and farm ownership. This shift in thinking prepared many people to accept Bishop Ireland's scheme, patterned on the older European model. It was a long time, however, before American welfare agencies in general, or American Catholics in particular, came around to endorse the systematic promotion of immigrant farming colonies.

As successive waves of immigration broke on the shores of the United States, more immigrant-aid organizations, sponsored by different nationalities, began to appear and in due course grew from dockside stations toward the status of labor unions. In a recent study James E. Roohan has remarked the rise of labor unions and accompanying decline of benevolent-aid societies in America. He is extremely cautious when he says that this phenomenon "may have been no more than coincidence." [27] Comparison of the constitutions drawn up by successive aid groups of different nationalities indicates that the societies which were able to survive for any length of time were those concerning themselves more and more with the task of securing jobs, good pay, and favorable working conditions for the immigrant.[28] Since

27. James Edmund Roohan, "American Catholics and the Social Question, 1865–1900" (unpublished doctoral dissertation, Yale University, 1952), pp. 238–9.

28. Thomas F. Meehan, "Emigrant Aid Societies," *The Catholic Encyclopedia* (1909), 5, 403. *Constitution of the Hibernian Society of New York*, New York, 1810. *Constitution de la Société Française de Bienfaisance*, New York, 1849. Eliot Norton, *Report to the Society for the Protection of Italian Immigrants*, New York, 1901. Copies of the printed constitutions are available in Sterling Library, Yale University.

labor unions have now become standard organizations in our society, which has long since cut off the annual influx of immigrants, the *raison d'être* of the aid group has been transferred partly to unions and partly to the expanded welfare facilities of the government.

The earliest record of an immigrant-aid society in this country is the constitution of the Charitable Irish Society of Boston, founded on March 17, 1737. Its formal purpose, to cultivate "an affectionate and compassionate concern for our countrymen in these parts, who may be reduced by sickness, shipwreck, old age, and other infirmities and unforeseen accidents" [29] is, in comparison to the later and more ambitious aid programs, merely a modest proposal to relieve indigent seamen and compatriots temporarily down on their luck. A surprising restriction in this document forbidding membership in the group to all Catholic Irishmen throws revealing light on the religious persuasion of Boston's Irish in 1737.

By the time Thomas Jefferson had entered on his first term as president, the number and needs of the Irish in the New World had grown so much that immigrant-aid programs of wider scope had to be devised. The constitution of the Hibernian Provident Society of New York, founded in 1802,[30] is a detailed and cogent piece of social legislation for the aid of distressed urban laborers. Articles viii, ix, and x provide respectively for monthly payments into a mutual fund, unemployment and sick benefits for those off the job, and annual compensation for the widows and orphans of deceased members. It would appear that by this time most of the Irish arriving in New York were Catholics, for one clause in this constitution forbids memberships to all "Orangemen."

Probably no other national group felt so profoundly the need for organization as did the Irish. From time to time small benevolent societies and Irish fraternal groups, disturbed by the growing numbers of destitute Irish in the eastern cities, proposed a national union of the Irish societies as a means to supply money and guidance to these needy immigrants. In January 1869 the Irish Immigrant Aid Society of St. Paul, Minnesota, directed by Father John

29. Meehan, p. 403.
30. See n. 28, above.

Ireland and Dillon O'Brien, issued a national appeal for such a federation to be organized. In response the St. Patrick's Society of Norfolk, Virginia, offered to act as host; and in that city on March 17, 1869, the Irish Catholic Benevolent Union held its first meeting.[31] The constitution of the new federation promised "to render assistance and information to the immigrant, and also [to] be the germ of . . . a general organization of the various beneficial societies of the country, under the State and National heads." [32] By this late date Irish Catholics were becoming increasingly aware of the benefits of organization being reaped by such national associations as the highly successful German Central Verein.[33]

The new Irish federation began the monthly publication of its own news organ, the *Irish Catholic Benevolent Union Journal,* from its headquarters in Philadelphia.[34] Each month in the columns of this paper lists were published giving the names of various aid societies which had applied for affiliation with the ICBU. Another service supplied by the *Journal* was the regular publication of letters from western settlers, describing the agricultural possibilities of rural regions from Michigan to Texas. Martin I. J. Griffin, secretary of the Union and editor of the *Journal,* encouraged his readers to send him any information they had on new lands opening for settlement. Under his direction the *ICBU Journal* became a monthly guide book for Catholic settlers going West. Griffin remembered the unsuccessful attempt made by Thomas D'Arcy McGee in 1856 to establish a nationwide Catholic colonization association and was constantly reminding his readers that the time had come to try McGee's ideas again.

At the fourth annual meeting of the ICBU in St. Louis, October 1873, Father Thomas Ambrose Butler, an Irish-born priest who was then working in the Archdiocese of St. Louis, proposed

31. *Proceedings of the Eighteenth Annual Convention of the Irish Catholic Benevolent Union* (Philadelphia, 1886), p. 21.

32. [Martin I. J. Griffin?] *Sketch of the History of the Irish Catholic Benevolent Union,* no date.

33. Colman J. Barry, O.S.B., *The Catholic Church and German Americans* (Milwaukee, 1953), pp. 27–43.

34. A complete file of this periodical (1869–93) is preserved in the archives of the American Catholic Historical Society of Philadelphia, St. Charles Seminary, Overbrook, Pa.

that a national bureau of immigration be established by the Union, to gather and disseminate information on how and where recent Irish arrivals in America might find land suitable for settlement.[35] The convention voted to sponsor such a bureau and named Butler its first chairman. Within a short time it became apparent to this committee that the immigrants needed more than information if they were to find their way to western lands. Hence at the convention of the ICBU held in Rochester, New York, December 1875, Father Butler and a Father John Fanning of Fairbury, Illinois, proposed to the delegates that the bureau of immigration be superseded by a new bureau of colonization and that the new bureau be given authority to buy land and organize colonies of Irish immigrants in the West. The delegates voted to accept the proposal and elected Father Butler chairman of the new bureau.[36]

During these years state welfare agencies also were beginning to realize and accept their responsibilities of caring for destitute immigrants in the port cities. In 1847 New York State had appointed a board of emigration commissioners and instructed this body to draw up a series of laws to regulate immigrant affairs.[37] A few years later the Emigrant Aid Society of Philadelphia, a private agency, appointed a committee to study the laws of New York State and City relative to the immigrants. The report of this committee was submitted to the Pennsylvania State Legislature in 1854 and a welfare program for that state was enacted, patterned after the New York model.[38] With the growth of such public welfare programs, private aid groups such as the ICBU were gradually relieved of the task of supplying the immediate wants of the immigrants and found themselves free to undertake larger projects for moving the settlers on to the land. In an editorial comment on this transition Martin I. J. Griffin reported, "The I.C.B.U. abandoned its immigration work of attending to

35. *ICBU Journal* (June 1874), p. 1.

36. Ibid. (December 1875), p. 6.

37. *Report on Emigration by a Special Committee of the Chamber of Commerce of the State of New York,* New York, 1865. Copy in Sterling Library, Yale University.

38. *A Report of the Delegation Appointed by the Philadelphia Emigrant Society to Enquire into the Nature and Operation of the Emigration Laws of the State of New York,* Philadelphia, 1854. Copy in Sterling Library, Yale University.

destitute immigrants arriving in this country; or rather, that work developed itself into the present colonization work." [39]

This shift away from immigrant aid toward formal colonization within the ICBU found support in the temperance societies and abstinence unions which were then seeking some positive method for combating intemperance among the immigrants. After his tour of America, even such an unquestionably loyal Irishman as John Francis Maguire could report: "I believe this fatal tendency to excessive indulgence to be the main cause of all the evils and miseries and disappointments that have strewed the cities of America with those wrecks of Irish honour, Irish virtue, and Irish promise, which every lover of Ireland has had, one time or another, bitter cause to deplore. Differences of race and religion are but a feather's weight in the balance." [40] The complaint was not peculiar to the Irish immigrants in America, although their greater numbers attracted more attention to their failings. In Liverpool Father James Nugent, editor of the *Catholic Times,* warned his fellow Irishmen and coreligionists that insobriety was their greatest vice. As a partial solution to the problem he recommended migration to and settlement on the western lands in America.[41]

In 1849 Ireland's famous temperance crusader Father Theobald Mathew came to the United States and during a two-year tour administered the total abstinence pledge to half a million persons. Catholic Total Abstinence Unions sprang up in all the cities he visited. In time many of these local societies, recognizing a connection between the poverty of urban immigrants and their tendency to overindulgence, turned their energy to the work of colonization. In his annual report to the Minnesota C.T.A.U. in 1875, Dillon O'Brien reminded his auditors that the task of settling immigrants on the land was a responsibility of their group, second only to the original task of promoting temperance. He regretted that the Minnesota chapter was not yet in a position financially to bring settlers to the West, but he affirmed that this was the goal toward which the group was working.[42]

39. *ICBU Journal* (July 1878), p. 4.
40. John Francis Maguire, *The Irish in America* (London, 1868), p. 281.
41. Quoted in the *ICBU Journal* (January 1883), p. 4.
42. *Northwestern Chronicle* (June 19, 1875), p. 4. As the weekly official news

This transition among the Irish from immigrant-aid societies and temperance unions to a larger colonization program does not have a parallel among the French and German Catholics. One obvious reason for such a difference is that the French and Germans often possessed enough initial capital to establish themselves on farms, without the help of benevolent societies. Probably of equal importance is the fact that the two latter groups had reaped the fruits of thriving agricultural economies in their old homes. To them life on the land was not a symbol of insecurity, as it was to the Irish. Moreover, the problem of intemperance, which was to make the Irish colony towns strongholds of teetotalism, had never been a problem with the French or German Catholics.[43]

At the time the idea of colonization in America was being launched and while it was still in a formative and precarious state, it met unexpected opposition from its source: the people of Ireland. In fact, the new land reforms in Ireland which followed Gladstone's Land Act of 1870 were destined to compete with American colonization plans for the allegiance of the Irish-American immigrants.

After the death of Daniel O'Connell the Young Ireland group had taken over the resistance movement in Ireland. Through the columns of such ardent Irish journals as *The Nation, The United Irishman,* and *The Irish Felon* [44] the Irish in America were kept aware of the quickened tempo in land reform circles at home. The passive resistance used by O'Connell had not brought reforms quickly enough to satisfy the demands of Young Ireland. It was no longer possible to convince the people "that they were the victims of God's famine, and not of landlordism or of English misrule." [45]

The Fenian Movement of the 1860's was one more step in the direction of increasingly radical agitation. If necessary, it was

organ of the Diocese of Saint Paul, from 1866 to 1900, this newspaper carried a detailed account of the immigrant colonies established in that diocese in that period. Cited below as *NWC.*

43. Barry, *The Catholic Church and German Americans,* pp. 192–3.
44. Michael Davitt, *The Fall of Feudalism in Ireland* (London, 1904), pp. 56–7.
45. Ibid., p. 53.

prepared to use armed violence to establish an Irish republic. At the end of the Civil War in the United States, Irishmen who had served as soldiers in its campaigns returned to Ireland to train the Fenian revolutionaries.[46] Gladstone later cited the intensity of Fenianism as the principal force behind his celebrated Land Act.[47] For almost a decade after the passage of this act agrarian peace returned to Ireland.[48] The number of evictions dropped, crops were good, prices for agricultural products were high, and land agitators such as Isaac Butt complained that they could no longer stir up the peasant farmers against the iniquity of the system.[49] The general prosperity of the times, however, even more than the tenure concessions of the Land Act, would seem to account for this brief respite of calm in Irish affairs. The peasant burden had not been appreciably lightened by the Act of 1870. Rather, the good times which then appeared gave the poor tenant increased means for discharging the same obligations which in bad times he had considered unbearable. But in 1877 the shadow of famine fell across the land again, and the suffering of the people broke out in overt acts of violence. In the wet seasons of '77, '78, and '79 potatoes rotted in the fields and there was not enough sunshine to dry the peat, virtually the only source of fuel for the majority of the people. At this time a benevolent Quaker, James Hack Tuke—who was later to visit and encourage the immigrant colonies of Bishop Ireland in Minnesota [50]—toured the distressed areas of Donegal and Connaught. His eloquent pamphlet, *Irish Distress and Its Remedies*, again aroused public discussion of the land question in Ireland.[51] The stage was set for Michael Davitt and his Irish Land League, an association of Irish tenants which was to improve the farmer's position in Ireland and at the same time undermine the colonization movement in America.

The Irish famine of 1879 was "the seed-time of the most formida-

46. Hooker, *Readjustments of Agricultural Tenure in Ireland*, p. 19.
47. Davitt, p. 77.
48. John E. Pomfret, *The Struggle for Land in Ireland, 1800–1923* (Princeton, 1930), p. 101.
49. Ibid.
50. Sir Edward Fry, *James Hack Tuke, a Memoir* (New York, 1899), pp. 135–7.
51. Norman Dunbar Palmer, *The Irish Land League Crisis* (New Haven, 1940), p. 75.

ble agitation in Irish history." [52] In this year the Irish social revolution, which Gladstone called "the storm in the West," began on October 21 with the formal organization of the Irish National Land League at the Imperial Hotel in Dublin, with Michael Davitt as its driving force and the more elegant and colorful Charles Stewart Parnell as its spokesman.[53] Sentiment in America was quickly marshaled in favor of the Land League by Patrick Ford's *Irish World* and the writings of Henry George. When the League sent Parnell to America in 1879 to appeal for funds, crowds thronged Madison Square Garden, Philadelphia's Academy of Music, and the Boston Music Hall to hear his plea, and vied with one another in contributing to his cause. In Brooklyn he was introduced by Henry Ward Beecher in glowing words: "I am in favor of the most serious, prolonged, and earnest agitation of public sentiment in America for the emancipation of the Irish peasantry from their present condition. There is no other subject that is more important to the great mass of mankind than the question of land." In New York, Parnell shared the platform with Thurlow Weed, and in Boston, Wendell Phillips told the crowd, "I come here, as you have done, from a keen desire to see the man who has forced John Bull to listen." [54] After a tour through the Midwest, which included a warm reception by Bishop Ireland in St. Paul, Parnell returned to Dublin with American contributions amounting to almost $250,000.[55]

It is significant that such American periodicals as the *ICBU Journal* carried enthusiastic letters and lists of generous donations to Parnell in the same issue with desperate pleas for more contributions to keep alive the colonies which that Union was then sponsoring in Kansas and Virginia.[56] The peculiar nature of Irish nationalism—as a bond capable of uniting the Irish in America behind every plea for helping the peasants in Ireland but utterly unable to secure majority support for any Irish-sponsored movement in America—was already appearing. In time this trait would promote the rapid assimilation of the Irish in America, but in

52. Ibid., p. 106.
53. Ibid., p. 142.
54. Davitt, pp. 193–5.
55. Ibid., p. 210.
56. *ICBU Journal* (August 1880), p. 5.

the early years it was often the means of killing sound proposals for bettering their condition here. The German Catholics could compromise their accidental differences and speak with one voice through their Central Verein, but the Irish groups found such coordinated activity impossible. Time has demonstrated that there are few positions in American society to which individual Irishmen cannot aspire, but heights demanding group cooperation have not been scaled by them. If the various factions within the Irish Catholic Benevolent Union had ever been able to settle their individual grievances and agree on a common course of action, the colonization plan devised in Minnesota by Bishop Ireland and proposed by him as a model for nationwide settlements might have achieved more of the great success envisioned by its sponsor.

CHAPTER THREE

The Catholic Plan for Minnesota

ON THE UPPER Mississippi the heyday of the steamboat was the two decades immediately preceding the Civil War. In these years the territory later to become Iowa and Minnesota enjoyed a strategic position at the intersection of the two most heavily traveled transcontinental routes in the country. The rail line from New York to Chicago gave the latter city somewhat the status of an immigrant receiving station. From here the immigrants moved down the Illinois River into the Mississippi, where their boats met the larger steamers plying between New Orleans and St. Paul. This pattern of transportation gave the region of the upper Mississippi Valley an unusually heavy French Catholic population. The French coming up river from New Orleans met the French Canadians who had left Quebec for the prairie provinces. For lack of roads and railroads in the Dominion the French Canadians were forced to pass south of the Great Lakes and back up into Canada, transferring from railroads to Mississippi steamboats and ending their journey in Red River ox carts. The greater number of early French settlers in the upper Mississippi Valley had come up the river and were well established long before the railroads reached the Mississippi.

On July 14, 1823, Rome had erected the new diocese of St. Louis to care for these French Catholics formerly under the care of the Bishop of New Orleans.[1] Fourteen years later a new diocese of Dubuque was erected to move with the frontier, and Father Mathias Loras, a native of Lyons, France, was named its first bishop.[2] Immediately after his episcopal consecration, Bishop Loras returned to France to enlist priests and collect money for his missionary diocese. He came back the following year with a

1. Donald C. Shearer, O.F.M., Cap., *Pontificia Americana* (Washington, 1933), p. 145.
2. Ibid., p. 198.

substantial grant from the Lyons Society for the Propagation of the Faith, accompanied by Father Joseph Cretin and four French seminarians, Lucien Galtier, who was later to name the city of St. Paul; Augustin Ravoux, who was to become the renowned missionary to the Sioux in Minnesota; James Causse; and Remigius Petiot.[3]

From Dubuque, Father Cretin made regular trips up the river to Prairie du Chien, to revive the Indian missions originally established by Father Louis Hennepin in his trip down the Mississippi in 1680. Prairie du Chien had for some time been an important fur depot for the Canadian *voyageurs,* situated as it was at the confluence of the Mississippi and Wisconsin Rivers. From this point the colorful *coureurs des bois* could paddle their enormous bateaux as far north as the Lake of the Woods, or as far east as Quebec. On his regular visits to this wilderness trading center, Father Cretin found the fur traders quite as glad to hear sermons in his exquisite French and as anxious to make their Easter confession to him as he was pleased to supply these sacred ministrations.[4]

In conferences back at Dubuque, Loras and Cretin outlined their plans for the future of the Catholic Church in the upper Mississippi region. We are indebted to the meticulous travel journal of a French Jesuit, Father Augustus Thebaud, for the details of this plan as revealed to him by Bishop Loras during Thebaud's visit to Dubuque in 1842. The first aim of the two missionaries was to secure permission from Rome for the erection of a new diocese up river, in the vicinity of Father Lucien Galtier's tiny mission station, St. Paul. Their second objective was a grand plan for "attracting European immigrants to the vast plains beyond the Mississippi." [5] Loras had sent Ravoux to the West to evangelize the Iowas, Sioux, Mandans, and Pawnees; but Cretin he had kept near him to help plan the settlement of the emigrants from Europe.

The exodus from Ireland, which was to take place four or five years later, was not then dreamed of. Still every week

3. Mathias M. Hoffman, *The Church Founders of the Northwest* (Milwaukee, 1937), p. 95.

4. Augustus J. Thebaud, S.J., *Forty Years in the United States of America, 1839–1885* (New York, 1904), p. 275.

5. Ibid., p. 276.

saw a great number of Irish immigrants landing on the Atlantic coast, chiefly at New York. The Germans also came in
constantly increasing numbers. So far most of them had remained in the East. The intention of Bishop Loras was to
draw them to the Great Lakes, and what was then called the
Far West, and particularly to settle them on farms as agricul-
turists.[6]

The first phase of Loras' plan was attained when Rome announced on July 19, 1850, that a new diocese was to be erected at
St. Paul in Minnesota Territory and that its first bishop would be
Dubuque's vicar general, Father Joseph Cretin.[7] After his arrival
in St. Paul in 1851, Bishop Cretin projected for his new diocese
a scheme of immigrant encouragement similar to the one which
he and Bishop Loras had planned for Dubuque.[8] For want of
priests, however, it was to be some time before he would be prepared to invite Catholic settlers to his frontier territory. By this
time Loras was engaged in a systematic program of propaganda
in favor of his plan in Iowa. He would regularly solicit financial
aid from the Leopoldine Society in Vienna for his German settlers,
and from the Lyons Society for the Propagation of the Faith on
behalf of his French settlers.[9] Each year he was acquiring a few
more priests from France and Germany and occasionally ordaining
one of his own candidates for the priesthood.

On July 15, 1854, the Boston *Pilot* carried a letter written by
Bishop Loras from Council Bluffs, Iowa, urging Catholic emigrants to consider the new lands being opened by the railroads
in Iowa. By return mail he received so many replies ("chiefly from
New England") asking for further details on the quality and price
of the Iowa lands that he was forced to answer them all with one
long letter, published in the *Pilot* on October 7. Federal land was
still available for the customary figure of $1.25 an acre; wages for
laborers were running up to $1.00 per day; and new settlers were
coming in every day. It would seem that these conditions war-

6. Ibid.
7. Shearer, p. 262.
8. James J. Reardon, *The Catholic Church in the Diocese of Saint Paul* (St.
Paul, 1952), p. 237.
9. Hoffman, *Church Founders of the Northwest*, pp. 369–79.

ranted an all-out effort on the part of the bishop to make his scheme attractive to the Catholic emigrants; but in this and his many subsequent letters there was always a note of quiet restraint. He would welcome any Catholics who came to Iowa, but he would not solicit them to come. In one major point his policy differed radically from that later employed by John Ireland in St. Paul: Loras would not promise a priest or a church or a school to any colony until the settlement was large enough to support this burden.

Often Loras' letters to the *Pilot* and to McMaster's *Freeman's Journal* warned the future settlers of the hardships of frontier life.[10] With commendable objectivity and no resorts to high-pressure salesmanship the bishop pointed out that mechanics and tradesmen need not come, since the West was already suffering from too many of these; "that others who have limited means ought not to venture to emigrate"; [11] that fear of the Know-Nothing movement in the East was not a sufficiently good reason for moving to the West; that anyone making a good living in the East should not think of migrating; and that those who came West should expect at least a year or two of serious privations. In two successive letters he cautioned his readers that he had been forced to take the resident pastor away from the Council Bluffs settlement because the people would not contribute to his support.[12] When and if they could support a priest, he would try to get one for them; but he made no promises, lest he "be blamed if some come too soon." [13] He had also counseled Father Laurent, former pastor at Council Bluffs, that he should not act as a land agent for any settlers. They were to make their own deals with the United States Land Office or with the railroad land commissioner's office.[14]

All of this is not to deny the enduring contribution made by Bishop Loras to the development of the Church in Iowa. It is rather to demonstrate by comparison that his plan was the product

10. Boston *Pilot*, January 13, February 24, April 21, and June 16, 1855. See also an item quoted from the New York *Freeman's Journal* and reprinted in the *Pilot* for July 15, 1854, without any date for the original quotation

11. Boston *Pilot*, April 21, 1855.

12. Ibid., January 13 and February 24, 1855.

13. Ibid., April 21, 1855.

14. Ibid., October 7, 1854.

of its age and as such less mature and far less positive than the
plan later invoked by Bishop Ireland in St. Paul. In Ireland's Minnesota colonies the first resident was the priest and the first building was the Catholic church; and in each colony the priest acted
as the official land agent of the railroad, selling lands, arranging
loans, breaking the first five acres before the settlers arrived, and
allotting space in the emigrant house for the earliest arrivals. In
contrast, the policy of Loras is crisply summarized in a letter of
his published in the *Pilot* for January 13, 1855:

> I must try . . . to correct a mistake under which many emi-
> grants are laboring. They say: "We must have Congress land;
> the land must be rich, well-watered and timbered; there
> must be a Catholic church and school in the vicinity; there
> must be a priest." And some would almost say "He must be
> supported by his Bishop. And besides that, there must be a
> market for our produce at a short distance from our land."
> Now, my dear sir, these conditions are incompatible in or-
> dinary cases. The emigrants must submit to some and many
> privations in the beginning, even in religious point of view,
> if they wish to settle in a new country, and, in course of time,
> make it Catholic. That motive is truly noble and worthy of
> the Apostles, whose function they, in some measure, perform,
> when by immigration from Catholic countries, they try, al-
> though mere laymen, to plant the faith of Jesus Christ in
> these wild regions. There is no doubt that the Almighty
> supplies, by His divine Providence, this want of churches
> and clergymen for a time. It is for not considering this that
> some of those who went last Fall to Council Bluffs came back
> dissatisfied. If they had put on a little more courage, they
> would have kept their priest. By giving a little support, they
> would have built a small church, and that great mission would
> not have been paralyzed for the present.

With the few priests at his disposal, Bishop Loras could not
reasonably have followed any other plan. He was forced to be
content with letters of description, regularly printed in the eastern Catholic press, citing the agricultural advantages of Iowa.
Considering that his diocese embraced the Iowa corn belt, the

richest farm land in the world, his modest claims on its behalf could certainly not be called exaggerations. The land was good; the railroads were coming; and priests would eventually follow. In time each of his careful predictions came true; but the Catholic settlement of Iowa was more the result of individual decision on the part of the pioneers than of any positive program sponsored by the Church. In the light of these facts, it is amazing to read in the recent popular work of Theodore Maynard, "[Of the American Bishops] only Loras of Dubuque can be said to have had much success [in the work of Catholic colonization]." [15]

The publicity work done by Bishop Loras in the eastern press should not be minimized. As early as 1841 he established correspondence with the Irish Emigrant Society in New York and delegated Catholic laymen in Dubuque to keep the New York group informed about the opportunities for Catholic settlers in Iowa. From his own pen countless letters poured out to the editors of the Boston *Pilot*, the New York *Freeman's Journal*, the Philadelphia *Catholic Herald*, *Public Ledger*, and *Truth Teller*, the St. Louis *Catholic Advocate* and the *Leader*, and the Cincinnati *Wahrheitsfreund*.[16] In 1856 Loras sent Father Jeremiah Trecy to McGee's colonization convention in Buffalo. In 1857 he commissioned the same Father Trecy to deliver a series of lectures to Catholics in eastern cities.

During this tour, on the evening of March 26, 1857, Father Trecy addressed a large audience in the Broadway Tabernacle auditorium in New York City. On that occasion he was seeking support and settlers for a proposed new settlement in northeastern Nebraska, then part of the territory under the jurisdiction of Dubuque. The surprise of Father Trecy was exceeded only by the delight of the newsmen present when at the conclusion of his speech a figure, unnoticed till then, stood up in the gallery to shout his disapproval of the priest and the plan. It was John Hughes, Archbishop of New York, wrapped in an overcoat and muffler. Father Trecy attempted to explain that he had come to plead his cause in New York with the approval of his own bishop

15. Theodore Maynard, *The Catholic Church and the American Idea* (New York, 1953), p. 121.
16. Hoffman, *Church Founders*, p. 352.

in Dubuque. Archbishop Hughes was insistent, however, that the western priest was recommending "Irish towns" which would at least impede and possibly prevent the assimilation into American society of the Catholic immigrants.[17] Warming to his attack, he went on to denounce "the discomforts, the afflictions, the mental and religious evils which were frequently the result of rude Western life." [18]

On the following morning, in reporting what it considered the "Singular Finale" of the colonization assembly, the New York *Daily Times* berated Hughes for this "latest instance of his blocking the improvement of the immigrant's lot." [19] The irony of the New York *Herald* editorial was even more devastating: "According to the Archbishop, the West is in a sad way for doctors, barbers, and other luxuries of eastern civilization, and it is wrong for anybody, more especially a priest to point it out as a place for systematic settlement." With his additional charge that Father Trecy's scheme was designed to enrich land speculators—a charge later shown to be completely untrue—the Archbishop completed his attack. In silence the bewildered members of the assembly left the hall one by one. Father Trecy made no more appeals in the Archdiocese of New York, though he continued to promote his plan for a colony at St. Patrick's, Nebraska, a site twelve miles west of Sioux City.

In extenuation of what some writers have considered unnecessary asperity in the charges of Archbishop Hughes,[20] it must be recorded that the colony at St. Patrick's never succeeded. At one time it numbered over three hundred Irish families, but after several severe winters and intermittent grasshopper plagues, it was abandoned. Undoubtedly the greatest single cause for its failure

17. Browne, "Archbishop Hughes and Western Colonization," pp. 274–5. Hughes' opposition to any such "distinctive" settlement plan earned for him at an earlier date the warm praise of Secretary of State William H. Seward: Seward to Hughes, Albany, November 10, 1841, preserved in the New York Archdiocesan Chancery Archives and quoted in Browne, p. 274.

18. Browne, p. 275.

19. New York *Daily Times*, March 27, 1857, quoted in Browne, p. 275.

20. Archbishop John Ireland, "Mathias Loras, First Bishop of Dubuque," *Catholic World*, 68 (October 1898), 3–4. Spalding, *The Religious Mission of the Irish People and Catholic Colonization*, p. 147. Kelly, *Catholic Immigrant Colonization Projects*, p. 219.

was the fact that Father Trecy was not in regular residence with his people. His missionary field covered most of the Nebraska Territory and it was necessary for him to leave St. Patrick's parish for long periods without the ministrations of a priest.[21] In a letter to the Boston *Pilot* one disgruntled settler revealed that seventeen persons had died in the settlement without receiving the last sacraments.[22] The very danger against which Archbishop Hughes had warned his people!

In further defense of Hughes it should be observed that the cautious claims and modest understatements in the eastern publicity released by Bishop Loras can be traced to the Iowa prelate's honest admission that *at that period* some of the charges made by the Archbishop of New York were actually true. The greater number of priests, the newly opened railroad lands, and the credit facilities which were to make Bishop Ireland's colonization plan much easier two decades later were not available to Loras. Obviously, Hughes was guilty of great shortsightedness in his views on western settlement, but his position was not entirely indefensible, considering the times and his own background.

In spite of such extenuating circumstances, however, Archbishop John Ireland never quite forgave Hughes for impeding the western program of colonization. Many years after the death of Hughes, Ireland reviewed the conflict between the Bishops of New York and Dubuque and cast his vote in support of the latter:

> The greatest misfortune that fell to the lot of Catholic immigrants coming to America forty or fifty years ago was that they were allowed to be huddled in cities where, as a rule, nothing was possible to them but to be made hewers of wood and drawers of water, instead of being induced to occupy the fertile lands of the Western States, where independent homes were to be won with little cost and little labor. . . . The leaders that were needed seldom came forward, and their efforts, such as they were, *often met with strong opposition even on the part of men whose position and intelligence should have promised better things.* It is today beyond

21. Kelly, pp. 248–57.
22. *Pilot,* July 11, 1857; August 28, 1857.

a doubt that had the enlightened views of D'Arcy McGee and those who took part with him in the famous Buffalo colonization convention of 1856 been duly encouraged and pushed to a favorable issue, the Catholic Church would be immensely more prosperous in all the Western States than ever again she can hope to be, and tens of thousands of Catholic families would have gained happy homes and an honorable competence upon the land, instead of having gone down to ruin in the fierce maelstrom of large cities.[23]

In the same article Ireland called the colonization efforts of Bishop Loras the surest way "to lay wide and deep the foundation of the Catholic Church in the West." It is important to notice that Ireland's insistence on building up the Church in the West was a primary motive in his plan of colonization. This aspect of his program is overlooked by those who consider his settlement work in Minnesota unsuccessful because it failed to relieve the pressure of labor unrest in the East.[24]

The most competent commentator on the history of the Catholic Church in Iowa has stated, "Because of a stronger Catholic immigration and colonization, the Church in Minnesota grew at a more rapid rate than it did in Iowa." [25] Joseph Cretin was to discover, soon after taking office as the first Bishop of St. Paul, that his young diocese was increasing in numbers each day, as a result of the earlier letters and lectures of Bishop Loras. The newcomers by this time (1851) were largely Irish. Cretin was amused by their "pompous celebration" of St. Patrick's Day, but he appreciated the fact that they did not object to his Sunday sermons being preached in both English and French.[26] The rapid growth of the Catholic population in his territory, in addition to the vast number of Indians already there, made it imperative that Cretin secure additional priests at once. He was disappointed when the Trappist monks at Dubuque declined his invitation to establish a monastery in his diocese, to be used as a center in catechizing

23. Ireland, "Mathias Loras, First Bishop of Dubuque," pp. 3–4.
24. Roohan, "American Catholics and the Social Question," pp. 212–13.
25. Hoffman, *Church Founders*, p. 329.
26. Ibid.

the Winnebago Indians.[27] His staff, almost entirely French priests at this time, was barely large enough to care for the parishes and schools already established. Because of this disability he was unwilling during his first two years in St. Paul to recommend it as a home for Catholic immigrants. Furthermore, his personal honesty demanded that he make a careful survey of the land, timber, and water resources in his territory before encouraging new settlers to come there. "In fact, he admitted early in 1853 that he had up to then refrained from answering requests for information regarding Minnesota, except to invite the writers to come and see for themselves, as he feared the descriptions of the advantages of the soil and climate of Minnesota had been exaggerated by speculators." [28]

A more extensive knowledge of his diocese, gained in his missionary trips, would later settle Cretin's doubts on this question. By August 28, 1853, he was prepared to announce in the New York *Freeman's Journal* that several rural settlements in his diocese now had resident pastors and that the fertility of the Minnesota soil, the average rate of rainfall, and the presence of timber sections for firewood promised willing workers a decent competence on the land. But ill health during the few remaining years of his life, lack of sufficient funds, and the small number of priests at his disposal prevented his ever carrying into operation in St. Paul the grand scheme of colonization which he and Bishop Loras had envisaged.

Shortly after Cretin arrived in St. Paul, the United States Government had concluded a treaty with the Sioux Indians at the famous Traverse des Sioux, in Minnesota Territory.[29] By the terms of this agreement the Sioux Indians, who owned all territory west of the upper Mississippi, ceded to the United States 21,000,000 acres. This land was immediately opened to white settlers. It was a great disappointment to Cretin that he could not claim some of it for a Catholic colony. For the most part, his active share in bringing about the settlement of this new tract was limited to the

27. Letter from Cretin to Loras, St. Paul, March 10, 1853 (preserved in the Dubuque Archdiocesan Chancery Archives); quoted in Hoffman, *Church Founders*, p. 332.

28. Kelly, p. 164.

29. Reardon, *Diocese of St. Paul*, p. 94.

letters he contributed to eastern papers. "What Bishop Loras was doing for colonization in Iowa, Bishop Cretin was doing in Minnesota." [30]

The greatest strides in the settlement of Minnesota at this time were being made by the remarkable Father Franz Pierz, a native of Austria, then in his sixty-seventh year, who had answered Bishop Cretin's call for volunteers in 1852.[31] Before coming to Minnesota, Father Pierz had been a missionary to the Indian tribes of upper Michigan. He hoped that he would be allowed to continue this apostolate by evangelizing the Chippewas of Minnesota. His great work in the new diocese, however, was to be that of encouraging German immigration to the farm lands west of the Mississippi.[32] In the columns of the Cincinnati *Wahrheitsfreund,* Pierz described the all but tropical splendor which German immigrants could expect to find on their arrival in Minnesota. As an appendix to his book *Die Indianer in Nord Amerika* he inserted a colorful piece of propaganda entitled "Eine kurze Beschreibung des Minnesota-Territoriums." [33] Within a year fifty German families had moved into the region which has since become Stearns County, Minnesota, probably the most solidly Catholic rural county in the United States today. The frequency, distance, and hardships of the missionary journeys undertaken by this remarkable priest to minister to his scattered parishioners recall the similar sacrifices made along *El Camino Real* by Junipero Serra, who had also reached the twilight of his life before he ever saw the New World. Within five years of his arrival in Minnesota, Pierz could summarize his achievements in a letter to a friend in Austria: "I have completed my seventieth year; the Lord has preserved me well; I am still in full vigor and enjoy good health. In three years I have established ten missions and built as many churches; two Indian, two French, and six larger ones for the Germans in the most beautiful country on the Sauk River." [34] The strong bonds of nationality and language aided the German set-

30. Ireland, "Mathias Loras, First Bishop of Dubuque," p. 6.
31. Kelly, pp. 165-6.
32. Ibid., pp. 166-7.
33. Antoine Ivan Resek, *History of the Diocese of Sault Ste. Marie and Marquette* (2 vols. Houghton, Mich., 1906-07), *1,* 353; quoted in Kelly, p. 168.
34. Barry, *The Catholic Church and German Americans,* pp. 8-9.

tlers materially in keeping their Catholic Faith in these new colonies, even though for long periods of time they lacked the ministrations of a resident pastor. In later years they were to be charged with an excessive attachment to the culture and traditions of their homeland, but in the early years of settlement such patriotic ties provided invaluable encouragement for the struggling immigrants.

When the first Catholic school in St. Paul opened its doors in the autumn of 1852, two of the boys enrolled were John Ireland and Thomas O'Gorman, destined to become respectively the first Archbishop of St. Paul and the first Bishop of Sioux Falls, South Dakota. John Ireland was almost fourteen years of age and Thomas O'Gorman was probably of about the same age, since they were assigned to the same class. Both boys had been born in County Kilkenny, Ireland, but had come with their families first to Chicago and later to St. Paul, after the Irish famine of 1848. Within a year the two youths were accepted by Bishop Cretin as candidates for the priesthood and were sent to the *petit seminaire* at Meximieux, in the Diocese of Belley in France where he had once studied.[35] Back in the United States, after eight years of classics, philosophy, and theology, their priestly ministrations in the Diocese of St. Paul were to be the means of realizing many of the plans Cretin had hoped to attain in his work with the immigrants. During their absence Joseph Cretin died on February 22, 1857, leaving a diocese which consisted of sixty-four parishes, twenty priests, and 50,000 Catholics.[36] His successor, the Dominican Father Thomas L. Grace, a native American from Charleston, South Carolina, was consecrated bishop in the Cathedral at St. Louis, July 24, 1859.[37]

The railroads had not yet reached Minnesota, but each day during those months that an ice-free Lake Pepin allowed passage proud sternwheelers like the *Northern Belle* brought new bands of home seekers up river to the young state of Minnesota, admitted to the Union in 1858. Under the press of many administrative problems—chiefly those of organizing Indian mission schools and

35. Moynihan, *The Life of Archbishop John Ireland,* p. 4.
36. Reardon, *Diocese of Saint Paul,* p. 119.
37. Ibid., p. 141.

providing parochial facilities for the recent arrivals—the new
bishop did nothing to encourage colonization until after Father
John Ireland had returned from duty as a chaplain in the Civil
War. It is still not clear whether the original impetus for formal
colonization projects in Minnesota at this time came from the
young priest or from his bishop. In any event, on May 12, 1864,
the Minnesota Irish Emigration Society was incorporated in St.
Paul by Bishop Grace.[38]

Father Ireland was named president of the new society and
Dillon O'Brien was appointed secretary. O'Brien, twenty years
John Ireland's senior, had been born in County Roscommon, Ireland, in 1818. Shortly after his marriage, the comfortable estate
and large family holdings which he had inherited from his father
were swept away by the agricultural famine and depression of
1848. Confident that his fine college training would enable him
to recoup his fortunes in America, he and his young wife and
four children left Ireland for the United States. His first years in
America were spent as a teacher in the Indian mission schools of
the region now embraced by Michigan and Wisconsin. In 1863
the family moved to St. Paul, where O'Brien became editor of
the *Northwestern Chronicle*, the Catholic paper of the Northwest.[39] His arrival in St. Paul coincided with John Ireland's return
from the war in the South; and from their first meeting until
O'Brien's sudden death in the Cathedral rectory in 1882 their
deep friendship and close cooperation were to bear fruit for the
Church in the Northwest.

By the time the new emigration society had organized in St.
Paul, the Catholic immigrant arrivals in Minnesota were mostly
Irish, as the name of the new group indicates. The prospectus
prepared by Dillon O'Brien spoke of Minnesota as the place for
Irish emigrants "to preserve unsullied the primitive coloring of
their good old Celtic nature." The fine Gaelic touch of John Ireland from Kilkenny and Dillon O'Brien from Roscommon was apparent in the first release of the young society.[40] The success

38. Howard Eston Egan, "Irish Immigration to Minnesota, 1865–1900," *Mid-
America, 12* (October 1929 and January 1930), p. 141.
39. Thomas D. O'Brien, "Dillon O'Brien," *Acta et Dicta, 6* (October 1933),
35–40.
40. One of the rare extant copies of this pamphlet is part of the Ignatius

which was to crown their later efforts in colonization, however, did not appear at the start of their careers. For a long time no tangible results were produced by the Irish Emigration Society.

As secretary of this bureau and editor of the *Northwestern Chronicle*, O'Brien lectured widely and wrote frequently on Minnesota's advantages for the immigrant.[41] Like John Ireland, he was also a strong believer in the temperance movement. "Give me temperance and a healthy immigration to land as levers and I will raise my people to the highest standards of citizenship." [42] There is little evidence that either Bishop Grace or Father Ireland gave much time to this program of encouraging immigration to Minnesota in these years, although O'Brien enjoyed their full support in his publicity campaign to convoke a national colonization convention in St. Louis in 1869. This meeting drew a distinguished audience of Irish-Americans. Mayor Edward O'Neil of Milwaukee was elected chairman, and O'Brien and William J. Onahan, of Chicago, were elected secretaries. The inevitable committees were appointed. A fine dinner and an excursion on a Mississippi steamer were enjoyed by everyone. "And that was all. Nothing came of it. The committees never met." [43] The times were still not propitious. O'Brien continued his lecture tours and succeeded in enlisting John Boyle O'Reilly, editor of the Boston *Pilot*, in the fight for colonization.[44] Undoubtedly O'Brien was later encouraged by the decision of the ICBU at its convention in 1875 to discontinue its tiny immigrant-aid program in favor of a full-scale colonization scheme.[45]

After the failure of the St. Louis convention, O'Brien used the pages of his *Northwestern Chronicle* to keep alive the message of immigrant-colonization. In each issue he solicited from his readers information concerning farms for sale, size of crops, and items

Donnelly Papers in the archives of the Minnesota Historical Society, St. Paul. It is attached to a letter from one A. D. McSweeney inviting Donnelly to become a member of the Emigration Society. See Ignatius Donnelly Papers, file October–November 1864, letter for October 11, 1864.

41. *NWC*, May 11 and 25, 1867.
42. "Dillon O'Brien," p. 40.
43. William J. Onahan, "A Chapter on Catholic Colonization," *Acta et Dicta*, 5 (July 1917), 69–70.
44. "Dillon O'Brien," p. 41.
45. *ICBU Journal* (December 1875), p. 6.

of interest to potential settlers.[46] The paper became a kind of bulletin board for immigrants seeking lands in the West. In his issue for April 3, 1875, O'Brien commented extensively on a brochure recently issued by the St. Paul and Sioux City Railroad entitled *Minnesota Homestead.* He called this guide book "the only literature of real value to the immigrants." A few weeks later he ran letters from seven different correspondents, each telling the virtues of a different county in western Minnesota.[47] In September of that year he left the *Chronicle* to join the staff of Ignatius Donnelly's *Anti-Monopolist,* for which, as a thorough Irish Nationalist, he wrote a column on Irish affairs.[48]

By this time the railroads were vying with one another in a race to attract settlers to the lands along their respective lines. By any standard, the Northern Pacific was out in front. With this fact in mind, admirers of John Ireland cannot justly assert that he initiated the plan of colonizing on railroad lands. It had been tried and found successful by both the Northern Pacific and the earlier Illinois Central before Ireland was a bishop.[49]

Once he became a bishop, however, the young prelate immediately set out to copy the plan he had seen working successfully for the Northern Pacific. On December 21, 1875, in the Cathedral of St. Paul, John Ireland was consecrated Coadjutor Bishop of that diocese.[50] Three weeks later the *Northwestern Chronicle* announced:

> Bishop Ireland has selected along the line of the Pacific Railroad [i.e. the St. Paul and Pacific, later to become part of James J. Hill's Great Northern] *seventy five thousand acres* of Railroad lands . . . and he is prepared to pilot *two thousand* Catholic immigrant families into Minnesota. He has an agreement with the road, that for the next two years none of this land shall be disposed of to any person without his written permission. This section Bishop Ireland has procured is sandwiched between another *seventy five thousand acres*

46. NWC (June 6, 1874), p. 1.
47. Ibid. (April 24, 1875), p. 1.
48. Ibid. (September 4, 1875), p. 4.
49. Gates, *The Illinois Central Railroad,* pp. 224–52.
50. Moynihan, *The Life of Archbishop John Ireland,* p. 13.

of Government Land, which can be settled under the Homestead Law; making a grand total of *one hundred and fifty thousand acres,* open to Catholic settlement.[51]

The same issue of this paper remarked that earlier attempts to erect colonies in the West had often been wrecked by land sharks. As soon as a few pioneer families had settled a new region, the very fact of its being settled gave the land an increased value which would attract land speculators, with the result that prices would be bid up beyond the range fellow colonists could pay.

To be sure from the start that such speculation would not blight his undertaking, Ireland had acquired complete control of all the railroad land in four townships in Swift County.[52] Even the town lots were to be protected from the dangers of an inflationary boom, because he was to plat out entirely the new townsites of De Graff and Clontarf. In acquiring control of this land and by doing so without any capital investment on his own part,[53] Ireland definitely improved the system of colonization finance originally suggested by Daniel O'Connell in 1841. Whatever its other weaknesses, the Minnesota plan was not shadowed by the specter of financial failure which had threatened land schemes since Colonial days.

By the terms of the original state and federal land grants, the railroads had been given alternate sections on each side of their right of way for a distance not to exceed three (or in some instances five) miles. Such grants gave each road a checkered swath of land from six to ten miles wide for the length of its trackage. The alternate sections were retained by the United States Government in the Federal territories and by the respective states within their limits. This land could still be claimed without charge by settlers who would agree to live on it for five years. Under the Homestead Act of 1862 such settlers were entitled to a maximum

51. *NWC* (January 15, 1876), p. 4.

52. Egan, "Irish Immigration to Minnesota," p. 145.

53. Great Northern Railroad Archives, Vault 602, Documents 17–12, Office of the Land Commissioner, St. Paul. This file does not contain a copy of the contract between the railroad and Ireland for this first section of 75,000 acres; but it does contain a copy of an agreement between them for an additional 26,000 acres in the same county, signed on June 28, 1879.

of eighty acres within ten miles of a land-grant railroad or 160 acres beyond this limit. Public land could also be acquired by settlers under timber-culture claims or pre-emption claims.[54] The former allowed settlers to acquire title to public lands, not to exceed 160 acres, on condition that within two years of claiming the land ten acres of trees would be planted for every 160 acres claimed (five acres of trees for eighty acres of land, 2½ of trees for forty acres, etc.);[55] whereas pre-emption claims allowed settlers to purchase public lands other than homesteads, not to exceed 160 acres, for a price of $2.50 per acre within ten miles of a land-grant railroad, or for $1.25 per acre beyond this limit.[56] By these provisions the danger of speculation in public lands was for the most part eliminated, though it was still at least theoretically possible for homesteaders to speculate on a small scale. One could, for example, homestead 160 acres and pre-empt a second quarter section (if he had the necessary $200 and would agree to farm the second quarter); or he could claim a second quarter section under the timber-culture claim by agreeing to plant ten acres of trees. But the physical limitations involved were almost certain safeguards against the danger of any single homesteader acquiring so much government land that he could trade in it. Hence when Bishop Ireland announced that he held exclusive control of all the railroad sections in Swift County, he could virtually assure his prospective colonists that no land shark would gain control of the remaining 75,000 acres of public land.

It was further arranged that settlers taking this land through Bishop Ireland could pay for it with the land certificates of the St. Paul and Pacific Railroad. Although these certificates were at that time selling far below their par value, it was agreed that when they were offered by settlers in payment for railroad lands, their face value would be allowed. This provision enabled the settlers (who could afford it) to purchase their land for as little as $1.40 per acre.[57] It would seem that most of the settlers in this early

54. Henry N. Copp, *The American Settler's Guide* (Washington, D.C., 1887), p. 25.
55. Ibid., p. 81.
56. Ibid., p. 66.
57. *NWC* (January 22, 1876), p. 5.

colony had the necessary money, for shortly after Bishop Ireland's announcement, the local press in Swift County reported a brisk trade in land certificates. One enterprising real estate dealer, J. E. Clausen, at Benson, the county seat, offered land buyers railroad certificates at 57½ cents on the dollar of their face value; [58] and the German American Bank of St. Paul carried advertisements in both the St. Paul and Swift County papers listing St. Paul and Pacific Railroad certificates at "sacrifice" prices.[59] According to the terms of Bishop Ireland's agreement with the railroad, he was at no time to own the lands himself: "The second party (John Ireland) shall send purchasers to the Land Department of the first party, where contracts shall be made with said purchasers." [60] With the exception of this method of finance, the settlements proposed for Minnesota in 1876 were the same as those suggested by Daniel O'Connell's Irish company for Ohio, Indiana, and Wisconsin in 1841.[61]

Shortly after the first colony was opened in Swift County, Father Thomas A. Butler of St. Louis, who was later to become a thorn in the side of Bishop Ireland, charged that Ireland's program was motivated merely by a desire to populate Minnesota and hence vitiated by a kind of self-interest.[62] Even before starting his colonies, Ireland had anticipated this objection and answered it in advance:

> In laboring to form Catholic settlements in Minnesota, my whole motive is the temporal and spiritual welfare of the immigrant. I must not be understood as advocating the claims of any Western one [sic] State over another. If at present I appear to speak exclusively of Minnesota, it is because I know the advantages it offers, while I am comparatively ignorant of the prospects that await our people in other States.

58. Benson *Times* (March 1, 1876), p. 1.
59. Ibid. (May 22, 1876), p. 3; *NWC*, April 11, 1874.
60. Great Northern Railroad Archives, Vault 602, Documents 17–12, agreement of June 28, 1879, p. 2.
61. Ireland's lengthy letter outlining his colonization plan was first published in *NWC*, January 22, 1876. For the details of Daniel O'Connell's plan see Chap. 2, above.
62. *ICBU Journal* (December 1876), p. 1.

If, in a special manner, I invite immigrants to Minnesota, it
is because here, and only here, I can be of service to them.[63]

The "service" of which he speaks here is that which any bishop
could offer his own people. Primarily, it meant that he could assure them a permanent resident pastor. This, more than any other
single factor, was to explain the success of his colonies: they were,
first of all, religious centers. Two years after the Minnesota movement began, Martin I. J. Griffin gave his opinion on why this venture had succeeded when others were failing: "The Minnesota
colonies are successful, because Bishop Ireland is in charge. As
Father Ireland, so much could not have been done." [64] Four years
later, the same writer, editorializing on the demise of the ICBU
colony in Virginia and the weakening of the one in Kansas, said
that their greatest deficiency was the lack of a bishop at their
head.[65] Even the plan for assisted emigration proposed by Daniel
O'Connell in 1841 had stressed episcopal direction as an absolute
necessity for any colonization plan. And time was to demonstrate
both that the patronage of a bishop was indispensable for the
Minnesota colonies and that the lack of it ensured the failure of
the ICBU colonies in Virginia and Kansas.[66]

At least in the beginning of the Minnesota operation Bishop
Ireland hoped to fill his lands with immigrant laborers drawn from
the industrial centers of the East. But it soon became clear that the
settlers rushing to take up his lands were seldom from large eastern cities. More often they were small farmers from Pennsylvania,
Ohio, and Indiana, who had left good farms to buy better ones.
Just after the Swift County lands were opened, Ireland was told by
his land agent, Major Ben Thompson, that several sections of the
land had been taken by a group of Irish-American farmers who
had sold their farms at Lake City, Minnesota, on the Mississippi
River and had then moved to the better soil of Swift County in
the West. Ireland tried to stem this tide with a stiff letter in the
next issue of the Chronicle: [67]

63. NWC (January 22, 1876), p. 5.
64. ICBU Journal (September 1878), p. 1.
65. Ibid. (July 1882), p. 4.
66. These colonies will be discussed in some detail in Chap. 9, below.
67. NWC (March 11, 1876), p. 5.

I have been informed that in several districts of Minnesota, Catholic farmers are preparing to sell their lands with the intention of moving to Swift County. I beg leave to say through your columns that no Minnesota farmer will from this date be admitted into the Swift County Colony. I have organized this colony for the benefit of men without homes, more especially for Eastern people, and I will rigidly adhere to my first plan. Minnesota farmers who would strive to locate in Swift County are defeating the good work which I have undertaken to do, and preventing their poorer fellow country-men from obtaining homes. Swift County has been open for settlement during many past years, and they did not care to secure lands within its limits. Now, however, when we wish to do some good by securing it for the poor and homeless, they insist on having their share in the division. I trust, we will hear no more of Minnesota farmers talking about Swift County.

Butler's charge that Ireland's lands were open only to those whose arrival would augment the population of his diocese and the young state of Minnesota was true; but such legitimate self-interest on the part of a frontier bishop, laboring to build his diocese, was probably not so reprehensible as Butler considered it. Many years later, Mother Seraphine Ireland, a sister of Bishop Ireland, was questioned about her brother's motives in organizing these colonies. She replied: "My brother had the interests of Minnesota at heart in colonizing this State. Next to his Church he loved America." [68] As originally conceived, Ireland's program had two purposes: to populate western Minnesota with Catholics, and to recruit these Catholics from eastern urban centers. Those aims were at first opposite sides of the same coin; but there can be no doubt that the Catholic settlement of Minnesota was Ireland's primary objective. The assumption that his colonies were failures, since they did not relieve the labor unrest caused by the Molly Maguires and the General Strike of 1877, is hardly tenable. Even after Ireland had seen that most of his settlers were not eastern laborers, he continued to solicit the members of that class. Un-

68. Egan, "Irish Immigration to Minnesota," p. 148.

doubtedly laborers and unemployed made up most of his audience when he addressed a mass meeting at Peter Cooper Union on June 26, 1879.[69] Talks such as this one and those of Bishop Spalding and Dillon O'Brien should not be underrated.

So shrewd an observer as Martin I. J. Griffin called one eastern lecture tour of Dillon O'Brien "eminently successful." Commenting on the same eastern tour, Griffin displayed his readiness to say a kind word about the Minnesota colonies: "So numerous have been the applications for land that the bounds of the colonies will be extended. But then Mr. O'Brien has a Bishop back of him— has a railroad company interested—has Government homestead lands in the State. He could not help being successful. Everyone cannot have the assistance of a Bishop." [70]

Although such eastern recruiting brought its rewards of small farmers and shopkeepers, such as a few families from Marlboro, Massachusetts, and a few from around Philadelphia, it did not attract large numbers of laborers from metropolitan areas. This is not surprising to us and should not have been to Ireland. In his letter announcing the first colony he warned his readers, "I wish no one to come into our settlement who will not have, after securing the land, at least four hundred dollars cash." [71] But the people to whom he explicitly directed such appeals were those families who were huddled in fifth floor, unheated, waterless tenements such as Gotham Court on New York's Lower East Side.[72] Railroad fare to Minnesota (even with the reduction offered by the railroad to incoming land buyers), a 10 per cent down payment on the land, and a four-hundred dollar cash reserve fund were beyond the wildest dreams of these people.

Certainly John Ireland was aware of the situation. Proof that he was is evident from the fact that he did not drop the colonizing effort in Minnesota when it became apparent that the incoming settlers were persons "possessing some means." [73] If he could have

69. From a clipping of *The Monitor*, a New Jersey Catholic newspaper, preserved in the Notre Dame University Archives, South Bend, Indiana, in a collection of private letters marked "Wisconsin, Illinois, Peoria."

70. *ICBU Journal* (April 1878), p. 1.

71. *NWC* (January 22, 1876), p. 5.

72. Oscar Handlin, *The Uprooted* (New York, 1951), p. 150.

73. P. J. Donohue, Secretary of the ICBU National Colonization Board, in a letter to the *ICBU Journal*, printed in the issue for March 1876, p. 1.

done so, he would have preferred to receive indigent laborers, but failing in this he was most happy to welcome to Minnesota the thousands of families "of some means" who came to him from the small towns and rural areas of New Hampshire, Massachusetts, Ohio, Pennsylvania, and Indiana. The final success or failure of his colonizing project deserves to be judged by the goal he hoped to achieve. This goal was the establishment of self-supporting Catholic parishes in western Minnesota. With the passage of time several features of his original plan had to be modified, but the primary objective remained, and the judgment of history is that it has been attained. In reviewing his achievement at this date it is important to realize that these settlements were intended primarily as rural religious parishes. It was never intended that their village trading centers should become thriving towns or cities. To this day these villages have remained small. Only three of the ten have populations in excess of 1,000 persons, and the average population for the ten villages is 650. As parochial religious centers, however, their number and success have measured up to the most sanguine predictions of their founder. In each of these settlements a common religion is still the principle of social cohesion.

CHAPTER FOUR

Invitation to the Land

WHEN BISHOP IRELAND first proposed to act as a land agent for the First Division St. Paul and Pacific Railroad in 1875, George L. Becker was managing that road for the Dutch and English creditors of the bankrupt Northern Pacific.[1] Anxious to revive the colonization scheme inaugurated by Jay Cooke and aware that Ireland's proposal would be just as beneficial to the railroad as to the settlers, Becker accepted the offer at once.

At no expense to the railroad save the usual land agent's commission, Ireland offered it a ready-made system of publicity to supplant its own defunct emigration bureau. As the words of a Catholic bishop, Ireland's advice to settlers would be carried in the Catholic press across the nation, and in foreign countries as well. As a prelate he could solicit the cooperation of other bishops, who in turn could recommend the project to their priests and people. In time this is exactly what happened. The Catholic press and episcopal letters did for the railroad land agency what it was not at that time able to do for itself. In later years Lord Strathcona (Donald A. Smith), who was by then a director in the Canadian Pacific syndicate, said to Archbishop Ireland, "In a manner unknown to yourself, you were a friend to [James J. Hill] and myself in a moment when we needed friends. Whatever I can do for you is but a return of thanks for what you and your colony once did for us."[2]

On January 22, 1876, Ireland publicly announced the establishment of the Catholic Colonization Bureau of St. Paul: a new agency, replacing the old Irish Emigration Society and administered by Dillon O'Brien.[3] At the same time he revealed that he had signed a contract with the St. Paul and Pacific Railroad, mak-

1. Folwell, *A History of Minnesota*, 3, 450.
2. Pyle, *The Life of James J. Hill*, 1, 206–7.
3. *NWC* (January 22, 1876), p. 1.

ing him the exclusive agent for all railroad lands in Swift County —the first of eleven such contracts signed by the bishop and five different Minnesota railroads within the next five years.[4] Ireland appointed Father John McDermot first pastor of the new Swift County colony and gave him authority to act as land agent in the new settlement.

The Swift County lands—embracing four townships, each six miles square and containing 23,040 acres—were taken up by Catholic settlers so quickly that it was soon necessary for Ireland to secure by a second contract an additional tract of 26,000 acres bordering the lands already settled.[5] Three years after its opening, the colony comprised 117,000 acres of railroad land in Swift County and probably an amount of state land almost as great. Within these limits the two towns of De Graff and Clontarf, four-teen miles apart, were platted by Bishop Ireland's agents. De Graff, named after a pioneer Minnesota railroad contractor, was hardly more than a railway station when the colony began; and Clontarf, named after the Irish townsland near Dublin, was built entirely by the colonists.

One year after the opening of the Swift County colonies, Ire-land negotiated a third contract with the St. Paul and Sioux City

4. For one such contract see below, Appendix.
5. There is some difference of opinion on the exact amount of land involved in this first agreement. The figure given here is that of Bishop Ireland's own statement. His agent, Dillon O'Brien, published a pamphlet (*Invitation to the Land*) in 1877, in which he said the Bishop controlled twelve townships (276,000 acres!)—an unlikely figure repeated by Howard Eston Egan. Undoubtedly this sanguine estimate was meant to include unsold government sections in between railroad sections. The actual amount of railroad land involved was probably about 75,000 acres. This figure allows for those sections of railroad land which might have been claimed by homesteaders before such land was given to the railroad. Monsignor Humphrey Moynihan sets the figure at 117,000 acres, probably by adding the original grant of January 1876 to the subsequent grant of June 28, 1879. A copy of the agreement for new lands on the latter date is on file in the Great Northern Railroad Archives, Vault 602, Documents 17–12. The figure of 75,000 acres for the original grant would also be in line with Bishop Ireland's announcement in the *ICBU Journal* for September 6, 1876, that he had sold most of his land (meaning 60,000 acres) by that date to 800 Catholic families. A copy of this agreement also is on file in Vault 602, Documents 17–12; the archives do not, however, contain a copy of the original contract of January 1876. This vital document, which served as a model for all of John Ireland's later railroad contracts, may possibly be among the James J. Hill Private Papers, which have not yet been opened to scholars.

Railroad Company, securing control of 70,000 acres of its railroad lands in Nobles County, in southwestern Minnesota.[6] Within this tract was the tiny village of Adrian, composed at that time of three houses and a railway station. In September 1877 Ireland sent the German-born Father C. J. Knauf to Adrian to establish a Catholic parish and to serve as the official agent for a new colony in that area. When Father Knauf arrived, he discovered that none of the town's residents was Catholic. Within seven months, however, it was necessary for the bishop to secure an additional 35,-000 acres of railroad land to accommodate the flood of Catholic settlers who came in answer to his publicity about the Adrian colony.[7] By May 1880 Ireland reported that only two farms remained unsold; and in 1882 Father Knauf stated that the Catholic families settled in the colony totaled 250.[8]

In 1877 the Black Hills branch of the St. Paul and Sioux City Railroad began construction through Murray County just north of Nobles County and the Adrian colony in southwestern Minnesota. In April 1878 Bishop Ireland was named exclusive agent for 52,000 acres of this road's lands in Murray County. He at once appointed Father Charles Koeberl to be resident pastor in the new colony, platted the town of Avoca, and erected a large emigrant house on Lime Lake. Between April and December of that year, Father Koeberl sold nearly 10,000 acres of railroad land in the Avoca colony.[9] More land than this would have been taken up had the colony been started early enough to enable the new farmers to get in a crop that year. Within two years 30,000 acres had been sold, and Father Koeberl announced that two new churches would be built within the colony lands, one at Iona and one at Fulda, to accommodate the extended congregation.[10] Addi-

6. Humphrey Moynihan, "Archbishop Ireland's Colonies," *Acta et Dicta*, 6 (October 1934), 222–3.

7. Worthington *Advance* (April 11, 1878), p. 2.

8. Moynihan, "Archbishop Ireland's Colonies," p. 223. A great portion of Father Knauf's detailed correspondence on the Adrian colony has been preserved in the archives of the St. Paul Seminary, St. Paul, Minn. It provides an unusually complete picture of life in this frontier community in the early 1880's and is used below, Chap. 8.

9. Moynihan, "Archbishop Ireland's Colonies," p. 226.

10. *The Colony of Avoca, Murray County, Southwestern Minnesota* (St. Paul,

tional lands bordering the colony but contained in the land grant of another railroad—the Winona and St. Peter—were secured by the bishop in the summer of 1879, through the assistance of Albert Keep, president of the latter road.[11]

At the time the Avoca colony was dividing into the new settlements of Iona, Fulda, and Currie in the southwest, Bishop Ireland commissioned Colonel J. R. King, a surveyor, to pick out suitable lands in Big Stone County for a new townsite and farm colony. Early in 1878 King bought a soldier's claim of 80 acres on the shores of Toqua Lakes, the continental divide for waters flowing to Hudson's Bay and the Gulf of Mexico. An additional 120 acres, then the property of one Colonel Dunlap, were added to the first 80 to provide the townsite for Graceville, named after Bishop Thomas L. Grace of St. Paul.[12] This site, in Minnesota's westernmost county, did not yet have a railroad. The first settlers who came took up homesteads and timber-culture claims. Before any of them arrived, however, Bishop Ireland had shipped five carloads of lumber overland from Morris, Minnesota, the closest railroad terminal, and ordered the immediate construction of a church on the shores of the lake. The church was completed within a month. Colonel King was commissioned by Bishop Ireland to act as an advisor for all incoming settlers, and Father A. V. Pelisson, a native of France, was named resident pastor. Eight months after the colony was started, Colonel King wrote, "From the roof of the church I can count today over 70 houses where last March

Catholic Colonization Bureau, 1880), p. 12. A copy of this pamphlet is part of the Griffin Papers, American Catholic Historical Society of Philadelphia, bound into a large volume entitled "Catholic Colonization Pamphlets."

11. Letter of Charles E. Simmons, land commissioner of the Winona and St. Peter, to Albert Keep, president of that road, July 16, 1879, copied into the railroad's Minute Book (Document 87-A), pp. 384–5, in Vault 15, Office of the Secretary, Chicago and North Western Railway System, 400 West Madison Avenue, Chicago, Illinois. It should be noted that the Winona and St. Peter, though now part of the Chicago and North Western system, has always retained its corporate identity. Its complete records are on file at the address given above.

12. *Catholic Colonization in Minnesota* (rev. ed. St. Paul, Catholic Colonization Bureau, 1879), p. 46. A copy of this rare pamphlet is among the Griffin Papers; another is preserved in the Coe Collection of Western Americana, Yale University.

there was nothing but a bare prairie." [13] In the meantime, James J. Hill had been named general manager of the reorganized and expanded St. Paul, Minneapolis, and Manitoba Railroad Company.[14] One of the assets then held by this Red River line was a parcel of railroad indemnity lands in Big Stone County. "Indemnity lands" or "lieu lands" were tracts given to railroads by Congress or state legislatures to compensate the roads for those portions of an original land grant that had already been settled by homesteaders when the railroads came through, or for those portions of an original land grant unsuited to tillage, such as lakes, alkali flats, or meander lands (lying between the high and low water lines of any lake or stream). After Hill became general manager of the St. Paul, Minneapolis, and Manitoba, he put 50,000 acres of such indemnity lands (in Big Stone and Traverse Counties) under Bishop Ireland's control for a period of two years, beginning December 31, 1879.[15] Colonel King, Bishop Ireland's aide, sold these lands at an average price of $4.00 per acre. During 1880, 100 Catholic families arrived in Graceville, and by September 1881 the colony consisted of 400 Catholic colonists.[16]

On May 1 and July 24, 1879, Bishop Ireland signed contracts with the Winona and St. Peter Railroad Company and extended these contracts by a new one on October 20, 1880, making him the exclusive agent for certain railroad lands in Lyon County, Minnesota.[17] The beginning of this contract coincided with the expiration date for some of the earlier contracts held with other roads. On July 12, 1879, Ireland announced the opening of this new tract of 45,000 acres for settlement.[18] He immediately installed Father M. J. Hanley as resident pastor in Minneota, a townsite just platted by the Winona and St. Peter. Father Hanley was to act as land agent for all Catholic settlers, and an employee of the

13. Ibid., p. 47.

14. Pyle, *The Life of James J. Hill*, 1, 289.

15. The original contract for these lands is not among those in the Great Northern Archives today, but there is a revision (Vault 602, Documents 17–12), signed on July 17, 1880.

16. Moynihan, "Archbishop Ireland's Colonies," p. 220.

17. Each of these contracts is on file in the Office of the Land and Tax Commissioner of the Chicago and North Western, in the Land Contracts Vault in a file box labeled "Minnesota."

18. *NWC* (July 12, 1879), pp. 8–9.

railroad at Marshall, Minnesota, was to sell lands to settlers other than Catholics. The cheap land, however, was passing quickly. Future settlements would have to be in Dakota Territory, now that Minnesota was nearly settled.

On June 1, 1880, the last major land contract for Catholic settlements in Minnesota was signed between John Sweetman—an Irish philanthropist from County Meath, Ireland—and the Winona and St. Peter Railroad. By its terms Sweetman bought outright 10,000 acres of railroad land in Murray County, Minnesota, around the village of Currie, at an average price of one pound sterling.[19] It was Sweetman's fond hope to settle indigent Irish emigrants on farms within this tract. Although the settlement of the colony did not follow the strict pattern established by Bishop Ireland for his other settlements, it may be listed as one of his colonies, since he was from the start active in its creation and expansion.[20]

As a result of all these land contracts, Ireland managed to secure for the Catholic Colonization Bureau in St. Paul control over 379,000 acres of Minnesota railroad lands, between January 1876 and June 1, 1880:

	acres
Swift County (De Graff and Clontarf)	117,000
Nobles County (Adrian)	105,000
Murray County (Avoca, Iona, Fulda)	52,000
Murray County (Currie)	10,000
Big Stone County (Graceville)	50,000
Lyon County (Minneota and Ghent)	45,000
Total	379,000

How much additional government land was settled by persons attracted to Minnesota by the advertising of Bishop Ireland cannot be established. That the number of acres was large, however, may be gathered from a study of the United States Land Office records in the vicinity of the colonies. For example, in the Swift County area, where John Ireland had announced his first colony in January 1876, the United States Land Office registered 932

19. John Sweetman, "The Sweetman Colony of Currie, Minnesota," *Acta et Dicta*, 3 (July 1911), 59.
20. Alice E. Smith, "The Sweetman Irish Colony," *Minnesota History*, 9 (December 1928), 333.

homestead, pre-emption, and timber-culture claim entries, covering 112,000 acres, within the three spring months of March, April, and May.[21] All of this was public land. That the pattern of settlement was similar near the other colony sites is demonstrated in a letter Bishop Ireland sent to Charles Simmons, Land Commissioner for the Winona and St. Peter Railroad, on October 18, 1883:

> I am well aware that I have not sold as much land for you as you had reason to expect. Two difficulties lay in my way in the setting up of the Minneota Colony. 1. I undertook it at a time when the harvests were turning out very badly; and 2. The old settlers on government land were too willing to sell to the new-comers. Around Ghent especially, nearly all the Norwegians and Americans sold out to our Belgians. I have brought into the country far more settlers than our sales of railroad land would indicate, and in one way at least I have been of use to the company—filling up the country along their line. I would be very sorry that any section of country should be reserved for me to the prejudice of the interests of the company. . . . The prospects of a larger emigration than we ever had are very good, and if you wish me to continue working, I will do so, in what manner may be agreeable to you. I am certainly anxious to bring [?] in as many of our people as I can along your lines—but I wish to do it in such a way that the Company will be quite satisfied with my efforts.[22]

The same pattern of settlement was reported by the Worthington *Advance* for the area surrounding the colonies in Nobles and Murray County. The editor of this paper returned to southwestern Minnesota in January 1878 after a business trip to the East. His first editorial reported that business was at a standstill in the East at that time and that many small businessmen were planning to settle on western lands in the spring.[23] A month later the sales

21. St. Paul *Pioneer-Press and Tribune* (June 9, 1876), p. 4; (July 1, 1876), p. 14.

22. This letter is on file, with the contracts referred to in n. 17, above.

23. Worthington *Advance* (January 10, 1879), p. 2.

of farm land and building sites in the town of Adrian were booming.[24] Three months after the Adrian colony began operations in
Nobles County, the St. Paul *Pioneer-Press* reported that the United
States land offices at Worthington and Benson were the two busi-
est ones in the state.[25] The former was the closest land office to
Ireland's colony at Adrian; the latter was in the very center of
his two Swift County colonies.

Surveyors for the western railroads were primarily interested
in laying out direct and economical routes between major freight
and passenger terminals. Hence not all the land granted by Congress to these roads was of equal fertility. In some places the rails
crossed alkali flats, other tracts were dried-up lake beds, and still
others were covered with glacial moraine and gravel too heavy for
cultivation. To avoid sending his colonists to such unpromising
land, John Ireland selected and secured from the railroads the
most fertile portions of their land grants. In person, or through his
agent, Major Ben Thompson, Ireland inspected every parcel of
land before recommending it to prospective settlers. After assur-
ing himself of the fertility and productivity of each tract, he commissioned Dillon O'Brien to prepare a brochure describing the location, average yield per acre, type of soil, and average yearly
rainfall characteristic of the area. While Ireland negotiated new
contracts with the various railroad land commissioners, O'Brien's
prolific pen turned out a series of settlers' guide books designed
to encourage and direct the Catholic migration into the West.
The rapidity with which interested persons answered these invitations to the land surprised even the most confident exponents
of western settlement.

In 1877, disturbed by "the magnitude of the recent strikes" and
hoping that his western lands would prove attractive to strike-
bound laborers in the East, Ireland instructed Dillon O'Brien to
write the first of these descriptive brochures—this one on the
Minnesota colonies which had been established one year earlier.

24. Ibid. (February 21, 1879), p. 3.
25. St. Paul *Pioneer-Press,* quoted in the Worthington *Advance* (December 20,
1877), p. 3. No date is given for the original.

O'Brien entitled it *An Invitation to the Land: Reasons and Figures.*[26]

More than once in the columns of the *Northwestern Chronicle* he had said that his writings would "remain undisguisedly true to those Democratic principles best enunciated by Thomas Jefferson";[27] true to his word, he opened his first pamphlet with a tag line in the best Jeffersonian tradition: "They who own the land own the country."[28] This publication was written to appeal explicitly to Catholics living in "dark, unhealthy tenement rooms, doing the slavish work of the docks and streets, with no hope of advancement." It would still be several years before Ireland and O'Brien realized that, by and large, persons in this category either could not or would not come west. For all their suffering at the time of the general strike in 1877, the Catholic laborers in the East preferred the ills they had to others that they knew not of. At this time O'Brien still felt that their hesitancy about coming west went back to the warnings of Archbishop Hughes against western colonies; hence his opening appeal anticipated their objections by agreeing that life in squalid urban tenements, with the benefit of church and priest nearby, was preferable to life on the open "prairie with herds and granary and free homesteads, without these blessings." However, he went on, with the additional priests provided by Bishop Ireland, Minnesota settlers could now enjoy both the opportunities of the land and the consolations of their religion.

In time Ireland even succeeded in winning some support for his colonization project from eastern Catholic leaders who had at first opposed the movement. The bishop's enthusiasm and O'Brien's tact finally managed to impress James A. McMaster—who had once officially reported and solidly endorsed in his *Freeman's Journal* the position of Archbishop Hughes. After a colonization rally in New York directed by Dr. Edward McGlynn, the enthusiastic disciple of Henry George, McMaster swung his editorial support behind the colonization enterprises of John Ireland. To

26. A copy is preserved in the Coe Collection of Western Americana, Yale University.

27. *NWC* (September 18, 1875), p. 1.

28. *Invitation to the Land,* p. 3.

those devoted followers of the Hughes tradition who reminded
him that this was a complete reversal of the intransigent position
he had taken in opposing McGee's Buffalo Convention in 1856,
McMaster replied, "There is no parity between the two movements." [29] The final compliment to the Minnesota plan was the
New York editor's assurance to his readers, "We are certain, were
Archbishop Hughes alive, now, he would offer no opposition to
the plan proposed by Bishop Ireland." [30] McMaster never became
an ardent booster of the Minnesota plan, and in later years he
spoke bitterly about the debacle of the Connemara settlers in
Ireland's Graceville colony,[31] but his few words of assurance early
in the campaign banished the shades of Hughes' opposition and
greatly encouraged Dillon O'Brien.

An important qualification voiced by O'Brien in his first appeal
for settlers was that only farmers or men who wanted farm life
should come west. His appeal to industrial workers in the East
presumed that many of these had been farmers before coming
to America. Such repeated injunctions in his pamphlet as "We
invite farmers only," and "The settler must absolutely have (in
addition to railroad fare) a sum of $400 in coming," and "If you
come without this capital you do so at your own risk," placed immediate restrictions on the number of people who were fitted for
the venture.[32] What had been merely objective description of the
difficulty of pioneer farm life in the earlier state and railroad publications became a grim painting of hardship in O'Brien's booklet.
His final section, "A Chapter for All to Read," is a sobering account
of the strenuous work, limited social life, primitive facilities, and
possible discouragements awaiting the settler on the frontier. If
a man were ready to brave these trials, he might, after a few years
of hard labor with very little gain to show for them, expect a comfortable return for his labor and the independence of being his
own boss. Following the style and argument of an earlier state
pamphlet by John Bond, O'Brien anticipated the stock objection

29. *Freeman's Journal* (June 14, 1879), p. 4.
30. Ibid.
31. Sister Mary Augustine Kwitchen, O.F.M., *James Alphonsus McMaster, a
Study in American Thought* (Washington, D.C., 1949), pp. 212–13. The failure
of the Graceville Colony will be discussed in detail below, Chap. 7.
32. *Invitation to the Land*, pp. 41, 30, 35.

that Minnesota winters were too cold. His reply, "It's a dry cold, and really quite bracing," has become a canonized cliché in Minnesota. In one of his lapses from factual reporting of hard prairie life O'Brien's Irish rhetoric revealed itself when he urged his readers to think of the Minnesota winter as a time for "warm robes, a light cutter, a fast horse, and tinkling sleigh-bells." [33] This pamphlet was printed in both English and German, and within ten months of its publication 13,000 copies were distributed by the St. Paul office. O'Brien and a German-born priest, one Father Berghold, toured the large eastern cities in the winter of 1878, lecturing in English and German respectively to the Catholic audiences of these cities, and distributing their brochures.[34]

In 1879 an enlarged and revised edition of the 1877 pamphlet was issued by the Catholic Colonization Bureau in St. Paul, with new material on the extent of the railroads, the records of recent harvests, and reports from the colonists already established in Swift, Big Stone, Nobles, and Murray Counties. The new edition reported that the Catholic press across the land had, in general, warmly endorsed the Minnesota plan. The editor of the *Catholic Review* had even come from New York to inspect the colonies, and had returned to that city to write a series of editorials vigorously recommending Minnesota to Catholics in the East.[35] In Liverpool, England, Father James Nugent, a priest of that diocese, had the boys in his industrial trade school run off several thousand copies of the Minnesota pamphlet, which he proceeded to distribute in England, Galway, and Belgium.[36] Nugent, who in Liverpool had founded an orphanage and trade school for boys, conducted a total abstinence crusade, and built a shelter for homeless women, had come to America in November 1870 to attend an immigration convention at Indianapolis, in the hope of discovering some place there for his homeless children.[37] After visit-

33. Ibid., p. 14.

34. John W. Bond, *Minnesota, the Empire State of the New Northwest* (St. Paul, 1878), p. 88.

35. *Catholic Colonization in Minnesota* (1879), p. 53.

36. Letter of Father James Nugent, Liverpool, England, to Bishop James O'Connor, Omaha, Nebraska, April 8, 1880, in Omaha Chancery Archives, Colonization File.

37. Canon Edward K. Bennett, *Father Nugent of Liverpool* (Liverpool, 1949), p. 100.

ing Texas and Minnesota (where he met Father Ireland), he returned to England, believing that western colonies might be the salvation of his indigent clients.

When John Ireland became a bishop and began his work of colonization five years later, he remembered the enthusiasm of his English friend and immediately commissioned Father Nugent

Fig. 3. An Emigrant Guide Book, ca. 1879

as his agent for emigration in England and Ireland. Nugent's office, at 50 Manchester Street, Liverpool, was called the Catholic Colonization Society.[38] From this information center thousands of pamphlets on the colonies in Minnesota were distributed across England, Ireland, and Belgium. Literally thousands of the settlers who eventually came to the Catholic colonies in Minnesota (and to similar settlements in Greeley County, Nebraska) were sent by Father Nugent. It was also through his influence that Canon Van Hee, a Belgian priest, brought about the establishment of a prosperous Belgian colony at Ghent, Minnesota, in 1881—the settlement which can without qualification be called John Ireland's most successful farming community.

Experience gained in settling the first six colonies confirmed O'Brien in the opinion that accurate factual description was the best way to advertise and sell western land. Acting on this premise he prepared a new pamphlet in 1880 entitled *Colony of Avoca, Murray County, Minnesota.* Avoca, established in 1878, was experiencing a steady expansion. But before listing its attractions, O'Brien cautioned his readers:

> The rapid growth and prosperity of our Catholic Colonies in Minnesota, more than keeping pace with the healthy growth and general prosperity of the State, make it necessary for the Catholic Colonization Bureau to continually revise, alter, and supplement the information it has already published for the benefit of *intending immigrants.* We wish to emphasize these words *intending immigrants,* for we have no desire that those with comfortable, respectable homes already, should break up those homes and come west, influenced [by the information we have given] for the benefit of the struggling, industrious many, who have no such homes nor any prospect of securing them in their present employments and locations. When persons of means . . . come to us . . . we welcome them . . . but we caution people, rich and poor alike, from making imaginary fancy pictures from the facts we lay before them. This caution is necessary for our protection and . . . it is to [such] cautions which we

38. See letterhead of Nugent's letter to Bishop O'Connor.

have given in every publication issued by the Bureau, that we attribute the gratifying fact, that among the thousands who have come here on our invitation, not more than one per cent returned dissatisfied: a most extraordinary fact to those experienced in immigration matters.[39]

O'Brien's obvious pride in reporting that less than one per cent of the Minnesota colonists had found their new homes disappointing is in keeping with his effort to tell the truth in the painfully realistic descriptions of frontier life often found in his later writings. And it must have cost this Irish editor (whose first published works—three novels, *The Dalys of Dalystown, Dead Broke,* and *Frank Blake*—were perilously close to the fashion of Horatio Alger's stories) some effort to keep his immigrant guides within the limits of accurate reporting. It is clear, however, that his publications measured up to the standards of precision and accuracy set by the earlier state-sponsored pamphlets of John Bond and Girard Hewitt, for in its general session for 1879 the Minnesota Legislature created a new State Board of Immigration and voted that this board be made up of "the Governor, Secretary of State, Clerk of the Supreme Court and Dillon O'Brien." [40]

It was during 1880, while O'Brien was preparing the material for his last pamphlet (on Avoca), that John Sweetman, the Irish philanthropist and friend of Parnell, came to St. Paul to find lands for his Irish neighbors who were then suffering from the distress of the famine of 1879.[41] Bishop Ireland encouraged Sweetman and offered to accommodate him with lands in any of the Minnesota settlements which met his approval. Sweetman and O'Brien set out on a tour of the colonies but gave their greatest attention to the Avoca settlement, in Murray County. At that time this colony was enjoying a mild boom. Sweetman was impressed by the good soil and the obvious success of the farmers who had settled there in 1878. But because most of Bishop Ireland's lands were taken, Sweetman ranged out beyond the colony lands and found nearby a promising tract of 10,000 acres, belonging to the Winona and

39. *The Colony of Avoca, Murray County, Southwestern Minnesota* (1880), p. 3.
40. *General Laws of Minnesota* (St. Paul, 1879), chap. 6, p. 237.
41. Sweetman, "The Sweetman Colony," p. 46.

St. Peter Railroad. It was his plan to return to Ireland to organize a joint-stock company and an Irish emigrant society; but to tie up the land he purchased the 10,000 acres (for 10,000 pounds sterling) with his own money before returning to Ireland to recruit settlers.[42] Back in Ireland, during the summer of 1880, he organized the Irish-American Colonization Company, Limited, with offices at 12 Frederick Street, Dublin. The provisional prospectus issued by this company explains its purpose:

> In the Western States of America vast tracts of magnificent tillage land are still unoccupied, affording a most favourable opening for capital and labour combined. These lands will not, however, long remain unsettled, owing to the large immigration from the Eastern States of America, and from Germany, Norway and Sweden. Great numbers of able-bodied men are now emigrating from Ireland, who, for want of capital, cannot settle on these lands. This company has been formed for the purpose of supplying this want of capital. It will purchase land in suitable localities, and place settlers on it, providing them with what they require for a fair start. A mortgage will be held on the land and on the implements, stock, and effects on the farm, until the settler has paid, by such installments as may be agreed on, the purchase-money, and sum advanced with a fair interest.[43]

After a second visit to America to confirm his arrangements for a colony in Minnesota, Sweetman returned to Dublin to solicit what subscriptions he could among his old Land League friends. In his own account of these years he relates that he was prepared to use his own fortune to promote the American venture and that he was not very confident of securing extensive aid from the Land Leaguers. They were at this time collecting funds in America themselves. And Sweetman, before coming to America, had broken with Parnell and Davitt on the means being used by the League to secure land reform in Ireland. Parnell had urged Sweet-

---

42. Ibid., p. 59.
43. *Provisional Prospectus of the Irish-American Colonization Company, Limited,* Dublin, 1880. A copy of this pamphlet is preserved among the John Sweetman–Currie Colony Papers at the Minnesota Historical Society, St. Paul.

man to stay with them,[44] but he refused and set out for the United States to seek Bishop Ireland's advice on how he might "go it alone" in helping his Irish neighbors.

In the spring of 1881 Sweetman decided to accompany his first band of Irish emigrants and settle with them in America. They arrived at Currie, Minnesota, a tiny village in Murray County, in time to plant crops for that year. Sweetman himself set up a model farm and purchased three purebred Shorthorn bulls as foundation stock for a combination beef and dairy herd. In 1881 he bought 10,000 additional acres of railroad land [45] and hired John P. O'Connor, a fellow Irishman, as manager of the colony affairs. In the beginning things went smoothly, but in 1883 Sweetman, somewhat disillusioned, published a short pamphlet, *Recent Experiences in the Emigration of Irish Families,*[46] spelling out the reasons for the partial failure of his original plan. Although his settlers had all been farmers in Ireland, it soon became apparent that very few of them wished to remain farmers in America. Several members of his original band left the colony as soon as they could arrange employment in the cities of St. Paul or Minneapolis. Others who were not prepared for the hardships of frontier farming gave up when these inevitable trials came upon them. Sweetman even charged that some of them had made their agreements with him in bad faith, intending to leave his group as soon as they arrived in America. Disappointed by the showing his compatriots had made, he announced a new policy for his company:

> Too much has been done for them [the settlers]—too much spoon feeding—and they became discontented like spoilt children. The Company has, therefore, been compelled to give up the idea of taking settlers who have absolutely no capital of their own. They will charge in future in the first

44. Sweetman, "The Sweetman Colony," pp. 41–3.

45. John Sweetman, *Farms for Sale in the Sweetman Catholic Colony of Murray County, Minnesota* (St. Paul, Irish-American Colonization Company, Ltd., 1885), p. 3. A copy of this extremely rare pamphlet is part of the Griffin Papers, bound into "Catholic Colonization Pamphlets."

46. A copy is preserved at the Minnesota Historical Society, St. Paul. For a detailed account of the Sweetman Colony, see below, Chap. 7.

instance one-tenth of the price of the land and of all the goods
advanced, allowing as before nine years for payment of the
balance with interest. They will not in future, advance oxen
or any live stock, nor will they advance food, fuel, nor perishable articles. It would therefore be necessary for a hard working farmer to have a capital of 100 pounds of his own.[47]

This is exactly the amount Bishop Ireland, in his first published
statement on the colonies, on January 22, 1876, had set as the necessary initial capital for prospective settlers.

Under its revised plan for recruiting settlers the Sweetman
colony began to show new signs of life in 1884, and at the end of
that year its benevolent founder was able to publish an account
of its modest success in a booklet which solicited further settlement. This pamphlet, *Farms for Sale in the Sweetman Catholic
Colony*,[48] was published in January 1885 and was followed later
in the same year by a larger edition, *The Sweetman Catholic Colony in Murray County, Minnesota*.[49] It was to be the last publication from the Catholic colonies of Minnesota. The first half of the
pamphlet reprinted a series called "Minnesota Letters," which
appeared in eastern papers during 1883 and 1884. The best of these
was a series of six written to the Boston *Pilot* by Father Martin
Mahoney, the pastor at Currie. For completeness of description
and accuracy of detail, these six letters are the best single summary
we have of life in a Minnesota colony during the early years. Rainfall, acreage yield, depth of water level, markets, transportation
facilities, schools, churches, housing problems, and the weather
are a few of the topics Father Mahoney covered. The last half
of the pamphlet is a revision of the stock description of Minnesota
which appeared in much the same form in all Minnesota emigrant
literature from 1853 to 1885.

A delicate problem which faced all the Irish Catholic colonizers
in general and Sweetman in particular was that of working effectively for the betterment of the Irish in America without antagoniz-

47. Sweetman, "The Sweetman Colony," p. 164.
48. See n. 45, above.
49. A copy is preserved in the Griffin Papers, bound into "Catholic Colonization Pamphlets."

ing those rising leaders in Ireland who regarded any plan of assisted emigration as a form of treason against the homeland. Even through the great famine year of 1879, when people were literally dying of hunger in the streets of Dublin, some Irish patriots, such as Father Thomas Ambrose Butler, continued to castigate anyone who suggested or encouraged emigration as a solution to Ireland's economic ills. Having worked intimately with Davitt and Parnell in the early years of the Land League, Sweetman was aware of this dilemma. His final decision to underwrite the emigration of some of his friends and tenants from County Meath in Ireland to Currie, Minnesota, was not motivated by any conscious desire to hurt Ireland or oppose her leaders; it was simply a practical decision dictated by the appalling suffering which he saw everywhere among his Irish neighbors. He had some money: Bishop Ireland offered lands. In the crisis of the times it seemed best to him to act at once by sending as many of his Irish tenants as possible to the open lands of Minnesota. Sweetman was realist enough to appreciate that whether or not he acted in this emergency, there were thousands of Irish leaving for America every month. Rather than ignore this mounting exodus, he decided to do what he could to direct it.

In his original prospectus (1880) he was careful to introduce the premise "Great numbers of able-bodied men are now emigrating from Ireland," [50] anticipating the objection from his former Land League friends that assisted emigration only alleviated surface symptoms and, by depleting Ireland's manpower, rendered the country less capable of solving her economic problems. Although the sponsors of Minnesota colonization did not hope for much financial or moral support from Irish leaders, they did hope to retain the good will of the Land League and the Irish hierarchy. Father Nugent in Liverpool and Bishop Ireland in St. Paul were most explicit in telling the public that they did not solicit people to leave Ireland. Through Dillon O'Brien's pamphlets the Minnesota bishop assured his Irish readers that his sole concern was to find homes in America for those who had already left Ireland and not, as his critics charged, to encourage emigration.

In a very shrill letter to the *ICBU Journal* on January 1, 1881,

50. See n. 43, above.

the irascible Father Butler attacked this mode of thinking. "I must declare my dissent here from everything that might induce our people to leave Ireland. . . . On this point I totally disagree with Bishop Ireland, Father Nugent, and others who favor emigration to the United States." There is a kernel of truth in Butler's description of John Ireland's method of recruiting settlers. The available evidence, however, is overwhelming that the Minnesota bishop did not want to encourage emigration from Ireland. That he allowed Nugent and Sweetman to set up offices in Liverpool and Dublin means only that he was trying to cope with the existing fact of large-scale emigration. The American bishops had nothing to gain by antagonizing the Irish hierarchy. The urban centers of our eastern states were easily capable of supplying all the Catholic settlers any western bishop could accept. There was really no need for the bishops to solicit emigrants from Europe, especially since the railroads were at this time carrying on extensive campaigns in Europe to obtain the volume of immigrants necessary to maintain America's labor force.

At the same time that the Winona and St. Peter Railroad signed its land agreement with John Ireland, it signed a contract with one John Martindale Farrar, a member of an English colony established in the 1860's at Fairmont, Martin County, Minnesota, commissioning him "to proceed to Europe and procure emigrants from the United Kingdom of Great Britain and Ireland to come to the United States and purchase and settle upon lands of the said railroad." [51] As agent for the railroad, Farrar was to receive a commission of 5 per cent on all land sales made through his efforts. In the same year, on September 30, Minnesota's Governor J. S. Pillsbury commissioned one Maurice Farrar (also of the English colony at Fairmont) "to act as Agent for the promotion of Immigration to this State by lecturing and otherwise diffusing information in Great Britain." [52] In 1880, to supplement his lectures in England, Farrar published a book soliciting English emigrants, entitled *Five Years in Minnesota*.

The Winona and St. Peter Railroad, on March 21, 1881, ap-

51. This agreement, dated October 11, 1879, is on file in the Chicago and North Western Land and Tax Office (Chicago), Land Contracts Vault, Minnesota.
52. Letter of Governor J. S. Pillsbury, St. Paul, September 30, 1879, to Maurice Farrar, reproduced in Maurice Farrar, *Five Years in Minnesota* (London, 1880), p. xii. Copy in Sterling Library, Yale University.

pointed one "John Everitt Commissioner of its Land Department in the United Kingdom of Great Britain and Ireland for the purpose of soliciting emigration to its Land Grant." [53] Everitt's main office was to be in the city of Liverpool, and he was to travel throughout the United Kingdom "to promote emigration" and "distribute the advertising matter of said company." He was empowered to hire subagents and to pay them (out of his own 5 per cent) a commission of 2½ per cent on all railroad lands in Minnesota sold through their efforts. He was also allowed an annual expense account of $2,250.[54] From the fact that this contract, originally made for one year, was renewed until August 1, 1882, it would appear that the company found the arrangement satisfactory.[55]

On April 5, 1882, the Chicago and North Western Railway System, which owned and operated the smaller Winona and St. Peter, signed a contract with the English land agents Swan and Leach, whose offices were at 1 Princess Street, Manchester, England, "to represent the said Railway Company in Great Britain in securing emigration to the regions of Minnesota and Dakota tributary to the lines operated by the Chicago and North Western Railway Company." [56] This contract was to last until July 1, 1883. It provided Swan and Leach with an expense account of $2,500 for the year, and promised a commission of 5 per cent on all railroad land sold through their agency, as well as "a commission of five percent (5%) on the Chicago and North Western Railway Company's proportion of the railway fare of all emigrants forwarded by Swan and Leach to Sleepy Eye, Minnesota and points west thereof."

It is also worthy of notice that the guide book which the settlers received from the Winona and St. Peter, once they arrived in Minnesota, recommended to all Catholic settlers the colonies of Bishop Ireland on that railroad's lands.[57] Hence, the railroad's system of international recruiting in a sense resulted in the estab-

53. This contract, signed on March 21, 1881, is on file in the Chicago and North Western Land and Tax Office (Chicago), Land Contracts Vault, Minnesota.

54. Ibid., p. 2.

55. Ibid. Attached to this contract as page 4 is a clause extending the contract from May 1, 1882, to August 1, 1882.

56. This contract, signed on April 5, 1882, is on file in the Chicago and North Western Land and Tax Office (Chicago), Land Contracts Vault, Minnesota.

57. *Guide to Homes in the New Northwest* (Chicago, Winona and St. Peter Railroad, 1880?), p. 29.

lishment of a feeder line for Bishop Ireland's Minnesota colonies. The degree to which the Catholic colonies profited from such publicity supports Butler's charge that the bishop was endorsing emigration from Europe. A more moderate view, however, would be that he was tolerating it but trying in every way to secure most of his settlers from among those Europeans who had already found their way to the United States. The evidence supplied by his speeches, pamphlets, and episcopal letters proves this latter point beyond doubt. Furthermore, his own letter to Land Commissioner Simmons, already cited,[58] states that the Catholics who came to his colonies did so as a result of his own advertising campaign.

Ever since the days of McGee's Buffalo Convention in 1856 John Ireland had cherished the hope of reviving the plan for a concerted nationwide effort at colonization. After his own diocesan project had been in operation long enough to prove its viability, he and Dillon O'Brien were convinced that the time was opportune to try again for a national colonization society such as they had unsuccessfully proposed at St. Louis in 1869. At Ireland's suggestion and with the assurance of his episcopal backing, William J. Onahan, then comptroller of the city of Chicago and secretary of Chicago's St. Patrick's Society, issued the invitations for interested laymen, priests, and bishops to assemble for a meeting in Chicago on March 17, 1879, to organize such a society.[59] By this time Ireland could count on the episcopal support of the newly consecrated bishops of Omaha and Peoria, James O'Connor and John Lancaster Spalding. Bishop O'Connor was even then negotiating with the Burlington and Missouri Railroad for part of its land in Greeley County, Nebraska, as a site for new Catholic colonies. And Spalding, who knew from his experience as a priest in New York the extent of suffering among the destitute immigrants, was also prepared to lend his episcopal endorsement to the western colonization movement.[60]

58. See above, p. 60, n. 22.
59. Sister M. Sevina Pahorezki, O.S.F., *The Social and Political Activities of William James Onahan* (Washington, D.C., 1942), pp. 85, 87.
60. Sister Mary Evangela Henthorne, B.V.M., *The Irish Catholic Colonization Association of the United States* (Champaign, Illinois, 1932), p. 25. This doctoral

The meeting in Chicago was a success, with many delegates in attendance from Iowa, Kansas, Nebraska, Dakota, and Minnesota. Bishop Ireland addressed the assembly and reported to them the encouraging story of his diocesan colonies, some of which were by then three years old. After several additional meetings, the Irish Catholic Colonization Association of the United States was formally organized and legally incorporated in Chicago on May 20, 1879. The articles of incorporation specified that a minimum capital fund of $100,000 would be necessary to undertake a national colonization effort; and it was agreed that this amount would be raised by the sale of stock certificates to be issued by the new corporation.[61]

Bishop John Lancaster Spalding was elected president of the board of directors. With him on the board were thirteen laymen and six bishops. The prelates were Archbishops Gibbons of Baltimore and Williams of Boston, and Bishops Ryan of Buffalo, Spalding of Peoria, Ireland of St. Paul, and O'Connor of Nebraska.[62] The decision to elect three eastern and three western prelates indicates that the founders of the movement realized that a national scheme of colonization demanded the cooperation of Catholics from both regions.

As an eastern priest and a western bishop, John Lancaster Spalding was admirably prepared to see both sides of the question of settling Catholics in the West, and as a writer of unusual clarity he was able to reconcile the apparent differences between the two positions. One year after being elected president of the new association, Spalding published his apologia for colonization, *The Religious Mission of the Irish People and Catholic Colonization.* This treatise, certainly the most distinguished piece of scholarly writing produced by the colonization movement, is still the classical statement of the theology behind Catholic colonization in the West. In its preface the Illinois prelate summarized his thesis:

---

dissertation, directed by Marcus Hansen, offers a detailed survey of the rise and fall of this association between 1879 and 1883. The opposition and support given it by various Catholic periodicals in both the East and the West are carefully analyzed.

61. Ibid., p. 51.
62. Ibid., p. 46.

The general truth which I have sought to develop is that the Irish Catholics are the most important single element in the Church in this country, and that their present surroundings and occupations are, for the most part, a hindrance to the fulfillment of the mission which God has given them [the spread of Catholicism in America]. It follows that all honest attempts to bring about a redistribution of our Catholic population are commendable. This is the object and aim of the Irish Catholic Colonization Association of the United States, which has also led me to write this book.[63]

With this statement Spalding developed a new idea in the literature on colonization—the suggestion that the Irish, numerically dominant in the Church in the United States, should consider themselves Catholic apostles in Protestant America, and that for religious as well as material reasons they should break up their urban concentration and spread out into the rural frontier. Since Illinois was already well settled and it was not possible for Spalding's own diocese to profit by any new colonies, his obvious altruism earned increased support for the new movement.

In bringing about the convocation of the national assembly in Chicago, Bishop Ireland had hoped to remedy the greatest single defect in his Minnesota colonization scheme. As a device for putting Catholics on the land his system was already a success; but he realized that some means had to be found for financing the purchase of western land for the really poor Catholics in the East. So far none of these people had been able to come west; and before they could make the trip some system of extensive, long-term credit had to be devised. After the meetings in Chicago, Bishops Ireland, Spalding, and O'Connor agreed to undertake a lecture tour of the eastern cities for the purpose of selling stock or eliciting gifts for the new association. They set out for New York early in June 1879.[64]

The occasion of their trip was the dedication of the new Cathedral of St. Patrick in New York. Bishop Spalding took advantage

63. Pages 13–14.
64. Henthorne, p. 51.

of the gathering of the nation's leading prelates and invited many of them to an informal meeting at St. Stephen's rectory, the home of Father Edward McGlynn, the popular New York priest whose subsequent espousal of the gospel of Henry George became a *cause célèbre*. Archbishop John J. Williams of Boston and Bishop Stephen V. Ryan of Buffalo were present at this meeting and endorsed the plan of colonization heartily.[65] Bishop Spalding also announced in the Brooklyn *Catholic Review* that the new association had the approval of the Archbishop of New York, Cardinal McCloskey.[66] Spalding's first public address in New York on this trip was delivered at the Young Men's Lyceum. Father McGlynn presided at the lecture, and Bishop Spalding explained the twofold purpose of his tour: to encourage Catholic laborers in the cities to come to the farms of the West, and to encourage Catholics who could afford it to purchase stock certificates in the company then being organized by the association to buy western land for poor settlers. The bishop assured his listeners that this was a respectable business venture which would give the investors a decent return on their money, and that it was not a charity.[67] In this, time proved him correct: none who invested in this association ever lost his capital, and dividend payments were always prompt. As far as it went, the association did good work. This work, however, was considerably limited by the unwillingness of the general public to purchase stock certificates in the new venture.

On June 4 Bishop Spalding addressed a mass meeting at Peter Cooper Union. The press reports of the address [68] indicate that even the New York *Herald,* which usually opposed western movements, was impressed by the plan which Spalding outlined. He discouraged those intending to move into the Deep South or the Far West on the grounds that in the former region Negro competition in the labor market was too formidable and in the latter, scarcity of rainfall made successful farming too hazardous. Hickey's *Catholic Review* was jubilant after the Cooper Union meeting. "Thank

65. Ibid., pp. 49–50.
66. *Catholic Review,* June 7, 1879.
67. New York *Irish Review,* June 7, 1879.
68. Reprinted in full in the *Catholic Review,* June 14, 1879.

heaven that the day [has] come when only the enemies of the Irish and Catholic people such as the New York *Herald,* the owners of New York tenement houses, and the projector of 4000 new tenement houses in Westchester county [are] opposed to Irish Catholic Colonization." [69] Horace Greeley was already dead, but his New York *Tribune,* traditionally fond of Minnesota as a home for those who would go west, commended the plan of Bishop Spalding and added only one constructive criticism—that he had set his sights too low in seeking only $100,000 as the initial capital stock for his association.[70]

After the New York meeting Spalding, accompanied by Ireland and O'Connor, accepted the invitation of Archbishop Williams to address a mass meeting in Boston. His lecture in Boston's Catholic Union auditorium was well attended by both clergy and laity. John Boyle O'Reilly's Boston *Pilot,* endorsing the plan, announced that the meeting had secured subscriptions of $10,000 in a single night.[71] The Boston *Pilot,* the Brooklyn *Catholic Review,* the New York *Irish-American,* and the Philadelphia *ICBU Journal* were the most vigorous supporters of the colonization plan. Regularly each week they reported its progress to their readers and generously offered their editorial columns to promote it.[72] In spite of such widespread endorsement by laity and clergy, however, the association was unable to raise its modest quota of $100,000. Bishop Spalding was keenly disappointed:

> It was thought that when the subject would be brought in all its fullness to the attention of the wealthier and more intelligent Catholics, public spirit and sympathy, however feeble, with the masses of their countrymen would lead them to take an interest in the question or to comprehend the urgent need of helping on the movement. Stronger evidence could not be desired of the dearth of large and enlightened views among wealthy Catholics on the work and wants of the Church in the United States. Even the better sort seem to have little idea of anything that reaches beyond a parish

69. New York *Tribune,* quoted in the *Catholic Review,* June 15, 1879.
70. Quoted in Henthorne, p. 53.
71. *Pilot,* July 12, 1879. See also *ICBU Journal,* August 1879, p. 6.
72. Henthorne, pp. 54–5.

charity. In order to raise the capital stock it was found necessary to hold mass meetings in various cities, so as to give the
poor an opportunity of subscribing for single shares.[73]

In an interview later given to the Dublin *Freeman's Journal,*
Bishop O'Connor stated that less than $10,000 had been subscribed
by men of means, and that the grand total amounted to only
$83,000.[74]

With part of this sum the association bought 10,000 acres of
railroad land in Nobles County, Minnesota, the last of John Ireland's 70,000 acres in that county. The balance of the $83,000
was used to buy 25,000 acres from the Burlington and Missouri
Railroad in Greeley County, Nebraska.[75] The business affairs of
the two settlements were left in the hands of William J. Onahan.
By remote control from his Chicago office this enterprising Irish
politician managed the two colonies with a degree of success.
The Minnesota group was quickly absorbed into the already
flourishing Adrian colony, then being guided by Father C. J.
Knauf. The Nebraska settlements, named Spalding (Spaulding)
and O'Connor, regularly complained to Bishop O'Connor in
Omaha that Onahan's direction of the colonies by mail from
Chicago seriously handicapped their advance.[76] Father Jules
Emile De Vos, pastor at O'Connor, warned Bishop O'Connor that
while Onahan slept, the Burlington line was by-passing the colonies. Onahan assured O'Connor this was mere phantasy: the railroads would definitely go through these settlements.[77] Fearful
that this benefit would be denied them, the Nebraska colonists
continued to appeal to Bishop O'Connor and to Onahan, urging
that land concessions and even large cash gifts should be made

73. Spalding, *The Religious Mission of the Irish People and Catholic Colonization,* pp. 195–6.
74. Dublin *Freeman's Journal,* June 14, 1885, quoted in Henthorne, p. 59.
75. Spalding, p. 196.
76. Letter of W. E. Hannon, cashier of the Spaulding Bank, Spaulding,
Nebraska, to Bishop O'Connor in Omaha, July 12, 1887, in Omaha Chancery
Archives, File 28. (The city was named after John Lancaster Spalding, Bishop
of Peoria, and on maps today is spelled "Spalding.")
77. Letter of William J. Onahan, Chicago, to Bishop O'Connor, Omaha; May
27, 1886, and Onahan to O'Connor, June 3, 1887: in Omaha Chancery Archives,
Colonization File.

to the Burlington and Missouri to get its line through the towns of Spalding and O'Connor.[78] When it finally dawned on Onahan that his vaunted influence with the railroad officials was an illusion, it was too late: in the end the rails went through Greeley Center, leaving the colony towns high and dry. This was very nearly the death blow to the Nebraska colonies, although as rural parishes both settlements survive to the present. Responsibility for the near failure of the Nebraska colonies must rest with Onahan, who kept the bishop convinced that the pastors and settlers were alarmists. If he had offered adequate inducements to the railroad builders early enough, or if at the beginning of the settlements the Nebraska colony planners had secured a promise from the railroads concerning the future route, all would have gone well. When it was announced that the railroad would go through Greeley Center, several merchants in the colony pulled stakes and moved to Greeley.

While Onahan was thus engaged in the task of managing the affairs of the association's colonies, Bishops Spalding, O'Connor, and Ireland were lecturing in cities across the land to secure financial backing for the venture. The popular enthusiasm generated by these gifted orators in the lecture halls of Chicago, Detroit, New York, Philadelphia, Baltimore, and Boston was deceptive. Their auditors regularly wished them well but seldom gave more than moral support.

It has often been remarked, in extenuation of the public reluctance to support this movement, that the Irish in the eastern centers at this time were too poor to buy stock in the plan. It is, of course, beyond doubt that these people had very little cash to spare, and many of them were actually destitute. Yet their failure to support colonization cannot be explained by saying that they simply lacked the necessary money, for they did have enough money to advance the modest amount proposed by Spalding and Ireland. The truth is, they were not convinced of the merits of colonization but on the other hand were deeply convinced of the worthiness of the land reform program then getting under way in Ireland, and their willingness to underwrite the expenses of that program

78. Letter of James R. Connell, a merchant in Spaulding, to Onahan in Chicago, May 21, 1886, in Omaha Chancery Archives, Colonization File.

is proof that they had some money but would expend it only on movements they considered deserving. During the very months that the American colonization subscription campaign for $100,000 fell short of its goal by $17,000, Charles Stewart Parnell toured the United States, speaking on behalf of the newly founded Irish Land League, and collected more than $250,000 from his en- thusiastic Irish-American audiences.[79] A particularly ironical illus- tration of this contrast is the fact that while the two American bishops stumped the East in the belief that the real money was there, the Irish Relief Committee of Rice County, Minnesota, sent Parnell a check for $1,325 to help settle dispossessed Irish cottiers on farms of their own in Ireland.[80] Exactly what the colonizers were trying to do for the Irish in America!

The issue at stake in the eastern lecture tours of Ireland and Spalding was the question of whether or not the rank and file of Catholics of the land were interested enough to buy stock in a settlement plan that had already been tested and proved in the Minnesota laboratory. By this time there was almost no govern- ment land left in Minnesota, and the railroad lands in that state were going rapidly. The settlement of Illinois had long been com- pleted. Hence when Bishop Spalding and one Father P. W. Rior- dan went through Arkansas and Texas in March 1881 prospecting for new colony sites, they were influenced by the purest kind of altruism, a genuine desire to help the really poor urban dwellers who had found no place in the earlier colonies where settlement demanded some capital.[81] If Bishop Spalding found in these re- gions the kind of land he considered suitable, it must have been a disappointment to learn that his financial backing was not ade- quate to cover the purchase price.

This attempt to establish a nationwide colonization association was not abandoned, however, until Ireland and Spalding were thoroughly convinced that the Catholic public would not support the venture. Spalding's biographer, summarizing the accomplish- ments of the association, states that "we must never consider

79. *ICBU Journal* (February 1880), p. 1.
80. Ibid. (August 1880), p. 5.
81. Letter of Onahan to O'Connor, March 21, 1881, in Omaha Chancery Archives, File 28.

the movement a failure." [82] Not the least of its contributions to Catholic immigrant settlement was its appointment of Father John J. Riordan as resident chaplain of Castle Garden and its pledge of $1,000 a year for his support.[83] To its further credit it should be remarked that "while the Association was not organized or carried on as a money-making enterprise, it . . . nevertheless paid the investors six per cent annually in dividends, and . . . at [its] close [returned] to the shareholders the full sum of their original investment with one year's additional interest." [84] An accountant examining the profit and loss ledgers of this organization would pronounce it a success, in that its final balance sheet showed a net profit of a few thousand dollars; similarly, the casual observer, seeing today the thriving parishes at O'Connor and Spalding in Nebraska and Adrian in Minnesota would probably consider the movement which established them a success. Judged from such limited vantage points, it did succeed. On the other hand, if it is compared with the magnificent project envisioned by its founders in 1879, its achievement must be classified as modest indeed.

From the experience Bishop Ireland had gained in Minnesota by 1879, most of the variables in the colonization formula had been determined. In his mode of operation there was no element of risk, no grappling with an unknown factor. But in the national undertaking of 1879 a crucial fact was still to be determined— whether there existed a readiness among Catholics in general to support a large-scale colonization movement by the purchase of stock certificates in the venture. It would appear that the evidence was all in by April 10, 1886, when Onahan, as secretary of the Irish Catholic Colonization Association, announced the annual meeting of that group and stated that the directors intended to close up the affairs of the association that year.[85] The story of the rise and decline of this national colonization venture has been

82. Henthorne, p. 101.

83. Letter of Onahan to O'Connor, October 9, 1883, in Omaha Chancery Archives, file for 1883.

84. Circular letter by W. J. Onahan, addressed to the stockholders, July 25, 1891, quoted in Henthorne, p. 101.

85. Onahan, circular letter to stockholders, April 10, 1886, in Omaha Chancery Archives, Colonization File.

told ably and completely in another place; [86] the summary of its progress here is given only as an illustration of the general principle that Catholic colonization schemes worked best on the diocesan level. On a smaller scale they failed for lack of episcopal backing. On a larger scale they became too unwieldy and too vulnerable to the multitude of internal pressures and organizational hazards that have plagued all nationwide associations since the founding of the federal union. Even the three colonies sponsored by the Irish Catholic Colonization Association (at Spalding and O'Connor, Nebraska, and at Adrian, Minnesota) managed to survive only because in each instance they were under the protection of a solicitous local bishop who gave them effective support after it had been demonstrated that the national association was unable to do so. There appears to be an optimum level within the Church for such settlements, namely the diocesan level. The failure of the national associations proposed in 1856 and 1869, and the short life span of the association begun in 1879, would seem to support this hypothesis.

86. In Henthorne. See n. 60, above.

CHAPTER FIVE

Finance on the Frontier

CRITICS were not lacking to accuse Bishop John Ireland of representing the "railroad interests" when he first encouraged Catholics to settle on the land grants of western rail lines. He was willing to accept such criticism, untrue though it was, because he saw in the railroad the only agency capable of offering credit facilities large enough to finance the western settlement he hoped to sponsor. He knew that previous experiments in colonization had regularly failed for lack of adequate financial resources. Well-meaning directors or priests had too often purchased in their own names large tracts of land, but when crop failures, plagues of locusts, summer droughts, or early frosts had robbed them of the income necessary to make good on their debts, they had been forced to disband their settlements in despair.

Long before the railroads invited Ireland to serve as a land agent, he was searching for some agency with sufficient capital and foresight to underwrite the colonization by white men of that fertile tract vacated by the Indians after the treaty of Traverse des Sioux; hence in 1875 he immediately recognized in the land grants a means of securing long-term financial backing from a well-disposed creditor without taking upon himself the responsibility for owning the lands to be colonized. Never before had any American colonizer been given such advantageous credit facilities, and never again would such opportunities be available after the western railroads completed their generous plan to subsidize wholesale settlement on the plains.

In the East railroads were a convenience; in the West they were a necessity. After 1873 the New York Central brought the welcome advantages of regular schedules, lower costs, and increased speed in freight shipments and passenger travel between Chicago and New York. Such improved transportation facilities, great though they were, represented but one portion of the railroad's contribution to the opening of the West. The western roads actually provided the personnel for permanent settlement beyond the Mississippi and in many places even financed the process of settlement.

The decennial census for 1890 was able to report that the frontier line (areas with a population of less than two persons per square mile) had disappeared in the United States; the principal reason was that the railroads had brought more men and heavy machinery west in two decades than had been carried across the Mississippi by all the wagon trains of the previous generation. In a very literal sense the rail lines were the instruments of western settlement.[1] In the East the rails had followed the established trade and travel routes of an earlier civilization. In the West, following the easy grade of natural water-level routes and mountain passes, or cutting directly across the trackless open prairies, they determined the path of subsequent settlement and dictated the location of farms, towns, and trading centers. "West of the Mississippi the railroads were built in comparatively new and unsettled country, and frequently anticipated by a generation the needs of the region tributary to them." [2]

This decisive role of the railroad in the West is especially apparent in the settling of the Catholic colonies in Minnesota. If the rail lines had not preceded the settlers in western Minnesota, all the agricultural advantages of that region would not have been able to offset the disadvantages of an isolated life and of farming on land-locked prairies without access to a market. In an era before the rails reached the West the plight of one western farmer who raised bumper crops in Minnesota's Red River Valley and then was forced to use them for fuel has already been described.[3] The railroad was the catalyst in the process of converting the po-

1. For a conflicting opinion see Frederick Jackson Turner, *The United States: 1830–1850, the Nation and Its Sections* (New York, 1935), p. 315, in which Turner cautions against overemphasizing the role of the railroad in settling the West. He believes that the railroads entered the West, just as they had the East, *after* being attracted by the economic success of those already on the land.

2. Hedges, "The Colonization Work of the Northern Pacific Railroad," p. 312; Casey and Douglas, *Pioneer Railroad*, p. 159. Both these works offer considerable evidence against the position of Turner mentioned in the preceding note.

3. See above, pp. 3–4.

tential value of prairie land to actual value by providing transportation for harvested crops and by bringing to the West the men who could produce the harvest. Of equal importance in Minnesota, at least for the Catholic colonies, were the credit facilities extended by the rail lines. Using land grant acreage as capital, the railroads in Minnesota after 1876 assumed the function of banks, underwriting the settlement of farmers drawn to that state by the publicity campaigns of the railroads and the Colonization Bureau established by Bishop Ireland in St. Paul.

In 1857 Congress granted 6,000,000 acres of land to four railroad companies in Minnesota Territory.[4] It was specified in the grant that unless the lines were completed in ten years the land would revert to the United States government. The grant was made at the time when Minnesota was experiencing its first financial boom and "all signs pointed to continued and increasing prosperity." [5] But on August 24 the Ohio Insurance and Trust Company of New York failed and the panic of 1857 immediately began. "Before sundown there were suspensions and failures in every considerable town in the whole country. The panic struck Minnesota with extreme violence." [6] City lots in St. Paul became virtually worthless, the population of that city fell almost 50 per cent, and the ambitious plans for railroad building came to a halt.[7]

The four newly chartered railroad companies "could not raise a dollar." One line, the Transit Company, "offered five hundred thousand acres at one dollar an acre, and found no buyers." [8] In the meantime the state of Minnesota had been admitted to the Union. As its contribution to the struggling railroads, the young state, forbidden by its constitution to *lend money* to corporations, devised a plan for *lending its credit* to the extent of $5,000,000.[9] Even this generous provision was not enough to salvage the four

4. Benson *Times* (June 9, 1877), p. 1. The four lines were the Minnesota and Pacific Railroad; the Transit Company; the Root River Railroad Company; and the Minnesota and Cedar Valley Railway. See Folwell, *A History of Minnesota*, 2, 328.

5. Folwell, *1*, 363-A.

6. Ibid.

7. T. M. Newsome, *Pen Pictures of St. Paul, Minnesota, and Biographical Sketches of Old Settlers* (St. Paul, 1886), pp. 675–6.

8. Folwell, *2*, 43.

9. Holmes, *Minnesota in Three Centuries, 4,* 346; Folwell, *2*, 44–5.

Fig. 4. An engine of the Minnesota Valley Railroad

companies. By July 1, 1859, the financial condition of the railroads was again so critical that construction was stopped on all
four lines. The Legislature of 1860 ordered Governor Alexander
Ramsey "to foreclose on behalf of the state all mortgages covering
the properties of the four land grant companies and in his discretion to bid them in for the state at the sale." [10] Ramsey ordered the
foreclosures and "when the transactions were consummated the
state was again in full control in trust of all lands granted for
railroads in 1857 and had to the good 240 miles of graded roadbed." [11]

Although the Transit Company had offered its lands during
the dark days of 1857 for one dollar an acre, it was generally agreed
that the railroad holdings were worth about five dollars an acre.[12]
By four separate statutes enacted on March 10, 1862, the Legislature conveyed all these railroad lands and the franchises of the
four defunct companies to four new corporations "which represented substantially the same interests" as the old companies.[13]
These were the assets which were to be used later in financing the
settlement of John Ireland's colonies.

Before Bishop Ireland began the work of colonization, the St.
Paul and Pacific (one of the beneficiaries of the new acts of 1862)
was selling its land in Swift County for five, six, and seven dollars

10. Folwell, 2, 328.

11. Ibid. At the time the five-million-dollar loan was authorized, the legislature
specified that the state would hold a mortgage on railroad land for any money
advanced. It was also agreed at this time that "upon the completion of any ten
miles of road, ready for superstructure, the governor on satisfactory evidence
thereof was to cause to be issued and delivered (to the railroad companies) bonds
to the amount of one hundred thousand dollars": ibid., p. 46. At this rate, the
240 miles of graded roadbed mentioned by Folwell would have cost the state
$2,400,000, or less, depending on whether or not any of it had been completed
before the loan was authorized.

12. Ibid., p. 43.

13. Ibid., p. 330. The corporate titles of the old railroads and those of their
successors were respectively:

Old	New
The Minnesota and Pacific	The St. Paul and Pacific
The Transit Company	The Winona and St. Peter
The Root River	The Southern Minnesota and the St. Paul and Sioux City
The Minnesota and Cedar Valley	The Minnesota Central

an acre, depending on its quality and proximity to the railroad. Settlers were expected to make a down payment of one year's interest (7 per cent) and were given ten years to pay the balance.[14] During this period the state of Minnesota was offering for sale its school lands in fourteen counties. Its terms were more severe than those of the railroad in that the state demanded an initial down payment of 15 per cent of the principal and 7 per cent interest on the balance, although the state plan gave settlers twenty years to pay.[15]

The credit plan announced by John Ireland for his first colony in 1876 was really the plan already being followed by the St. Paul and Pacific. Catholic colonists taking up these lands may have enjoyed some slight advantage in that Ireland agreed to arrange "the lowest market figure" for any settlers who wished to purchase St. Paul and Pacific Railroad bonds, which were then selling considerably below par but were accepted at face value when offered in payment for railroad lands. Settlers who could take advantage of this arrangement got their land for about $1.50 an acre.[16] Because the bishop himself never owned the land but merely acted as agent for various railroads, the credit terms varied between different colonies, depending on which railroad owned the land and how brisk the land trade was in the different regions.

In Nobles County the Adrian colony lands were on the Sioux Falls Branch of the Sioux City and St. Paul Railroad. And because this land was unusually rich, the trade was brisk. Prices were no higher than in Swift County ($5.00 to $7.50 an acre), but the terms were more stringent. The wealthier settlers were given the great advantage of a 20 per cent discount for cash. For time contracts the terms were one-tenth of the principal and one year's interest on the balance (at 7 per cent) to be paid at the time of settlement; one year's interest (7 per cent) to be paid in advance at the beginning of the second year; one-fourth of the principal plus one year's interest to be paid during the third year and for three ensuing years.[17] In the same colony school lands offered in

14. NWC (February 16, 1876), p. 4.
15. Ibid. (October 23, 1875), p. 5.
16. Ibid.
17. Catholic Colonization in Minnesota (1879), p. 50.

public sale in the spring of 1878 brought from $7.50 to $17.00 an acre.[18]

In Avoca colony, Murray County, on the lands of the Black Hills Branch of the St. Paul and Sioux City Railroad, Ireland arranged a much more lenient credit plan. In this settlement land was offered at from $5.50 to $7.00 an acre. Those who were prepared to pay cash were given a 20 per cent discount. All those who signed time contracts were expected to pay the first year's interest (7 per cent) in advance; the second year's interest in advance; at the end of two years, one-tenth of the principal and a year's interest on the balance; at the end of three years, the same; and at the end of each year thereafter, 20 per cent of the principal and interest on the balance until the entire debt was paid.[19] The advantage of this plan was that it postponed payments on the principal of the debt until after the farmer had harvested his second crop. After Ireland had negotiated this arrangement, Dillon O'Brien predicted that "a quarter-section of land will support a family, pay for itself, leave after seven years a balance in cash, and be worth more than twice its original value." [20]

In the Lyon County colonies (Minneota and Ghent), the Winona and St. Peter Railroad charged a lower rate of interest but expected final payment in a shorter time. Settlers along this route had to pay in advance 10 per cent of the purchase price of the land and 6 per cent interest for one year on the balance; 6 per cent interest for one year, in advance, at the start of the second year; 10 per cent of the purchase price (not the unpaid balance) plus 6 per cent interest during the third year; and 20 per cent of the unpaid balance plus 6 per cent interest each subsequent year.[21]

The most favorable credit terms enjoyed by any of the settlers were those to be found in Big Stone County. Before the railroad

18. Ibid.

19. *The Colony of Avoca, Murray County, Southwestern Minnesota* (1880), p. 13.

20. Ibid., p. 14.

21. Charles E. Simmons to Albert Keep, Chicago (April 2, 1879), p. 2. Simmons was land commissioner for the Winona and St. Peter, and Keep was president of the Chicago and North Western. This letter is on file in the Chicago and North Western Land and Tax Office, Land Contracts Vault, Minnesota.

reached this westernmost county and while its land was still open for claiming under the Homestead, Timber-Culture, and Preemption Acts, the Catholic Colonization Bureau settled 175 families in and around the town of Graceville.[22] After the railroad line entered Big Stone County, James J. Hill, by then general manager of the St. Paul, Minneapolis, and Manitoba Railway Co. (formerly the St. Paul and Pacific), turned over to Bishop Ireland all the indemnity lands of his road in that vicinity, with the understanding that the settlers would not be called on for payment until the railroad could guarantee them full title. In making such liberal terms Hill undoubtedly knew the many legal delays which customarily followed the granting of indemnity lands. In this instance the delay was unusually long. Ten years elapsed before the St. Paul, Minneapolis, and Manitoba acquired clear title to these lands from the federal government.[23] "The settlers, meanwhile, paid no taxes, and finally purchased their lands for a small price, although these had increased in value more than fivefold." [24] When the railroad patents were finally cleared and registered with the state auditor, J. P. O'Connor warned M. J. McDonnell, the bureau's agent in Graceville, against land speculators who might seek to claim some of the bureau's cheap lands ($4.00 an acre) with the intention of reselling them at their real value.[25]

In effect the railroads were acting as bankers for the colonies. Instead of holding mortgages on the land, the railroads merely delayed transferring their own title until the settlers had paid for the land. And because the railroads had a deep interest in multiplying the number of settlers in the West, they were inclined to be lenient with tardy debtors.[26] In contrast, the state of Minnesota ruled that all school lands sold to private settlers would revert to the state as soon as one interest payment was missed.[27]

In addition to subsidizing directly the settlers on colony lands,

22. *Catholic Colonization in Minnesota* (1879), p. 44.
23. J. P. O'Connor to M. J. McDonnell, May 8, 1889, St. Paul Chancery Archives, Diocesan Letters, 1888–89, pp. 161–3.
24. Pyle, *Life of Hill*, 2, 207.
25. J. P. O'Connor to M. J. McDonnell, March 29, 1889, Diocesan Letters, 1888–89, pp. 105–6.
26. Swift County *Advocate* (November 30, 1877), p. 1.
27. NWC (October 23, 1875), p. 5.

the Minnesota railroads indirectly financed the Catholic Colonization Bureau itself. Through Bishop Ireland, who served as a land agent for the railroads, the bureau received a commission of 10 per cent on all lands sold to its colonists. Moreover, the railroads gave the bureau "liberal donations" of town lots in the various colony centers.[28] Some of these sites were used for churches, schools, and rectories, but many of them were held until prices rose and were then sold.[29]

After the death of Dillon O'Brien in 1882, John P. O'Connor, who had until then been manager of the Sweetman colony in Currie, became the executive secretary of the diocesan Colonization Bureau. And with his coming a decided change occurred in the administration of this organization. O'Brien had been a writer, lecturer, and public relations man. O'Connor was a businessman to his fingertips. He could quote railroad regulations to railroad presidents and knew at any given moment the exact status of diocesan finances. The beginning of his term in office came at the end of the active colonization period. By 1882 most of the land in western Minnesota had already been taken up. Moreover, Bishop Ireland was by this time becoming increasingly concerned with the task of building new schools and parishes for the expanding Catholic population in the city of St. Paul.[30] O'Connor was quick to see that a boom in town lots in the western colonies would

28. Letter from Charles E. Simmons to Albert Keep, Chicago (April 2, 1879), p. 2, in Chicago and North Western Land and Tax Office, Land Contracts Vault, Minnesota. See also the land contract signed on April 22, 1876, by Herman Trott, land commissioner for the First Division St. Paul and Pacific, and Benjamin Thompson, agent for Bishop Ireland, in Great Northern Archives, Land Commissioner's office, St. Paul, Vault 602, Documents 17–12. For separate lists of these town lots, see St. Paul Chancery Archives, Diocesan Letters, 1887–88, p. 212, and 1888–89, pp. 201, 214, 233.

29. It will be recalled that this procedure of holding some lots off the market until they had increased in value was proposed as a means of supporting the original colonization scheme endorsed by Daniel O'Connell in Ireland. See above, p. 16.

30. Diocesan Letters, 1887–88, p. 165, in which O'Connor notes that Archbishop Ireland has just paid $32,000 for land in Bryant's Subdivision of the Palace Addition in St. Paul. In the same volume (p. 287) see O'Connor's letter to one "P.J.," stating that Archbishop Ireland is trying to borrow $50,000 on some land he owns in the Midway District. The land is assessed at $300,000 and the Archbishop is willing to pay 8 per cent on his loan.

be a decided advantage to diocesan expansion in the Twin Cities. Money obtained from the sale of business sites in the colonies could be used to build schools, orphanages, and churches in the more populous eastern portion of the diocese. In itself this shift in administrative policy was significant. The colonies were regarded no longer as ends in themselves but as means of meeting diocesan obligations on other fronts. Ireland himself never quite accepted this new mode of thought, but neither did he restrain O'Connor's relentless subordination of colony affairs to diocesan needs.

Whenever a Catholic settler whose lands bordered a colony town line indicated a desire to sell out or surrender his farm, O'Connor would take over the property in the name of the diocese rather than let it revert to the railroad.[31] In a few years he acquired sizable holdings in this fashion, with town lots for sale in Graceville, Currie, Clontarf, Adrian, and Fulda.[32] The biggest business in town lots was conducted at Fulda. Near this town the bureau purchased seven eighty-acre parcels of land in 1887, and as the population of the town grew, quarter sections of farm land at the edge of town were platted into city lots.[33] From time to time O'Connor would suggest to his subagents in the West that circumstances were propitious for starting a "building boom" in their respective towns.[34] At one time when the bureau owned more than 100 lots in Fulda, he wrote to the agent for that colony, "Cannot we work up the matter and give the place a boom?

31. By thus assuming the debt of an individual farmer O'Connor did not primarily intend to underwrite needy settlers, but rather to acquire for the bureau title to land which in the near future could be platted into town lots and sold at a profit.

32. St. Paul Chancery Archives, Diocesan Letters, 1887–88, a deed conveying 106 lots in Clontarf to Father Anatole Oster, p. 1; a letter from J. P. O'Connor to M. J. McDonnell, July 15, 1887, regarding the sale of lots in Graceville, p. 9; a list by J. P. O'Connor of 39 lots in Graceville owned by Bishop Ireland, pp. 159–60; a list by J. P. O'Connor of more than 100 lots owned by Bishop Ireland in Fulda and 12 in Currie, p. 212; a letter from J. P. O'Connor to Father Knauf in Adrian, asking for the tax charges on 5 city lots owned by Bishop Ireland, p. 213.

33. J. P. O'Connor to A. Boysen and Co., May 29, 1888, Diocesan Letters, 1887–88, p. 224.

34. Diocesan Letters, 1887–88, p. 212; also J. P. O'Connor to M. J. McDonnell, July 15, 1887, p. 9; (1888–89), J. P. O'Connor to M. J. McDonnell, April 1, 1889, pp. 109–10.

We will have circulars posted along the line of the Southern Minnesota Railway and advertise in some of the papers." [35] When the Fulda boom was on, O'Connor wrote to the same agent that diocesan funds were low and that any ready cash obtained from the sale of town lots in Fulda would be welcomed in the chancery office.[36] In correspondence of this type O'Connor was always careful to state that these were orders from Bishop Ireland, but because Ireland left more and more of the colony affairs to his manager it is difficult to say just how much of this shift in policy was endorsed by the bishop. It is at least worthy of note, however, that the period of O'Connor's administration coincides with John Ireland's waning interest in the colonies. On occasion the bishop intervened to soften O'Connor's directives (such as the one ordering all delinquent colonists to pay up or be evicted [37]), but in the daily administration of colony affairs the manager's policy prevailed. Undoubtedly in the end O'Connor's business-like methods made the colonization program pay its own way. He came on the scene after the period of settlement; his task was the unpleasant one of supervising collections in the final stages of the colonization project. Had it not been for the sales of town lots engineered by him, the Colonization Bureau would never have been able to meet such extraordinary expenses as those attending the Connemara debacle in Graceville. Some additional income was realized from the five-dollar contribution Bishop Ireland asked from each person settling 160 acres or more,[38] but the great bulk of income must have come from O'Connor's astute marketing of town lots and business sites.

If Bishop Ireland and O'Connor had kept colonization finances separate from general diocesan expenses, it would be possible to report conclusively on the ultimate costs of the colonization program. Since this was not done, it is only possible to say that considering the generous commissions and grants of town lots pro-

35. J. P. O'Connor to William D. Sheehan, April 7, 1888, Diocesan Letters, 1887–88, p. 182. Sheehan, who resided at Madison, Dakota Territory, was the Colonization Bureau's land agent for southwestern Minnesota.

36. J. P. O'Connor to William D. Sheehan, Diocesan Letters, 1887–88, p. 244.

37. J. P. O'Connor to M. J. McDonnell, April 24, 1889, Diocesan Letters, 1888–89, p. 145.

38. Benson *Times* (February 16, 1876), p. 4.

vided by the railroad and the additional lots bought and sold by O'Connor, and considering also that John Sweetman, lacking such liberal railroad subsidies, finally managed to make his colonization program pay its own way,[39] it is more than likely that the larger diocesan project was at least equally successful.

John Ireland could hardly have chosen a less promising time for starting his western colonies than the spring of 1876. This was a period of general discontent in agricultural areas; and in western Minnesota the farmers were just recovering from the disastrous locust plagues of 1873 and 1874 which had cut farm crops so drastically that Governor Davis sent state funds to aid the stricken area.[40] Against such odds it is remarkable that Ireland was able to convince any farmers that the West held a promising future for them. But in his favor there were several other helpful forces, not the least of which were the efforts of the western rail lines to win and hold the good will of the people.

The few small rail lines in Minnesota at that time were hard pressed to protect themselves against the wave of popular antipathy which had already denounced the "big" eastern railroads and was moving west slowly each year. For almost a decade after 1875 the ingenuity of Minnesota's railroad builders in devising ways to counter such popular hostility on the local level was remarkable.

The Granger laws passed by the Minnesota legislature in 1871 and amplified in 1874 were described by Folwell as laws "which the most radical of reformers could hardly have expected." [41] When the first permanent Grange was organized in Minnesota on September 2, 1868,[42] "the leaders of the movement had not contemplated an assault upon railroad abuses." [43] Within the next three years, however, the railroads in that state had received so much adverse publicity that the citizens were aroused and the

39. Several volumes of business ledgers, covering the entire operation of the Sweetman colony, are among the Sweetman Papers in the manuscript division of the Minnesota Historical Society, St. Paul; but a careful search of the St. Paul Chancery Archives has failed to produce similar records for the diocesan Colonization Bureau.

40. Folwell, *A History of Minnesota*, 3, 97–8.

41. Ibid., p. 40.

42. Ibid., p. 38.

43. Ibid., p. 39.

Grange proposed new legislation to regulate the carriers. Extortion, unjust discrimination on rates, abuse of franchises, tax evasion, and restraint of trade were some of the charges made by investigators against the few small roads operating in Minnesota in 1871.[44] In his report the following year, the state railroad commissioner revealed that the railroads had flagrantly violated the laws enacted against them in 1871.[45] That the Legislature had made extraordinary and almost extralegal efforts to help the railroads with the five-million dollar loan of 1858 only increased popular antagonism against the carriers. In 1873 the St. Paul and Pacific defaulted on its bonds, and the general suspicion which had been building up across the country against the much publicized abuses among the big railroads turned to malevolence, and one result of this hostility was the passing by the Minnesota Legislature of its second series of Granger laws in 1874.[46]

These laws, together with the repercussions of the panic of 1873, effectively restrained the extension of railroads in Minnesota for at least three years. At the end of this time most of the local roads were under different management, and the new leaders were well aware of the popular antipathy toward them among the people.[47] Hence, in addition to reorganizing the finances of the various companies, this new leadership sought to win back the good will and confidence of the people. In that program the St. Paul and Pacific led the way. Three of Bishop Ireland's colonies were on their route, and his settlers arrived in the West just as the new policy of conciliation was being adopted by the railroad. The credit advantages that were extended to the settlers and the diocesan bureau were without qualification the greatest of all the accommodations offered by the railroads; but in addition to such financial assistance, the new colonists received countless minor benefits which made their life in the West much more pleasant.

During their first summer on the land very few of the colonists were able to lay in a supply of firewood. It was an exceptional farm which had a sufficient stand of native timber to provide fuel

44. Ibid., p. 40.
45. Ibid., p. 42.
46. Ibid., p. 51.
47. *NWC* (September 11, 1875), p. 6.

for an entire winter. As an accommodation to the settlers the St. Paul and Pacific purchased twenty-five carloads of maple cord-wood in St. Paul and ran a special train to Benson, the most central town in Swift County.[48] There the wood was sold to the colonists for $5.50 a cord, the market price which the railroad had paid for it in St. Paul.[49]

Both the government and the Colonization Bureau had urged the settlers to plant trees on their prairie farms. In addition to serving as windbreaks around western farm buildings, trees were helpful in conserving ground water during dry spells. The editor of the Benson *Times* recommended that each settler plant at least 1,000 saplings. When it became evident that the farmers were convinced of the value of tree planting, the St. Paul and Pacific advertised in the western press that it would transport free of charge from St. Paul to the colonies all the saplings the colonists would plant, and posted the current prices for tree plantings in the St. Paul area:

White willow	$1.50 per 1,000
Cottonwood	3.00 per 1,000
Lombardy poplars	2.40 per 1,000
Yearling box elder	3.00 per 1,000
Yearling soft maple	3.00 per 1,000
1–2 year-old ash	3.50 per 1,000
1–2 year-old poplar	3.50 per 1,000 [50]

A common problem in all early western towns was that of muddy, unpaved streets. The level land did not drain rapidly; long after rainstorms had passed, the black prairie loam held the rain water, and streets and sidewalks became impassable mires. To help the towns along its route to build better streets, the St. Paul and Pacific offered to load its empty "deadhead" freight cars with sand and gravel and agreed to deposit these materials free of charge at the depots along the line.[51]

After the grasshopper invasion of 1877 the same railroad sent

48. Benson *Times* (August 28, 1876), p. 1.
49. Ibid. (September 11, 1876), p. 4.
50. Ibid. (March 22, 1876), p. 4. At this remarkably low rate, some tree plantings cost only ⅓¢ apiece. Even though the species mentioned in this list are all native to Minnesota, the prices quoted are extremely low for such seedlings.
51. Ibid. (July 21, 1877), p. 1.

its agricultural agents into the stricken counties to advise farmers and to direct the operations undertaken to destroy the larvae left by the insects. The road also offered to transport without cost whatever materials the farmers needed to clean up their fields.[52] When J. P. Farley, general manager of this road, notified the settlers that in view of the plague, payments on railroad land would be postponed until the next harvest, the western press and the state government both commended the railroad for its spirit of cooperation.[53]

Loneliness and social isolation were two of the greatest burdens of western life. Travel by ox cart was slow and tedious and few of the settlers owned riding horses. Hence the railroad policy of offering reduced fare tickets to the settlers on national holidays, during State Fair Week, and on other special occasions was received with considerable enthusiasm.[54] To encourage additional good will among the settlers the St. Paul and Pacific also staged a grand ball each year during the winter months, at the Ryan Hotel in St. Paul. The leading citizens in each colony were invited to this affair as guests of the road. Such social highlights in the winter season were eagerly anticipated and widely publicized in the western press after the fortunate guests returned to their respective settlements.[55]

Since it was often one of the largest buildings in town, the railroad depot frequently served as a community center in the earliest years of the colonies. At Ghent, Sunday mass was offered in the depot for some months before the first church could be completed. In De Graff the depot served as a school classroom until the first community school was built. On one occasion a western depot even served temporarily as a grain storage warehouse. After their first harvest in Swift County the colonists lacked sufficient space to store their grain. Private capital and railroad interests were building grain elevators in the West as fast as they could.[56] By June 1876 the St. Paul and Pacific had large elevators at Litch-

52. Ibid. (May 26, 1877), p. 4.
53. Swift County *Advocate* (November 30, 1877), p. 1.
54. Benson *Times* (September 8, 1877), p. 4; (June 23, 1877), p. 4; Worthington *Advance* (November 1, 1877), p. 3.
55. Benson *Times* (February 2, 1877), p. 1.
56. Ibid. (June 12, 1876), p. 4.

field, Delano, Cokato, Atwater, Willmar, Kerkhoven, Benson, and Herman, but the harvests increased faster than the storage space. Hence when the single elevator in Benson was filled with grain from the crop of 1877, railroad officials notified the farmers that the town depot would be boarded up and used to store the excess grain until other dry storage space could be found.[57] In time the railroad control of grain terminal facilities was to lead to the infamous abuses of the "wheat ring," [58] but during the first years of colonization the settlers learned to look on the local railroads as their benefactors.[59] By their enlightened policies of serving the public, Minnesota railroad builders after 1875 provided many small financial advantages and even a few social amenities that were a significant contribution to the stability of the frontier colonies.

Signs of the agrarian revolt in the West were apparent in Minnesota as early as 1880, but because of several peculiar economic advantages the western counties of this state did not join in the chorus of rural discontent until after 1885. Even in the late 70's Minnesota wheat farmers were aware that discriminatory freight rates, market pools, and deliberate undergrading of their product were cheating them of part of their deserved income.[60] However, during the same years other economic factors were working to the advantage of the farmers who had just taken up "new" land in the western counties.

Until 1875 the center of wheat growing in Minnesota had been the eight southeastern counties,[61] but after this date the western counties took the lead. Soil in the older area had been depleted by continuous wheat growing, whereas the virgin soil of the west

57. Ibid. (October 20, 1877), p. 1.

58. Henrietta M. Larson, *The Wheat Market and the Farmer in Minnesota, 1858–1900*, Columbia University Studies in History, Economics, and Public Law, 122, No. 2 (1926), p. 80. This work is an extremely detailed study of the many complex forces which affected the wheat market in Minnesota during the last four decades of the 19th century. It is the source from which almost all of the material in this section is taken.

59. Swift County *Advocate* (November 30, 1877), p. 1.

60. Larson, pp. 116–17.

61. *Annual Report of the Minnesota Commissioner of Statistics* (1876), p. 56, quoted in Larson, p. 119, n. 4.

promised a succession of several bumper crops before it reached
a similar stage of exhaustion. Diversified farming was being forced
on the eastern counties at this time. Fortunately, the conversion
to dairy farming, stock raising, and planting of oats and corn in
this region coincided with an improved market for these products
in the new cities that were then making their appearance in eastern Minnesota. Because of such happy circumstances, "the change
[from wheat farming to diversified farming] was not a hardship
for the [southeastern] farmers." [62]

At precisely the same time that this shift in the wheat-growing
area occurred in Minnesota, the main outline of the railway
system in that state was also being completed. One of the most
obvious advantages of this new rail network was the lower freight
rates which resulted from the greater efficiency and heavier pay
loads. Between 1875 and 1885 in Minnesota "there was a significant decrease in [railroad freight] rates. The average for all roads
in the state fell from 2.523 cents a ton mile in 1875 to 1.460 cents
in 1885." [63] Not only were rates lower, but almost every farmer
in the newly opened western counties had immediate access to
a steady market. By 1881 the state railroad commissioner reported "that there was hardly a cultivated farm in the state
from which the farmer could not drive to the railroad station and
return in a day." [64] As a result of such improved transportation
facilities Minneapolis and Duluth became primary wheat markets.
Before 1880 Minnesota farmers had to rely on Milwaukee and
Chicago as the closest dependable wheat markets for their grain.
However, "by 1880 Minneapolis was the largest milling center in
the United States," [65] and in the opinion of the best authority on
this subject, "The change which more than any other affected
Minnesota's wheat trade in the late seventies and eighties was the
rise to a position of importance of the local primary markets,
Minneapolis and Duluth." [66]

62. Larson, p. 119.
63. Ibid., p. 122.
64. *Annual Report of the Minnesota Railroad Commissioner, 1881,* in *Minnesota
Executive Documents, 1881, 1,* 15; quoted in Larson, p. 121, n. 3.
65. *Internal Commerce of the United States, 1884,* p. 116, quoted in Larson,
p. 127, n. 4.
66. Larson, p. 126.

The proximity of the new western wheat lands, the increased railroad facilities, and the abundant supply of water power from St. Anthony Falls all helped make Minneapolis the new milling center of the nation at the time when Bishop Ireland's colonists were harvesting their first crops. The deciding factor in the rise of this Minnesota city to its leading rank in flour production, however, was the new milling process which was invented and perfected by three or four Minnesota millers after 1870.[67] "The new-process milling, which was developed in the state [Minnesota], made a change in the relative value of winter and spring wheat in favor of Minnesota, the great spring-wheat state." [68]

At that time almost the entire wheat crop in Minnesota was sown to spring wheat. On the market, however, spring wheat regularly brought less than the tougher winter wheat, which was considered superior for milling purposes. The difference in value was due largely to the imperfect milling methods then in vogue. Henrietta Larson, in her detailed study of wheat marketing in Minnesota, has summarized the complexities of this technical problem and its economic consequences.

> Spring wheat has a brittle bran which is easily broken. The bran of winter wheat, on the contrary, is tough and resists grinding. The skin of the former, owing to the ease with which it is pulverized, was separated with difficulty by the old milling methods. As a result, spring-wheat flour was darker and gathered moisture more readily than that made of winter-wheat; its bread-making and keeping qualities were, therefore, lower. Consequently, its price was less than the price of winter-wheat flour.[69]

Any improvement in milling technique that would advance the market value of spring wheat, Minnesota's leading crop, would have been a great advantage to the western grain growers. During the 60's a miller named Archibald at Dundas, Minnesota, experi-

67. Ibid., p. 118.
68. Ibid.
69. *Report of the Minnesota Bureau of Labor Statistics, 1891–92,* quoted in Larson, p. 128, n. 3. See also W. C. Edgard, *The Story of a Grain of Wheat* (New York, 1903), for further details on the new-process milling techniques. See also Folwell, *A History of Minnesota, 3,* 135–8.

mented with a new process for grinding spring wheat. He discovered that by grinding slowly and loosely, by keeping the millstones smooth, and by regrinding the flour, he could produce a superior grade of white flour from spring wheat. "The value of this method lay in the slow and loose grinding, which did not pulverize the bran but broke it into larger particles so that it could be separated from the rest." [70] Using this method, Archibald was the first miller to market white flour made from Minnesota spring wheat at a price higher than for winter wheat flour.[71]

As the reputation for the Minneapolis-produced flour increased, together with exports from that city, Minnesota growers of spring wheat found that competition among western wheat buyers also increased. In 1878 Minneapolis shipped its first direct exports of flour (109,183 barrels) to foreign countries.[72] By 1879 English, German, Belgian, and Dutch bakers were importing thousands of barrels of Minnesota flour each year, in spite of the opposition of native millers in these countries. "By 1884 one fifth of the total flour exports of the United States were shipped from Minneapolis." [73]

The competition among wheat buyers in Minnesota became so great that in 1876 the Minneapolis Millers' Association (which had existed before but had been small and ineffective) was formally reorganized.[74] This agency was called into activity to supervise the purchase, grading, and storage of Minnesota wheat on a systematic basis, so that the Minneapolis mills would be assured a regular and adequate supply of wheat. This association was to operate for an entire decade (1876–86), in which period it brought to the farmers of western Minnesota the advantages of a standard grading system and the assurance of a steady and reliable local market. Unfortunately, the increased efficiency of the new system eventually began to work against the wheat producers and to eliminate almost all competition in the buying of Minnesota wheat. But before this stage was reached, the Minneapolis millers had a

70. *Northwestern Miller* (September 7, 1883), p. 22, quoted in Larson, p. 129, n. 2.
71. Larson, p. 129.
72. Ibid., p. 133.
73. Ibid.
74. Ibid.

decade of huge profits and the wheat farmers, while conscious
that the milling interests were taking advantage of them, were
receiving larger checks each year for their wheat crops and were
not sufficiently aware of the ultimate consequences of the unfair
price system to raise a public clamor, although throughout these
years there were occasional individual protests against the association's monopoly.

In time the western counties came of age. Their land was injured by several years of successive wheat cropping; movements
which began as efficiency measures to systematize wheat buying
ended by restraining competition, to the great loss of the wheat
producer; railroads, chastened by the memory of the Granger laws
in the early 70's, hesitated to enter the grain business themselves
but were forced to make liberal rate concessions and rebates to
hold the trade of the big milling interests; and in periods of restricted credit farmers with bumper crops but no storage space
realized their utter dependence upon the milling and grain-
handling interests which owned the elevators and mills along
the western rail lines. However, it took time—in this instance at
least ten years—before the wheat farmers in Minnesota began to
feel the effects of these harmful forces in the market.[75]

After 1885 there was strong popular demand that the Millers'
Association be replaced by an open market and grain exchange
under the direction of the Minneapolis Chamber of Commerce.
The wave of agrarian discontent that had hit other areas of the
West as early as 1875 finally rolled into Minnesota, but not until
the western wheat farmers had had a decade of good going, with
reasonable if not handsome wheat prices, rapidly increasing land
values, and a succession of good harvests. The Catholic colonists
sponsored by Bishop Ireland were in a peculiar position to enjoy
these advantages. They came into the West just as the railroads
arrived, purchased virgin land at minimal prices, were given
all the advantages of a lenient credit system, and in general enjoyed a bull market for their main crop during their first decade
on the prairie. Grasshoppers, blizzards, early frosts, and dry spells

75. Swift County *Monitor*, December 28, 1899, quoted in Stanley Holte Anonsen, *A History of Swift County* (Benson, Minn., 1929), p. 23. Folwell, *A History
of Minnesota, 3,* 160–1, 211.

notwithstanding, the Catholic Colonization Bureau of St. Paul sponsored its program of western settlement at a singularly propitious time.

It took John Ireland a long time to realize, and an even longer time to admit, that poor people could not join his colonies. He had arranged a most favorable credit system for the purchase of land from the railroad, he had assigned competent agricultural and financial advisers to direct the colonists, and he had picked well-qualified pastors to assist the settlers in the many problems contingent on moving families into the West. But he was never able to secure enough funds to underwrite the many additional but necessary expenses of poor people who applied to him for aid. He could only accept in the colonies those farmers who were able to meet these additional expenses from their own capital resources.

The first and by no means least expense encountered by farmers moving west was that of railroad transportation. Within Minnesota the colonizing railroads agreed to grant free transportation over their lines to any family settling on their lands. Persons coming from out of state, however, had to pay their own fares to the Minnesota border.[76] When the Avoca colony opened in 1879, Dillon O'Brien issued a printed list of railroad fares for passage from eastern cities to St. Paul:

From New York	to St. Paul		$24.00
" Philadelphia	" "	"	24.00
" Montreal	" "	"	26.00
" Toronto	" "	"	23.00
" Buffalo	" "	"	23.00
" Cleveland	" "	"	20.00
" Chicago	" "	"	12.00
" Milwaukee	" "	"	9.00 [77]

A family of four could hardly expect to spend less than $100 in getting to its land in Minnesota. At the opening of the colonies

76. There was one exception to this rule. The Chicago and North Western System extended from Chicago, through LaCrosse, to Dakota Territory. Settlers taking any of its lands in Minnesota were allowed free passage from Chicago to their destination. See John Sweetman's pamphlet *Farms for Sale.*

77. *The Colony of Avoca, Murray County, Southwestern Minnesota* (1880), p. 22.

Bishop Ireland, as noted above, had suggested that no settlers should move west without a minimum capital of $400.[78] Later, John Sweetman announced that he had discovered through experience that settlers needed between $400 and $500 before they could hope to succeed on the land.[79] Neither Ireland nor Sweetman considered transportation costs as part of this basic figure, hence both estimates should have been increased by at least $100; but even then they would have been drastically lower than the amount really needed for a modicum of comfort and a reasonable amount of farm machinery.

In an attempt to bring the official estimates of settlement costs into line with the bishop's announcement, Dillon O'Brien prepared an itemized account of expenses; even after paring each item to the lowest possible figure, his calculations were still slightly in excess of $400. This budget allowed no money for land payments, seed, clothing, medicines, or luxuries, and it assumed that the farmer would do all his own work, including that of building his house. Even the convenience of having one of the association's $200 prefabricated houses was denied those settlers who hoped to get through their first year on $400. "The poor man's temporary house" that went with this budget was a frame shanty (16 × 18) and was estimated by O'Brien to cost $38.75.

1600 feet of lumber	$25.00
2 windows, 2 doors	6.50
Shingles	7.25
Total	$38.75 [80]

The interior furnishings of such a house were expected to cost $43.00, or slightly more than the house itself:

Cooking stove	$25.00
Crockery	5.00
Chairs	2.00
Table	2.00
3 bedsteads	9.00
Total	$43.00

Draft oxen and farming implements were even more expensive:

78. *NWC* (January 22, 1876), p. 1.
79. Sweetman, "The Sweetman Colony," p. 63.
80. *Catholic Colonization in Minnesota* (1879), p. 35. The next five tables of expenditures are taken from the same source, pp. 34 f., 38.

Yoke of oxen weighing from 3,200 to 3,400 lbs.	$100.00
Breaking plow	23.00
Wagon	75.00
Total	$198.00

The cost of feeding a family of four and of heating their house for a year was computed by O'Brien at $100:

30 bushels of wheat ground into flour at $1.00 a bushel	$ 30.00
Groceries	15.00
1 cow for milk	25.00
Fuel	30.00
Total	$100.00

According to this severely limited estimate no settler could hope to spend less than $409.75 for the bare necessities of life in the West during his first year:

House	$ 38.75
Fuel	30.00
Furniture	43.00
Oxen and tools	198.00
Food and cow	100.00
Total	$409.75

In working out such a table of expenses O'Brien was still under the impression that poor people, chiefly unemployed eastern laborers, might somehow manage to move west if only the costs were low enough. It is unlikely that many of the settlers who did come were willing to accept the mean living conditions and increased manual labor which were corollaries of this "poor man's budget." O'Brien recognized this and published a second budget entitled "What a Man with Moderate Capital Can Do":

Three horses	$ 375.00
One sulky plow	70.00
Seeder	65.00
Harrow	12.00
Harvester and self-binder	285.00
Horse rake and mower	125.00
Wagon	75.00
Total	$1,007.00

When the Irish Catholic Benevolent Union in Philadelphia began its colonization program in southwestern Virginia in the spring of 1878, it recommended that all prospective settlers should have a cash reserve of at least $500. One year after the foundation of the colony, a settler wrote back to the parent society and suggested that future colonists should come with no less than $1,000 in cash reserves.[81] John Sweetman, after five years in Minnesota, reached the same conclusion. "We do not recommend anyone who has a family to attempt settling here unless he has capital of $1000." [82] In his last colonization brochure Sweetman warned that a minimum of seven hundred dollars was necessary for any man intending to take up farming in the West.

1st payment on 80 acres	$ 80.00
Frame house, 14 × 18	150.00
Lumber for barn roof	10.00
No. 9 cooking stove and furniture	22.00
House furniture	30.00
Breaking plow	16.00
Wagon	52.00
Harrow	7.50
Small tools and sundries	32.50
Yoke of oxen	120.00
Cow	30.00
Food and fuel for one year	150.00
Total	$700.00 [83]

Considering the economic status of the Minnesota colonists and the types of homes they had left in the East, it is unlikely that many of them would have been satisfied with the unplastered frame shanties which O'Brien said could be built for $38.75. One enterprising settler in the Avoca colony contracted for a more substantial home 16 × 24, "a story and a half high, with a T. addition, and a cellar 12 × 16." This house, with three rooms upstairs, a hall, two rooms downstairs, a hall and a pantry, and finished in plaster, cost $355. Of this sum $280 was for materials and $75 was for labor.[84]

81. *ICBU Journal* (May 1879), p. 1.
82. *Farms for Sale*, p. 4.
83. Ibid.
84. *The Colony of Avoca* (1880), p. 19.

The scanty budget of $400 originally suggested by John Ireland and Dillon O'Brien was intended for poor laborers; but few poor laborers reached Minnesota. The farmers who did come were in search of bigger farms and were prepared to buy the machinery necessary to cultivate large acreages. Hence Sweetman's revised table of expenses or O'Brien's estimate for a "Man with Moderate Capital," each demanding $1,000, is a reliable approximation of the costs of settlement during the first year on the land.

The immediate profits to be reaped from prairie wheat farming were available to all who had enough initial capital to take up land in the West. But for every small farmer or laborer who could afford this move there were dozens who could not. Each day's mail brought Dillon O'Brien requests from the "deserving poor" for help in getting to the western colonies. Referring to such letters Bishop Ireland wrote to Martin Griffin, editor of the *ICBU Journal*, on January 28, 1877, "I regret that I cannot advise very poor people to come to our colony. Perhaps some day in the near future." [85] Unlike other colonization efforts sponsored by Catholic societies, the Catholic Colonization Bureau of St. Paul was not a joint-stock company. Its modest budget, obtained from land-sale commissions and the small assessment levied on each settler, was sufficient to cover only office expenses, salaries, and the printing costs entailed in administering the program. The task of supplying credit for the purchase of land was left to the railroads, banks, and individual settlers.

As soon as reports drifted back to St. Paul concerning the good harvests in Swift County in 1876, public confidence in Bishop Ireland's first colony rapidly increased. It was generally recognized that the new railroad and wheat-shipping facilities in western Minnesota had already enhanced the chances for success in the settlement project. Speculators were not wanting who would readily have paid more than the asking price for colony lands; [86]

85. John Ireland to Martin I. J. Griffin, St. Paul. January 28, 1877, Griffin Papers. The present study is greatly indebted to Sister Joan Marie Donohoe, S.N.D., for her kindness in referring the writer to many such helpful references among the Griffin Papers.

86. J. P. O'Connor to M. J. McDonnell, March 29, 1889, St. Paul Chancery Archives, Diocesan Letters, 1888–89, pp. 105–6.

but Ireland and O'Brien refused to do business with them. At this time a public-spirited citizen of Rochester, Minnesota, one William O'Mulcahy, proposed the organization of a joint-stock company as a means of underwriting the settlement of indigent people on some of the colony lands still not claimed in Swift County. O'Mulcahy reasoned that poor persons who were willing to work hard could quickly repay any backers who were prepared to advance them the initial capital necessary for starting a wheat farm in Swift County. Undoubtedly the impetus for this project came to O'Mulcahy when he attended the Irish Catholic Benevolent Union convention in Cleveland in the fall of 1876. At that meeting plans had been discussed for financing the rural settlement of needy Irish immigrants.[87]

O'Mulcahy was well known in Irish circles in Minnesota. His project was endorsed by both Bishop Grace and Bishop Ireland. In undertakings of this type it was never hard to secure attendance at the first two or three grandiloquent convocations; and after a few months of preliminary organization a convention of Minnesota's leading Irish Catholics was assembled in Minneapolis in January 1877, with Bishop Ireland presiding. The bishop and Father Swift, pastor in the Swift County colony, were the principal speakers. They addressed the delegates on the regulations governing their colonization program and recommended O'Mulcahy's project as a worthy means of subsidizing those needy settlers who could not be accommodated by the existing plan.

As a result of this meeting the Minnesota Colonization Company was organized and on February 15, 1877, was incorporated under the general laws of Minnesota.[88] The articles of incorporation specified that "the general nature of the business of said Corporation shall be the buying and selling of tracts of land in said State of Minnesota and assisting needy and deserving persons in settling thereon." [89] The capital stock of the new company was set at $25,000 and was to be obtained by the public sale of 2500

87. *ICBU Journal* (December 1876), p. 1.
88. *NWC* (March 31, 1877), p. 3. Although this new corporation (The Minnesota Colonization Company) took a name similar to Bishop Ireland's organization (The Catholic Colonization Bureau of St. Paul), the two were entirely separate organizations. See Moynihan, "Archbishop Ireland's Colonies," p. 216.
89. *NWC* (March 31, 1877), p. 3.

stock certificates at $10 each.[90] Bishops Grace and Ireland each
purchased ten shares of stock in the new company.[91] *McGee's
Illustrated Weekly* (New York) ran a feature article on the new
project and offered to take up fifty shares of stock as its vote of
confidence in the undertaking.[92] In general the new company
enjoyed a favorable press throughout the nation.[93]

Then came the routine work of turning such voluble public en-
dorsements into cash subscriptions. This was another matter.
Following the standard procedure adopted in such public campaigns for funds, the *Northwestern Chronicle* promised to supply
its readers with periodic lists of new stockholders. For a few
months the lists were published as promised; but as the scarcity
of subscriptions became more embarrassing, the lists were dropped.
By June 1 a total of 345 shares (worth $3450) had been pur-
chased.[94] The promoters of the new company saw in the Molly
Maguire riots and in the violence attending the Baltimore and
Ohio strike in July graphic reasons why public support should
come to the aid of the laboring class. These "deeds of blood and
arson will leave [a] red mark upon the brow of labor forever." [95]
Much of the publicity at this time was directed toward the unemployed eastern laborers themselves, enumerating the injustices
under which they suffered and contrasting the benefits of independent farm life in the West.[96] The directors of the new company never properly appreciated the fact that there was no need
to convince poor people of the advantages of becoming independent land owners. The persons who were to benefit by the plan
of resettlement were not the people who were in a position to buy
stock. The Minnesota Colonization Company, like so many of its
contemporaries, dissipated its energies by not defining clearly
the direction of its sales appeal.

This appeal was always confused. None of the leaders was quite
sure whose help he was trying to enlist. When the company was

90. Ibid.
91. Ibid. (May 26, 1877), p. 5.
92. Ibid. (August 25, 1877), p. 4.
93. Ibid.
94. Ibid. (May 26, 1877), p. 5.
95. Ibid. (August 25, 1877), p. 4.
96. Ibid. (August 11, 1877), p. 4; (August 25, 1877), p. 4.

organized, the price of stock certificates was kept low, so that persons in modest circumstances could buy shares; [97] and subsequent experience was to demonstrate that persons in this category supplied the bulk of the capital for ventures like this. But as it became apparent in the summer of 1877 that the stock was not selling fast enough, the *Northwestern Chronicle* reminded that often mentioned but seldom seen group of "wealthy Catholics," "We have a great number of well to do Catholics who can and should lend their active aid to the colonization movement." [98] To impress possible investors from this group with the soundness of the project, it was solemnly announced that dividends on company stock would "not exceed twelve per cent per annum." [99] Inquirers who wondered what would happen if the poor settlers tired of farm life were assured, "Should the person so located, for any reason, fail to fulfil his contract, the improved land is always worth more than the actual outlay, and in this manner, shareholders are protected from the loss of stock invested." [100] In spite of such assurances that this was to be a sound business investment and not a charity, stock sales continued to be disappointingly slow. Subsequent lists of contributors showed that the "well to do Catholics" were not interested in the project. Purchases of one, three, or five shares were most common; only four persons bought more than ten shares. The two largest blocks of stock (twenty-five shares each) were purchased by Anthony and P. H. Kelly, two brothers who were prominent wholesale grocers in St. Paul and Minneapolis.[101] The sharp-tongued Martin Griffin, disappointed at the slow sales and irritated by the emptiness of earlier convention promises, reminded "the sleepy-headed organizers and Convention delegates [to] stop nodding and bobbing and open their eyes wide enough to see that the colonization movement is getting successful and popular." [102] Unfortunately,

97. Ibid. (April 14, 1877), p. 4.
98. Ibid. (August 11, 1877), p. 4.
99. Ibid. (October 27, 1877), p. 8.
100. Ibid. (May 26, 1877), p. 5.
101. Ibid. (May 26, 1877), p. 5.
102. *ICBU Journal* (April 1877), p. 1. Griffin is here speaking explicitly of the ICBU delegates who spoke so eloquently at the 1876 convention and then failed to bring in the promised subscriptions for the colonization stock company in Philadelphia.

its popularity was considerably greater than the success mentioned
by Griffin.

In an address to the newly formed "Friends of Ireland" Dillon
O'Brien warned his audience that their excessive concern for conditions in the homeland weakened their ability to meet the more
immediate problems of fashioning a new life for themselves in
America.[103] Commenting on the same division of loyalty, an editorial in the *Northwestern Chronicle* noted rather bitterly that
the Fenian "Skirmishing Fund" then being collected among Irish-
Americans had already passed the $36,000 mark, while the deserv-
ing cause of colonization went begging for support.[104] The same
writer caustically admonished his Irish confreres, "the sums an-
nually wasted in useless parades might be turned to a far better
account in settling poor men on the land." In October 1877, in
order to bolster the selling campaign, Dillon O'Brien, although
he was not an official in the new company, agreed to deliver a
series of lectures in Minnesota recommending the venture to the
Irish in that state.[105]

In spite of the slow sale on stock certificates the company went
ahead with its plans. By July 1877 it had purchased 4,046 acres
of railroad land in Swift County.[106] By the very fact that it was
allowed to purchase railroad lands at the old price arranged two
years previously by Bishop Ireland (less than $5.00 an acre in
this instance), the young company considerably improved its
weak financial condition. Only a down payment was needed to
gain possession of the land; and no matter what other troubles
arose, these lands could always be sold for more than the purchase
price.[107]

During the summer of 1877 the company began settling its
families of indigent colonists on eighty-acre tracts in Swift County.
In several respects the terms of settlement were more generous
than those prevailing in Bishop Ireland's colonization program.

103. *NWC* (September 1, 1877), p. 6.
104. Ibid. (August 11, 1877), p. 4.
105. Ibid. (October 27, 1877), p. 4.
106. Ibid. (July 7, 1877), p. 4.
107. Ibid. (October 27, 1877), p. 4. In this article, written one year after the
opening of the Swift County colony, the writer stated that the lands in that colony
had doubled in value in twelve months.

He loaned no money for houses. O'Mulcahy's group advanced each settler thirty dollars' worth of lumber for his house. Ireland, as agent for the railroad, asked a down payment of one year's interest at the time of settlement. The new company asked the settler for no money on land or lumber "until the first day of December following his second harvest." [108] However, as a protection for its investment O'Mulcahy's company insisted that "during each one of the two summers . . . preceding his second harvest, the settler will be obliged to break upon his land twenty additional acres for which he agrees to ask no payment should he afterward fail to complete his contract for the final purchase of the land." [109] The task of breaking twenty acres each summer was a sizable one and prevented the company settlers from taking on such occasional part-time jobs around the colony as were open to the other colonists.

There is no exact record of how many poor families took advantage of this plan offered by the Minnesota Colonization Company. One commentator gives twenty families as the total.[110] The final official report on the company's operations was published in July 1879. In it the secretary stated that the company had only 480 acres of unsold land.[111] Presumably this meant that 3566 acres had been sold (out of the original tract of 4046). Since each family was given an eighty-acre tract, it would follow that about 45 families had been settled between July 1877 and July 1879. There is no record that the company ever bought any other tract of land. And although the stock sold by the group never approached the proposed amount of $25,000,[112] the company was enabled to pay

108. *ICBU Journal* (February 1878), p. 7.
109. Ibid.
110. Sister Joan Marie Donohoe, S.N.D., *The Irish Catholic Benevolent Union* (Washington, D.C., 1953), p. 129. This work is a recently published dissertation, covering in great detail the entire life span of the ICBU. For the most part its material has been gathered from the files of the *ICBU Journal* in Philadelphia. The extent of Sister Joan Marie's research can be appreciated only by one who has tried to synthesize the far-ranging interests of this very articulate journal. I am greatly indebted to Sister Joan Marie for her several helpful letters and countless valuable suggestions on where pertinent material might be found for the present study.
111. *ICBU Journal* (July 1879), quoted in Donohoe, p. 130.
112. Donohoe, p. 125, adds an extra digit in saying that "stock to the amount of 25,000 shares at ten dollars a share was sold." In reality there were only 2500

its way and give its shareholders a good profit because of the generous credit terms afforded by the railroad. All the company had to do was collect enough money to make the down payment and one interest payment on the land. After that the automatic increase in the value of western lands, the breaking supplied by the settlers (worth $2.50 per acre and not charged against the company), and the annual crops all assured the solvency of the parent group.

Writing in 1880, Bishop Spalding called the company a success and cited it as a modest example of what could be achieved on a much larger scale by the projected Irish Catholic Colonization Association: "A joint-stock company, similar in every respect to the one of which I have spoken, except that its capital is smaller and its aims local, was organized in St. Paul three years ago; and the colony which it has founded is thoroughly successful, while the property which it now holds represents more than double the amount of capital originally invested in the business." [113] Within these limits, the Minnesota Company was completely successful. But the unpleasant fact is that this company was originally established in order to settle poor people on the land, and after two years of work it had settled only forty-five families at most. How many of these left the land later cannot be estimated. On the basis of the heavy mortality rate in similar settlements of assisted immigrants, it is reasonable to assume that the number who turned back from the plow was much higher than among other types of settlers. In the spring of 1879 the Catholic Colonization Bureau in St. Paul ran several newspaper advertisements, trying to rent "one thousand acres of land, well-ploughed, all ready for seed, situated near elevators and churches in Swift County." [114] This was Dillon O'Brien's bureau, the group which never farmed any land in its own name. How did it acquire a thousand acres of broken and ploughed land? It is highly probable that these were farms which were originally claimed by the assisted settlers of

shares authorized by the articles of incorporation (*NWC*, March 31, 1877, p. 3); and less than half this amount was ever sold.

113. Spalding, *The Religious Mission of The Irish People*, pp. 196–7.

114. *NWC* (March 1, 1879), p. 16; (March 8, 1879), p. 16; (March 15, 1879), p. 16.

the Minnesota Colonization Company and which had now re-
verted to the sponsors of that project. In spite of its admirable and
charitable motivation, the project made an extremely modest contribution to the total pattern of colonization in Minnesota.[115]

The failure of this company underscores in a way the fact that
the general success of the Minnesota colonies lay in the recruit-
ment of capable farmers who were able to advance without outside help. The history of this short-lived company, however, is
chiefly significant as an illustration of the reluctance with which
churchmen and Catholic lay leaders came to realize that the Irish
in America were very unimpressed by all the plans to get them or
their money into western colonies. Such shrewd observers as John
Boyle O'Reilly and Martin Griffin, who knew the history and the
character of the Irish better than most of their contemporaries,
concluded very early in the colonization movement that trained
farmers with a little capital were the best prospects for western
settlements. Both these writers urged the leaders of colonization
to give up their fond hope of recruiting poor laborers as colonists.
In the end the colonizers were forced to admit the wisdom of this
advice, but not until several such failures as O'Mulcahy's had
demonstrated the impossibility of getting popular support for the
benevolent type of colony.

In one important respect the colonies founded by Bishop Ireland resembled the earlier settlements of Brigham Young in Utah.
Both foundations combined a strong and specifically religious appeal with a more general appeal, secular in nature, in the form
of unusually attractive land. Historians have not failed to comment on the dual motives, religious and economic, which drew so
many Mormons to the watered valleys of the Wasatch Range after
1847. A similar combination of motives, spiritual and material,
inclined many Catholics of a later day to answer the call of Bishop
Ireland to western Minnesota. He was, it is true, offering them
unparalleled opportunities to practice their religion close to a
Catholic church; but he was also inviting them to occupy some

115. For a much more sanguine view of the achievements of this company see
Donohoe, p. 128.

of the richest land on the continent, and at a price far below its potential value.

Wheat, the key to the western economy, could not be planted on prairie lands until a year after the virgin sod was first turned. It was possible, however, for settlers in their first year to plant flax seed without breaking the surface of the soil.[116] Dillon O'Brien estimated, on the basis of previous yields, that if ten acres of flax were sown the first spring, a cash crop of $100 could be harvested in the fall. This was the only money income a settler could expect from the land in his first year. His vegetable garden, while it produced valuable staples for the family diet, brought in no cash. During harvest time a man might also earn between $40 and $60 working for neighbors with larger fields under cultivation.[117]

Many unmarried farmers and occasionally even families left their colony farms after the harvest season and spent the winter months in St. Paul.[118] This arrangement gave the farmers the financial benefits of working as laborers and gave their families the welcome advantages of better schools and the comforts of urban living for at least part of the year. Even within the colonies themselves, day laboring jobs on the railroads were open during the first years of western settlement. Work on the track-laying crew paid $1.50 per day; [119] once the rails were down, many other jobs opened up in each colony. The Irish settlers around De Graff were especially quick to take up railroad jobs as station masters, telegraph operators, and grain elevator managers.[120] The Irish settlements were also the ones in which business establishments sprang up most quickly.[121] Within one year of its establishment, the De Graff colony had a depot, flour mill, elevator, brick yard, four

116. Anonsen, *History of Swift County*, pp. 16–17.
117. *Catholic Colonization in Minnesota* (1879), p. 35; *The Colony of Avoca* (1880), p. 17.
118. Benson *Times* (April 24, 1877), p. 1; (September 8, 1877), p. 4; (November 24, 1877), p. 4.
119. Anonsen, p. 22, quoting the Swift County *Advocate* for September 7, 1877.
120. Benson *Times* (May 22, 1876), p. 4; (March 31, 1877), p. 1; (May 26, 1877), p. 4.
121. Swift County *Advocate* (September 28, 1877), p. 1; (May 31, 1878), p. 1; (August 23, 1878), p. 4.

general stores, two hardware stores, two blacksmith shops, a hotel, and an emigrant house.[122]

Such occupations, however, were ancillary to the real business of the western colonists. Indeed all other businesses depended in the last analysis on the primary industry of wheat raising. Until a man had his land broken, he might take an occasional odd job at other work, but his final intention was to see his entire farm sowed to the "yellow gold" that was prairie wheat. It took time to prepare the soil for a wheat crop. Only the most industrious could count on having forty acres broken and seeded at the end of two years. And in addition to the labor involved, forty acres of wheat demanded an investment of at least $200.

Seed for forty acres	$ 60.00
Rent for a drag to put in the crop	12.00
Fee for automatic reaper	60.00
Machine threshing at 5¢ bu.	40.00
Total	$172.00 [123]

Crop yields in the virgin soil often went over twenty bushels of wheat to the acre; and in the decade following the opening of the colonies the price of wheat fluctuated between $1.05 and $.90 a bushel.[124] Before 1880 the wheat farmer could count on at least $.90 a bushel.[125] At this price forty acres of wheat harvested in Minnesota between 1876 and 1880 would give the farmer a gross return of about $800. By breaking an additional ten acres each year the settler was adding $2.50 an acre to the value of his farm and increasing his annual gross production by $200. At this rate his total income over a period of five years would be more than $5,000.

122. Benson *Times* (May 26, 1877), p. 4.

123. *The Colony of Avoca,* p. 17.

124. Between 1866 and 1875 the average annual price for wheat in the United States was $1.053 per bushel. Between 1876 and 1885, the price dropped steadily and its average for the decade was $.92 per bushel. In the 80's India, Russia, and Australia entered the world wheat markets and American farm prices "dropped like rockets": Hacker and Kendrick, *The United States since 1865,* pp. 142–3.

125. Up until 1880 the American wheat market held fairly steady. Even in that year O'Brien's colonization pamphlets—always cautious in their claims for western advantages—continued to list $1.00 as the going price for Minnesota No. 1 hard wheat. See *The Colony of Avoca,* pp. 17–18.

His total expenses, after the initial outlay of $1,000 would have been about $2300 for food, fuel, seed, and planting and harvesting expenses.[126] If the land had originally cost $7.00 (and much of it sold for less), an eighty-acre tract would have cost $560. Thus after five years a western settler, under ordinary conditions, could present an impressive financial statement:

Expenditures		*Income*	
80 acres of land at $7.00 an acre	$ 560.00	6,000 bushels of wheat (15 bushels per acre) at 85¢ per bushel	$5100.00
Initial expenses (house and machinery)	1000.00	Yield from flax	100.00
Food and fuel	750.00	Earning from harvest jobs ($40 each year)	200.00
Seeding and harvesting	1290.00	Value added to 80 acres after breaking at $2.50 per acre	200.00
Total	$3600.00	Total	$5600.00

Even allowing for the grasshopper plagues and the gradually falling price of wheat, western farmers in this decade could easily pay for their land and the cost of settlement within five years.[127]

The Russo-Turkish War of 1877 had given American wheat producers a vastly increased foreign market [128] at precisely the time they were harvesting the heaviest crops on record.[129] In the

126. Computed on the basis of Dillon O'Brien's list of living costs given above.
127. In his estimates on farm income for these years Dillon O'Brien always listed wheat at $1.00 a bushel. Henrietta Larson's exhaustive study of the Minnesota wheat market in these years in general agrees with O'Brien: "The annual average price of the highest grade of wheat in Minneapolis shows that in only one year in the period from 1876 to 1883, inclusive, did the price fall below $1 a bushel—in 1878 the price was 92 cents" (*The Wheat Market in Minnesota,* p. 161). However, the farmer in western Minnesota collected not the full Minneapolis market price for his wheat but that price less freight charges to the market. These charges probably averaged less than ten cents a bushel (see Larson, p. 123). The table above has been altered to include this cost. It should also be mentioned that the figure given here is for No. 1 wheat. No. 2 brought about 5¢ a bushel less, and No. 3 about 15¢ less. In the virgin soil of western Minnesota, however, No. 1 wheat was the rule. An attempt has been made in preparing the above table to inflate the items in the expense column and to deflate those in the income column, on the assumption that most written accounts of farm operations, and especially those in colonization literature, err in the opposite direction.
128. Swift County *Advocate* (November 9, 1877), p. 2.
129. NWC (September 22, 1877), p. 4.

same year the Minneapolis Board of Trade announced that of 50,000 bushels of Minnesota wheat graded in one day in that city less than 300 bushels were listed as No. 2 grade.[130] Wheat buyers had already posted premium prices for Minnesota No. 1 wheat and had moved their buying operations from Milwaukee to Minneapolis.[131] In 1876 the mills along St. Anthony Falls turned out 1,700,000 barrels of flour.[132] New land seekers along the St. Paul and Pacific were so numerous that men were sleeping on the hay in livery stables for lack of hotel accommodations.[133] The Swift County *Advocate* recorded on October 19, 1877, that "the prodigious wheat crop of Minnesota this year has produced an immense demand for farms." Farther south the Worthington *Journal* reported in the same month: "Settlers are coming into Nobles county by the dozens, fifties, and hundreds, yet the stream continues to swell rather than diminish." [134]

The rising wheat market in these years was strong enough to attract investment capital from many persons who had no interest in settling on the lands themselves. One John H. Camp, a St. Paul investor, advertised in the Benson *Times* that he had "five improved farms to let on shares." [135] Each farm had a new house and from 100 to 150 acres already broken and ready for seeding. Camp was prepared to furnish the seed, pay the tenant for his labor in the fall plowing, and promised as well to give the tenant half the crop. A Chicago real estate agent bought 44,000 acres in Nobles County in January 1877.[136] In the same year a wealthy Irishman from Dublin bought a whole section of Swift County land as the site for a commercial stock-raising farm.[137]

In the decade after 1875 the good yield and high price realized by wheat farmers blinded most of them to the dangers of a one-crop economy. "Everywhere along the new railways the immigrants followed one unfailing policy. It was almost a religion

130. Worthington *Advance* (September 22, 1877), p. 1.
131. Benson *Times* (February 23, 1876), p. 4.
132. Ibid. (January 6, 1877), p. 4.
133. Ibid. (May 8, 1876), p. 1.
134. Quoted in *NWC* (October 27, 1877), p. 4.
135. Benson *Times* (December 9, 1876), p. 5.
136. Worthington *Advance* (January 25, 1877), p. 3.
137. Benson *Times* (March 17, 1877), p. 1.

with them. They took up virgin soil, broke it, planted it to wheat, and continued to raise that one crop year after year until the yield became so poor that they had to move away." [138] After the grasshopper plagues of 1874, 1876, and 1877, farsighted farmers turned some of their acreage to grass and hay crops and started dairy herds as a protection against future grasshopper invasions and grain blights. The land around the Clontarf settlement was lighter than that of the other colonies. Taking advantage of this soil condition, some of the Swift County farmers began the commercial production of hay and blue grass.[139] Seed from their farms was soon being shipped to Kentucky labeled "Kentucky blue grass." This commercial seed and hay business is still a large and thriving operation in the Clontarf settlement. As early as 1880 Dillon O'Brien advised settlers to divert some of their time and money to stock and sheep farming, which he predicted would "bring in the most reliable profit . . . in the coming years." [140] To encourage such diversification John Sweetman provided a foundation herd of purebred Shorthorn cows and bulls on his Currie farm and offered breeding services free to any settlers who were interested in starting beef herds.[141]

Before the advent of hybrid corn, stock growers had to rely on grasslands and hay to fatten their cattle. This meant that cattle had to grow to maturity before they were marketable as beef. In that day cornfed "baby beef" was unheard of. In October 1876 Nobles County shipped its first carload of grass-fat cattle to St. Paul.[142] By this time Minnesota dairy products had also been successfully shipped to England, and the dairy industry had learned that during grasshopper plagues grazing lands and hay meadows were left untouched by the insects. In 1877 spokesmen for the Minneapolis Board of Trade and the St. Paul Chamber of Commerce urged Minnesota farmers to enlarge their dairy herds and turn more of their acreage into grazing lands.[143] The next year a commercial farmer at Benson, in Swift County, shipped to St.

138. Pyle, *The Life of James J. Hill*, 1, 362.
139. Benson *Times* (September 11, 1876), p. 1.
140. *The Colony of Avoca*, p. 20.
141. *Farms for Sale*, p. 6.
142. Benson *Times* (October 22, 1876), p. 2.
143. Swift County *Advocate* (September 28, 1877), p. 2.

Paul two carloads of grass-fat steers. Among these were "a pair of six year olds [which] weighed 4120 pounds and they had never had anything to eat but grass." [144] After the bumper wheat crop of 1879 was harvested, the market took its customary drop. On this occasion a columnist for the *Northwestern Chronicle,* citing the recent increase in beef production and the steady prices prevailing in the cattle market, urged the farmers to spend more money improving their beef and dairy herds and to cut down their wheat planting.[145] But in spite of such enlightened advice, the farmers in Minnesota continued to plant and crop their wheat at a furious pace until they were forced by foreign competition and tariff barriers to change their methods.[146]

John Ireland's Jeffersonian ideal of placing every citizen on a farm of his own was qualified by his realistic Hamiltonian conviction that no settlement would succeed unless it could attract sufficient private capital to provide the commercial and mercantile facilities necessary for trade and exchange. In the beginning he had erected a colony lumber yard in Swift County at Benson, midway between the settlements of Clontarf and De Graff. As soon as Benson, the county seat, gave evidence of enough growth to warrant a second lumber yard, however, Ireland moved his to Clontarf and left the Benson area to be developed by local business interests.[147] Before the first settlers arrived in De Graff, Ireland commissioned one William O'Gorman to inspect the size and location of the colony tract and report on the commercial and mercantile possibilities of the new settlement. O'Gorman's report, printed in the *Northwestern Chronicle,* advertised that the new colony would need a lawyer, a machinery dealer, and a hotel keeper at once.[148] In a later issue of the same paper Dillon O'Brien advised his readers that "De Graff needs a general store." [149] Every effort was made to welcome entrepreneurs to the new settlements and to enhance the possibilities for their success. In none of Ire-

144. Ibid. (May 3, 1878), p. 4.
145. NWC (January 18, 1879), p. 10.
146. Hacker and Kendrick, *The United States since 1865,* pp. 142-3.
147. Benson *Times* (June 12, 1876), p. 1.
148. NWC (February 26, 1876), p. 6.
149. Ibid. (October 27, 1877), p. 8.

land's colonies was there a cooperative or community store, such as Brigham Young had organized for his followers at an earlier time. Ireland's belief in the private ownership of land was a corollary of his equally firm belief in the importance of private enterprise in industry and commerce.

Confident that healthy competition is the life of trade, Ireland often donated portions of town land, purchased by himself from a land-grant railroad, to another competing rail line crossing his lands in another direction. He realized the economic advantage of having several carriers serving the same area. In Graceville, where James J. Hill had sold him some St. Paul, Minneapolis, and Manitoba indemnity lands, Ireland donated to the Chicago, Milwaukee, and St. Paul Railway Company "a strip of land . . . 100 ft. wide, and 50 ft. on each side of the centre line of the Company's Railway," thus granting the north-south spur of the Milwaukee Road depot facilities on land once granted to Hill's east-west St. Paul and Pacific.[150] Similarly in Fulda, on land once granted to the St. Paul and Sioux City Railroad, Ireland donated depot space and trackage rights to the Milwaukee Road,[151] hoping thereby to increase the facilities for freight and passenger traffic in this new German settlement.

At Tyler, in Lincoln County, he was even more generous. Although this was not one of his colony towns, he purchased platted portions of the town lands from the St. Paul and Sioux City Railway. From these holdings he donated to the town of Tyler a site for a grain elevator, and to the Milwaukee Road sufficient land for a depot and switching tracks.[152] Since Tyler was not even in

150. Letter of J. P. O'Connor to the Milwaukee Railroad Land Department, St. Paul Chancery Archives, Diocesan Letters 1887–88, p. 158.

151. See letters of J. P. O'Connor, secretary of the Catholic Colonization Bureau of St. Paul, to the Hon. S. J. Earling, president of the Chicago, Milwaukee, and St. Paul Railway, October 2, 1908; and the reply by the secretary of the railroad to O'Connor, October 7, 1908. Both letters are on file in the office of the secretary of the railroad, Union Station Building, Chicago, Illinois. They were made available to me by Mr. John Roche, the present secretary. See also the master map for the Milwaukee Railroad right-of-way through Murray County, Minnesota. This map records the transfer of lands from John Ireland to the railroad. It is filed in the Industrial Department of the Milwaukee Railroad General Offices, Room 286, Union Station Building, Chicago.

152. J. P. O'Connor to Milwaukee Railroad, February 24, 1888, St. Paul Chancery Archives, Diocesan Letters, 1887–88, p. 77.

Fig. 5. Lake Benton, Lincoln County, Minnesota in 1879

the same county as any of his other settlements, he must have extended his donations this far west in the hope that soon his settlers in the nearby counties of Lyon and Murray would be spreading out into the adjoining lands.

Ireland's encouragement of competition among merchants and commercial agents probably did not extend into the field of promoting the erection of "competing" churches in his colonies; but the record is clear that on November 4, 1882, he conveyed to one W. M. Davis and his wife "Lots 6 & 7, Block 13, Davis Addition, Fulda," which lots were conveyed on the same day by Mr. and Mrs. Davis to the "Trustees of the Methodist Episcopal Church." [153] This fact offers interesting avenues for speculation.

153. A photostatic copy of the county abstract title book on these lands is now filed in the Industrial Department of the Milwaukee Railroad. This photostat reproduces the official Murray County Abstract Title Book (1883): Book B, p. 265; Book C, p. 342. The originals are preserved in the Office of the Registrar.

There were, of course, growing numbers of Protestant settlers in all of John Ireland's colonies. Was he willing to help provide houses of worship for them? Were Mr. and Mrs. Davis merely convenient agents between the bishop and his Protestant neighbors? The abstract title book in which this transaction is recorded reveals that the land which Ireland sold to them for $5.00 was in turn sold by them for $32.50. Had they been merely his intermediaries, it is unlikely that they would have taken a profit on the transaction. On the other hand, if the Davises had been engaged in any subterfuge they would certainly not have made the second transfer of title on the same day as their purchase from the bishop. Considering his lifelong friendliness toward Protestants,[154] it is more than likely that Ireland, anxious to accommodate his Protestant neighbors, knew all along what was to become of these lots and only used Mr. and Mrs. Davis as agents to absolve himself from any possible future charges that he had engaged actively in fostering the growth of the Protestant religion.

Ireland's policy toward the various railroads and municipal administrations in the instances mentioned above contrasts strikingly with the economy practiced by William J. Onahan in his administration of the Irish Catholic Colonization Association lands in Greeley County, Nebraska. In the petitions sent to Bishop O'Connor by the pastor, merchants, and bankers in the Nebraska settlements, free depot sites, trackage rights, and even cash bonuses were proposed as the means to woo the railroad.[155] However, as has been mentioned,[156] Onahan's power in colony affairs blocked any such concessions for Nebraska. John Ireland, on the other hand, once the east-west rail lines were through his colonies, did all in his power to secure additional routes running north

of Deeds for Murray County, Slayton, Minnesota, and the photostat is on file in the Industrial Department of the Milwaukee Railroad.

154. For his kindly disposition on this point see letter describing his experiences as a chaplain in the Civil War, "Miscellany," ed. James P. Shannon, *Catholic Historical Review* (October 1953), p. 303.

155. Omaha Chancery Archives, Colonization File. See letters of James R. Connell, Spaulding, to Onahan, May 21, 1886; W. E. Hannon, Spaulding, to Onahan, July 12, 1887; and Onahan's replies to Bishop O'Connor, ranging from extreme confidence, through the first stages of doubt, to crushing disappointment: May 27, 1886; March 31, 1887; June 3, 1887.

156. See above, pp. 79–80.

and south through his lands. To this end he bought and gave away several business and industrial sites, confident that he was contributing to the future of the settlements. His plan paid off handsomely, while Onahan's "inland" colonies nearly died on the vine.

CHAPTER SIX

Who Went West?

SINCE the majority of American immigrants came from the traditionally stable society of western Europe, it might have been expected that the new social order which they created would reflect the established pattern of the lands from which they came. On the contrary, the great shock which was necessary to uproot the European peasant from his native land continued to influence his life in the New World and made subsequent shifts in space and residence relatively easy, after the initial painful break with his fatherland. "Americans are always moving on." [1]

Among the thousands of farmers and prospective farmers in New York, Ohio, and Illinois during the last quarter of the 19th century there were many successful operators of small farms who recognized the greater opportunities offered by the newly opened wheat lands of Minnesota. These men knew what they wanted: rich land, lying level, serviced by railroads, and available in large tracts at a low price per acre. They were the men who settled rural western Minnesota after 1875; and the Catholic members of this tide were the men who settled John Ireland's colonies. Again and again their letters of inquiry to Bishop Ireland, Bishop O'Connor, or the ICBU in Philadelphia asked whether or not the colonies could offer good land near a Catholic church and school.[2] The warning against western settlement originally sounded by Bishop Hughes and often echoed by other eastern clergymen in these years had reached the Catholic immigrants in the middle states. To go west without the assurance of a resident priest was tantamount to risking the loss of their Faith. This the Catholic immigrants were not willing to do.

1. Stephen Vincent Benet, *Western Star* (New York, 1943), p. 3.
2. See esp. the Adrian Colony Papers and the correspondence of Father Knauf in the archives of the St. Paul Seminary; *ICBU Journal* (March 1876), p. 1; (August 1878), p. 5; *NWC* (March 8, 1879), p. 10; and the bound volumes of Diocesan Letters, St. Paul Chancery Archives.

These same people, however, in addition to being Catholics were often reasonably successful farmers or small businessmen and were shrewd enough to realize that the wheat lands of Minnesota offered unusual opportunities to those who would claim them. The weekly market reports, listing Minnesota hard wheat at a premium price of $1.00 a bushel,[3] together with the railroad land booklets quoting farmlands at prices from $1.50 to $5.00 per acre, were compelling inducements to any farmer who wished to improve his fortune. And once Bishop Ireland announced to Catholic settlers that they could be assured a local priest and a church in every colony, the Catholic portion of the westward tide moved more and more toward Minnesota. Ireland had warned that he did not want farmers in other states to sell their farms to come to Minnesota for better ones. He hoped to recruit laborers from the industrial centers of the East. But while these laborers remained at their jobs, either through choice or necessity, thousands of small businessmen and farmers from New England to Wisconsin sold their business or their land and headed for Minnesota.

During his eastern speaking tour of 1879 Ireland delivered a series of six lectures on western colonization to the Catholics in Marlboro, Massachusetts. From this urban parish he recruited six families for the Graceville colony. The father of one such family, Maurice Greene, was an Irish-born immigrant who had been in this country long enough to have established a modest business of his own as a shoemaker. Impressed by the future described by the bishop, Greene sold his house and shop and moved to Graceville, where he was able on arrival to buy outright 100 acres of land at $5.00 an acre. In company with Greene at this time were five other families from Marlboro and seven whom Ireland had recruited in Philadelphia.[4]

A few years later one Daniel J. Walsh wrote from Philadelphia to Bishop O'Connor in Nebraska inquiring about the conditions for settling in one of the new western colonies of the Irish Catholic

3. *NWC* (February 8, 1879), p. 11.

4. These statements are based on an interview with Sister Grace Aurelia, C.S.J., September 5, 1953. Sister Grace Aurelia, who has since died, was the daughter of Maurice Greene.

Colonization Association.[5] The letter, written on his own business stationery, reveals that he was the proprietor of a wholesale woolen and cotton rag warehouse: "I write to you to ascertain in what manner I can join your colony opened some two years ago. . . . I am as you see by my letter heading in business here and just about making a living and I have a wife and 4 children. I am 38 years old, my oldest child, a boy, 10 years. I have had a desire for some years to take up a farm when lands are cheap and growing in value and I write you for advice. . . . I presume I could bring with me nearly four thousand dollars." Walsh was no illiterate. He wrote a fine Spenserian hand, owned his own business, and could bring "four thousand dollars." [6] He and Maurice Greene are typical of hundreds of farmers and small businessmen from the East who came to John Ireland's Minnesota colonies. The rising price of western lands, contrasted with the uncertainties of business competition in the East, convinced them that a better economic future awaited them in the West.

On January 25, 1879, an unemployed miner in Brady's Bend, Pennsylvania, wrote to Dillon O'Brien, "This place, once famous for its iron works, [is] now abandoned by every body that can leave. . . . Brady's Bend once had the largest blast furnaces and rolling-mill in Pennsylvania, giving employment to five or six thousand men, but, through the incompetence and mismanagement of its officers, it has gone under, never to rise again, leaving a debt of $75,000 due the poor workingmen employed in and around here." [7] The writer assured O'Brien that several of the unemployed steel workers were anxious to come to the Minnesota colonies, if some means could be provided for their transportation and subsidization. As in so many similar instances, O'Brien most likely extended his sympathy and explained that his bureau still lacked sufficient funds to underwrite such worthy pleas.

In contrast to the plight of the steel worker in Brady's Bend is the story of John Gorman, the boss puddler in a steel mill at Oxford,

5. Daniel J. Walsh, Philadelphia, to Bishop James O'Connor, June 14, 1881, Omaha Chancery Archives, Colonization File.
6. Ibid.
7. *NWC* (February 8, 1879), p. 11.

Warren County, New Jersey. Gorman was told by his doctor that the intense heat of the blast furnaces had injured his lungs so much that it was imperative for him to change to some kind of job that would keep him out in the fresh air. The doctor had read some of the railroad publicity recommending the "salubrity" of the climate in Minnesota for any persons suffering from respiratory illnesses. He suggested that Gorman write to Bishop Ireland in St. Paul. On his foreman's salary, Gorman had saved a sufficient sum to enable him to buy outright three forty-acre tracts near Sweetman's Currie settlement in Minnesota. In 1883 he brought his family to Murray County, Minnesota, and his great-grand-children still live in the Currie settlement.[8]

During the first year of operations in Bishop Ireland's Swift County colony, Ignatius Donnelly reported in his *Anti-Monopolist* that several delegations "from the workshops of Boston and the coal and iron mines of Pennsylvania have visited Swift County and secured land. They will be followed by others. If the stream of idle mechanics and miners of the East, *many of whom have considerable sums in savings banks,* can be turned to the fertile plains of Minnesota, the welfare of the immigrants and the growth of the state will both be secured in an eminent degree. Success to the great and charitable enterprise." [9] Many of the settlers who first came to the colony in Swift County were precisely men of this category, miners or shop workers who had sufficient savings to move west and buy their own land. They were enterprising fellows who recognized the limitations of their positions in the East and who grasped at the same time the opportunities to be found on farms in the West.

That these particular instances are typical of the status of settlers coming to western Minnesota in these years is demonstrated by Secretary Young's report to the Minnesota State Board of Immigration for 1879. During eight months of that year 40,000 immigrants had entered the state and had brought with them a sum exceeding $4,000,000. "Those with most means were the German

8. Based on an interview (June 15, 1953) granted me by Charles Gorman, a present-day resident of Currie, Minnesota, and a son of John Gorman. He came to Minnesota as a small boy with his father and their family in 1883, and is today the oldest living member of the Currie colony.

9. Quoted in the Benson *Times* (March 8, 1876), p. 4.

and French; less, English; least, Irish. Many had from $1000 to $10,000. Seven from Germany arrived at one time with drafts of $20,000; one came with $9,000, and possessed property in Germany; it was common for them to have $500–$8000 with them." [10]

Patrick Donohue, Secretary of the ICBU National Colonization Board, reported to the members of the union in March 1876 that most of the inquiries about colonization came from Catholic farmers and small-town residents in New England, and he added, "Most of the correspondents represent themselves as possessing 'some means.'" [11] A few years later Martin Griffin mentioned in an editorial in his *Journal*, "Very few correspondents of the Philadelphia Colonization Society are from the large cities, but nearly all are from the small towns and villages of the country." [12]

Eighteen months after the opening of the colony at Adrian, Minnesota, a settler name O'Hearn wrote to the *Northwestern Chronicle* that all the government land and all but a few parcels of railroad (colony) lands had been sold in Nobles County and that most of the new residents had come to that colony from other farms in eastern Minnesota. "Nearly all the colony land that has been bought here is [sic] by farmers from the eastern and northern parts of Minnesota, generally old Minnesotians, most of them pretty comfortable, many of them buying half-sections, and several of them buying more." [13] O'Hearn explicitly stated in this letter that the great attraction in Nobles County was the bumper crops of flax and wheat that had been harvested during the three previous seasons. The harvest of 1878 had in some parts of the colony yielded forty bushels of wheat to the acre, and the average had

10. St. Paul *Pioneer Press*, undated clipping in William J. Onahan's Scrapbook for 1879, quoted by Sister Mary Evangela Henthorne, *The Irish Catholic Colonization Association*, p. 13, n. See also the Benson *Times* (April 28, 1877), p. 1: "Pennsylvania has sent quite a number of well-to-do farmers to De Graff." See also the Worthington *Advance* (March 21, 1878), p. 3, "Arrivals," a news story relating the fact that a scouting party had surveyed the Nobles County land (near Adrian) and that "100 families from Red Wing and vicinity will come here this spring and one or two hundred more in the future. *The parties who were here are men of means, one or two of them being worth $100,000 to $200,000. They intend to break a large quantity of ground this season*" (italics mine).

11. *ICBU Journal* (March 1876), p. 1.

12. Ibid. (August 1878), p. 5.

13. *NWC* (March 8, 1879), p. 10.

been "from 25 to 30" bushels. Given these facts, the migration within Minnesota in these years can be explained primarily by the greater economic advantages to be found in the West. Men who knew farm values moved into the areas of agricultural opportunity, and of these men, the Catholic members settled in the townships which had a church and school. Even to the present day the parish of St. Adrian, with its parochial elementary and high school, has the largest enrollment of Catholic students in Nobles County. Men who came west for realistic reasons found what they wanted, and the subsequent history of their settlement has been characterized by great stability. For the most part the residents in Nobles County today are essentially the same kind of people who came when the land there was first opened for settlement.

Bishop Ireland had warned Minnesota farmers that he would sell his colony lands only to persons coming from out of the state. He had been disturbed to read in his own diocesan paper an account of three farmers from Watertown (eastern Minnesota) who had arranged to sell their eighty-acre farms (with log houses and thirty acres under the plow) for $1600 each, with the intention of moving into his Swift County colony (western Minnesota), where this sum would purchase four times as much land.[14] His stern warning against this practice had little effect; there were too many ways of getting around his regulations.

For example, one Thomas McSorley, a wealthy farmer from Red Wing (on the extreme eastern boundary of Minnesota), arranged to purchase several colony farms from the railroad and brought Catholic families from New York to farm them for him. He was, in a way, complying with Ireland's plan of accepting only out-of-state settlers; but in a larger sense he was circumventing the bishop's plan by introducing the unwelcome features of tenant farming. Apparently Ireland tolerated such arrangements as this in the hope that such tenants would eventually acquire their own farms. However, because the organization of the colonies gave him no control over the economic and social affairs of the settlers, he was unable to do more than voice his disapproval in situations of this kind. Such men as McSorley could not

14. Ibid. (March 4, 1879), p. 1.

be effectively restrained from investing their surplus capital in colony lands if they so desired.[15]

It was also possible for farmers from other parts of Minnesota to enter the colony lands by buying their land from one of the earlier settlers. In this way it was not necessary for them to deal with Bishop Ireland's agent. The Scandinavian settlers who had preceded the colonists were often ready to sell their improved farms at a profit and move on to open lands farther west,[16] and occasionally the Catholic colonists themselves would agree to sell some Minnesota farmer a portion of their land. Shortly after Bishop Ireland announced that he would not sell land to any Minnesota resident, one of his De Graff colonists, John Doyle, sold his improved colony farm to a Mr. Kelly from Red Wing, Minnesota.[17]

It was always to be a disappointment to John Ireland that he never succeeded in bringing poor people into his colonies; but by the very nature of the enterprise, and especially because of its timing, capital was a necessary part of its success. By this time the design of bonanza-type farm machinery had advanced sufficiently to enable one farmer and his family to cultivate huge tracts of land which formerly could have been worked only by several farmers. Automatic grain binders had been patented as early as 1850, but 1877 marked the year that the McCormick "Old Reliable" wire self-binder first appeared on the market. Four thousand of these machines were sold in that year. Within a year three similar models were produced by competing manufacturers, and

15. Ibid. (August 4, 1877), p. 4; Swift County *Advocate* (June 14, 1878), p. 4.

16. This was especially true in the two Lyon County settlements at Ghent and Minneota. In these colonies the Belgian immigrants wanted improved farms and usually had the money to pay for them. Leo Hennen and John Brewers, both original members of the Ghent settlement, informed the present writer in an interview on June 21, 1953, that many of the improved farms taken up by the early Belgians were purchased from Norwegian and Swedish farmers who wished to move farther west in 1880. See also Arthur P. Rose, "We the People," in the Marshall *Messenger*, March 10, 1953; also the letter of Bishop Ireland to Charles Simmons, Land Commissioner for the Winona and St. Paul, printed above, p. 60. Note also that the Catholic settlers in Lyon County took over the townships of Nordland, Eidsvold, and Westerheim, originally named by Scandinavians: A. P. Rose, in the Marshall *Messenger*, March 19, 1953.

17. Swift County *Advocate* (February 1, 1878), p. 4.

by the harvest time of 1878, 20,000 self-binding, automatic grain reapers were in use in this country.[18] Heavy breaking plows, sufficiently strong to turn the thick prairie sod, were a necessity for every settler who did not wish to pay the commercial rate of two to three dollars per acre for breaking. The extent of the prairie farms made the old broadcast method of seeding too laborious and too inefficient and prompted the rapid conversion to large-scale drill seeders. The first patent for a machine of this type had been granted in 1841; by 1874, more than half the winter wheat seeded in the Mississippi Valley region was planted with this new type of drill.[19]

At a time when "the drill was still practically unknown in New England," the prairie states "witnessed a very rapid transition from broadcasting to drilling." The United States Department of Agriculture summarized the merits of this new machine in its annual report for 1874. "The drill is used for seeding in connection with thorough culture, especially in winter wheat growing; the broadcast seeder for imperfect culture and rough surfaces; and sowing by hand is the method adopted for small patches and first efforts of impecunious pioneers." [20]

The Minnesota settlers of this period were far from impecunious pioneers. Just a few months after the opening of Ireland's first colony in Swift County, a farm machinery distributor in Benson reported that the larger areas of these western farm lands made the new type of machinery imperative for the settlers. "The farmer who would stop to sow his wheat broadcast, or to reap it with a cradle, would be laughed at by his neighbors." [21]

Such elaborate machinery, however, required a considerable investment from the prairie farmers. That they were for the most part prepared to meet such an outlay would appear from such notices as they printed in the Benson *Times* for June 5, 1876:

18. Leo Rogin, *The Introduction of Farm Machinery: in Its Relation to the Productivity of Labor in the Agriculture of the United States during the Nineteenth Century,* University of California Publications in Economics, 9 (Berkeley, 1931), p. 111.

19. "Wheat Drilling vs. Broadcasting," U.S. Department of Agriculture Report (1874), pp. 60–7, quoted in Rogin, p. 197.

20. Ibid., p. 197.

21. Benson *Times* (March 8, 1876), p. 1.

"There are some 35,000 bushels of wheat in our elevators, mostly owned by the farmers in the vicinity of Morris who are not disposed to part with it at the present prices. They are rich enough to pay storage and wait for a rise in the market. Not so bad for a frontier community." [22]

In an era of industrial growth, American agriculture, while it became increasingly lucrative, resembled the rest of American business in that it demanded ever increasing amounts of capital. The family of one M. Daly, after arriving in Bishop Ireland's De Graff colony, found to its dismay that this was no place for poor people. Being unable to find open government land near the railroad, they all packed up and returned to their home in Buffalo, New York.[23] Even on this new frontier a modicum of capital was necessary for success. Payments on the land, seed, livestock, and farm machinery of recent design, not to mention cash reserves sufficient to supply a family with food and clothing for at least two years, effectively limited the number of persons who were in a position to take up colony lands.

It is more difficult to determine the political sympathies of the new colonists than to describe their economic status, although the two factors were certainly not unrelated. It is clear, as might have been expected, that many of the incoming settlers voted the straight Democratic ticket.[24] However, there is good reason for believing that the financial position of many of the colonists influenced their political allegiance and inclined them to share their episcopal patron's loyalty to the Republican party.

In these years John Ireland was already becoming famous as one of Minnesota's leading Republicans. His party ties, which were to bring him international prominence under the Republican administrations of McKinley, Roosevelt, and Taft,[25] were

22. Ibid. (June 5, 1876), p. 4.
23. Ibid. (October 6, 1877), p. 4.
24. Sister Grace Aurelia, in an interview on September 5, 1953, indicated that many of the first settlers in Graceville were Democrats. In an interview on October 15, 1953, Father Melvin Blais, pastor of St. Bridget's parish, De Graff, stated that the Catholic settlers in that parish have traditionally voted the Democratic ticket since the beginning of the colony settlement.
25. Moynihan, *The Life of Archbishop John Ireland*, pp. 258–63.

already widely known; and although he did not openly campaign in Minnesota for Republican candidates, he was able to write to one Angela Ewing on March 26, 1885, that he was confident the Irish vote in Minnesota had supported James G. Blaine against Grover Cleveland.[26]

It may have been that some Catholics—normally Democrats—voted for the Republican Blaine, prompted by the knowledge that Blaine had at one time practiced the Catholic Faith. In a private letter to Austin Ford, editor of the New York *Irish World*, Ireland spoke of having tried to bring Blaine back to the practice of his religion.[27] Whatever the motives behind the vote of 1884, the bishop was satisfied that the Irish Catholics in Minnesota had voted for the Republican candidate. On the other hand, Dillon O'Brien, who was in more immediate contact with the Catholic settlers on the land, was an equally loyal member of the Democratic party all the years he lived in Minnesota.[28] As often as he was called on, though, to address political and civic gatherings, O'Brien "gave little attention to politics." [29] Certainly in comparison to the acknowledged Republican sympathies of Bishop Ireland, O'Brien's quiet and enduring loyalty to the Democratic party was not likely to influence the Catholic vote in Minnesota substantially.

Exactly what part the Catholic vote played in the western counties at this period remains uncertain. If ballot returns by township were available, it would be possible to determine precisely the influence of the Catholic vote, at least for those ten townships which were almost solidly Catholic in population.[30] The first year in which the returns were recorded by township was 1888, and in this campaign six of the Catholic townships sup-

26. John Ireland to Angela Ewing, March 26, 1885, Notre Dame University Archives, Private Letter Collection, Minnesota (St. Paul), 1860–90.

27. John Ireland to Austin Ford, December 20, 1892, Notre Dame University Archives, Austin Ford Papers, I and II, 1885–97.

28. O'Brien, "Dillon O'Brien," p. 42.

29. Ibid.

30. In Swift County these were the townships of Cashel, Kildare, Dublin, Clontarf, and Tara, named by the Irish settlers to commemorate the famous sites of Ireland; and in Lyon County, the five townships of Eidsvold, Nordland, Westerheim, Vallers, and Grandview were occupied mostly by Catholics. See Rose, "We the People," Marshall *Messenger*, March 19, 1953.

ported Cleveland and four preferred Harrison.[31] Possibly John Ireland had reliable sources for his statement (made *after* the election of 1884) that the Irish Catholics in Minnesota had supported Blaine. From the extant voting returns, however, it can only be said that for 1888 the Catholics in western Minnesota cast a surprisingly heavy Republican vote. In these returns the Irish in Swift County favored Democratic candidates, whereas the Belgians in Lyon County preferred the Republican candidate.[32] In most of the ten townships, however, the vote was fairly well divided between the Republicans and Democrats (with a remarkably large vote cast by the Belgians in Lyon County for Clinton B. Fisk, the Prohibition party candidate). No candidate received a landslide vote from the Catholics of western Minnesota. On the basis of such limited evidence it can only be said that there was no discernible Catholic bloc of votes among the colonists. Apparently, immigrants who had been assimilated to American ways were already beginning to vote according to their economic interests and not primarily according to their religious or Old World ties.

When the first colony opened in Swift County in 1876, most of the settlers who came to it were Irish-born or the children of parents born in Ireland.[33] With the passage of time Irish names became less and less numerous in the various colonies.[34] It would be a serious mistake, however, to assume that even in the beginning these colonies were exclusively Irish settlements. In some instances, as at Ghent, they were from the start almost entirely

31. See election returns for Minnesota printed in the New York *Tribune Almanac* for 1889.

32. Ibid.

33. In 1876 the first ten babies baptized at St. Bridget's parish, De Graff, were named Moran, McInerney, Buta, Kehoe, Killeen, Ferguson, Kennedy, Ganley, Kenedy, and McGuire. In 1880 the first ten names were: McConley, Collins, Duffy, Brady, Hughes, Kennedy, Hoban, McNelis, Hynes, and Reynolds. See parish baptismal register, St. Bridget's Rectory, De Graff, Minnesota.

34. Ibid. See the same register for the years 1900, 1920, and 1930, to note the growing number of non-Irish names among the first ten baptisms in each of these years. In 1950 the first ten names were Laughlin, Matthews, Chevalier, Krattenmaker, Dahl, Johnson, Byrne, Cain, Miller, and Wersinger. The disappearance of Irish names is almost complete in the comparable parish records at St. Edward's Rectory, Minneota, Lyon County, Minnesota.

non-Irish. So much has been written on the Irish portion of this
westward movement that the non-Irish element (which eventually inherited at least the earth in western Minnesota) has been
greatly neglected.

Many French, Belgian, German, and English—and a few Polish
—Catholics answered Bishop Ireland's invitation to Minnesota.
In every colony there were representatives of each of these national groups, although each colony had its own dominant national strain. In De Graff, Clontarf, Graceville, Avoca, Currie,
and Adrian, Irish names predominated on the parish rosters. From
the beginning until now the names in Ghent have been almost
exclusively Belgian; and in Fulda, German. A significant, if not
dominant, number of French families came early and are still
prominent in the vicinity of Clontarf. The large numbers of French
who came to Ghent and Currie have for the most part sold their
lands and moved to the city. The English who came to Minneota, Adrian, and Swift County have demonstrated the staying
power that has been traditional with the colonial representatives
of their nation.

For several reasons German settlers were never numerous in
John Ireland's colonies. Long before the bishop announced his
first colony, German Catholic settlers had established their own
thriving rural centers at New Ulm in Brown County and at St.
Cloud in Stearns County. These centers continued to grow
throughout the years of his episcopate, although they were in no
sense part of his colonization endeavor. There were, of course,
many settlers of German origin who finally settled on his lands,[35]
although there was never anything like a mass movement of German settlers to his western colony sites.

The rise of Bismarck's new German empire, with its established order of militarism, increased taxes, and the systematic
elimination of "uneconomical" small farmers gave many loyal
German sons the incentive necessary to seek new homes across
the Atlantic.[36] German Catholics in particular had reason to leave

35. In Minnesota, Fulda, Ghent, and Marshall benefited chiefly by the arrival
of German immigrants. See NWC (March 1, 1879), p. 1; and Rose, "We the
People," Marshall Messenger, March 19, 1953.
36. Barry, The Catholic Church and German Americans, pp. 4–5.

their native land after the rigors of the *Kulturkampf* pressed down upon them. One Catholic tenant in the Rhineland, when asked the reason for his going to America in 1883, replied "My acquaintances write from there that they have such good conditions, and on Sundays as many as wish may go to Church. My children shall not imitate my slavery." [37] For the two decades immediately following the enactment of Bismarck's rigorous May Laws (1870), German immigrants to America were more numerous than those from any other nation, but the vast majority of those headed for the "German triangle of the West." [38] Very few of them got as far as western Minnesota. The Germans who came to Bishop Ireland's colonies following the Civil War usually came from the neighboring states of Iowa, Illinois, Indiana, and Ohio, and in the present study rank as German-Americans who had already acquired American ways. Like the Irish-Americans already mentioned, they adopted the American creed that westward expansion and commercial agriculture were twin phases of a manifest destiny.

Moreover, since "the peak of the German emigration was attained in 1853 and 1854," [39] the Minnesota Catholic colonies were more properly timed to receive the Irish portion of the Atlantic migration than the German element. There is also a possibility that during the years 1875–80, the period of the colonization program in Minnesota, the total number of German-born residents in that state actually declined.[40]

Another phase of the internal migration which occurred in North America at this time was the shift in population from the eastern provinces of Canada to the middle western United States. The panic of 1873 worked a serious hardship on the economy of Canada and served to stimulate migration from the eastern provinces of

37. Ibid., p. 5.

38. That is, the area described by imaginary lines drawn between St. Louis, Cincinnati, and Milwaukee.

39. Marcus Lee Hansen, *The Atlantic Migration* (Cambridge, Mass., 1951), p. 287.

40. Folwell, *A History of Minnesota*, 3, 73, 140, cites the Minnesota State Census for 1875 as recording 67,030 German and Austrian born residents of the state, whereas the tenth decennial federal census for 1880 lists only 66,592. However, it should be noted that this comparison is between the more reliable federal census figures of 1880 and the more questionable state census figures of 1875.

the Dominion into the United States. It was not the danger of destitution that prompted so many Canadian families to leave home at this time, but an unwillingness to accept the limitations placed on their chance of future advancement by the dangers of overpopulation or of a depressed national economy. "As early as 1851 there could be detected in eastern Canada clear signs that some counties had become 'overpopulated'; that is, had reached their maximum density in terms of the unwillingness of some inhabitants to accept a lower standard of living." [41]

Scores of American land agents swarmed over the eastern provinces at this time, encouraging the emigration of the youthful Canadians. "Every American land-grant railroad had representatives in Canada." [42] Resentment against these foreign agitators reached such heights in Canada that an attempt was made in the Canadian Parliament to secure legislation to curb their activities.[43]

> But the real incitement to emigration was not found in advertisement and propaganda. It lay deeper, in the fundamental changes then affecting the agriculture of the province. The farms in the old settled parts were small. Usually the future of only one child could be provided for. The other children had traditionally moved away, striking off into the backlands of the community or into the new townships that opened up to the west and north. But now the limit of desirable agricultural settlement within Ontario seemed to have been reached and the present phase of the migration was different only in that the young people were obliged to go farther from home, crossing the international boundary on the way.[44]

Among the Canadian emigrés, French-Canadian Catholics had additional reason for seeking homes in the prairie states. In some of the provinces action had been taken by the early Anglo-Saxon

41. Marcus Lee Hansen, *The Mingling of the Canadian and American Peoples* (New Haven, 1940), p. 183.
42. Ibid., p. 185.
43. *Dominion of Canada, Debates, House of Commons,* Session 1881, X, 1303, quoted by Hansen, p. 186.
44. Hansen, p. 186.

residents to enact statutes prohibiting Catholics from membership in the provincial legislature. Such political disability in their native land, contrasted with the political freedom and agricultural opportunities of the American West, promoted the emigration of countless French-Canadian Catholic families.[45] Several French families had already settled in Swift County before John Ireland opened his De Graff and Clontarf colonies in that area. The first of these was Firmin Bedard, who settled at Benson, Minnesota, in 1871 [46] and who became the trustee and leader of the great French settlement which was established after Bishop Ireland announced his plans to build Catholic churches in Swift County. One of the later French settlers, Arsidas Benoit, sold his 132 acres of farm land in the parish of St. Jude, Quebec, and moved to Minnesota in 1876, where he "bought a 240-acre farm about five miles from Benson." [47]

By January 1, 1877, there were at least twenty-one French Catholic families in Swift County. Bishop Ireland sent a French-speaking priest, one Father P. Lebret, into the Swift County colony in that month to offer Mass and administer the sacraments to these newcomers.[48] A few months later Ireland announced that the parish in Clontarf, heretofore a mission from the church in De Graff, would become an independent parish with its own resident pastor, Father L. l'Hiver. The new pastor found a thriving parish, with a spacious church and several "enterprising and worthy families arriving daily from the Eastern and other states in large numbers." [49] Like the Belgians who came later, these French settlers were skilled farmers. They had sold small farms in the eastern provinces of Canada and had come to the States with sufficient capital to purchase larger farms. During the following two decades, the resident pastor at Clontarf (nominally an Irish settlement) was a French-speaking priest, Father Anatole Oster.[50]

45. *NWC* (June 3, 1876), p. 1.
46. *Dedication of St. Francis Xavier School,* a memorial pamphlet issued by the parish of St. Francis, Benson, Minn. (August 28, 1953), pp. 9, 11.
47. Ibid., p. 11.
48. *NWC* (April 7, 1877), p. 5.
49. Ibid.
50. Reardon, *Diocese of St. Paul,* p. 630.

And because the French Catholics who came to Swift County found what they sought—good land near a parish church—they have stayed on the land till the present day.

In two other Minnesota colonies, Ghent and Currie, French Canadian Catholics were well represented. Some French-Canadians from Kankakee, Illinois, were among those "American" farmers who answered John Sweetman's final advertisement for Catholic settlers in his Currie colony. French from Kankakee were also prominent in the later Belgian settlements at Ghent and Minneota in Lyon County, Minnesota,[51] although they have since sold their lands to the Belgian farmers in both these settlements.

By any standard the two Belgian colonies at Ghent and Minneota were Bishop Ireland's most successful foundations; yet they have been the two settlements most neglected by subsequent historians. It may be that students of immigration have tended to overlook the Belgian immigration because of its small numbers.[52] In no single year has the movement from Belgium to the United States accounted for even one per cent of the total received here.[53] Those few writers who have touched on the Belgians in America have treated the topic either as a minor phase of the German migrations [54] or as an insignificant portion of the French movement.[55]

In contrast to this attitude among students of history, American immigration and land settlement agents have realized for a long time that Belgian farmers were especially good prospects for colonization schemes. In its early years as a territory Minnesota sent one Eugene Burnand to solicit emigrants from Belgium to the upper Mississippi Valley. Long before Hans Mattson turned

51. For more on this group of French settlers, see below, pp. 147–8.

52. Francis J. Brown and Joseph S. Roucek, *One America* (New York, 1945), pp. 90–6. In this chapter Professor Brown advances the opinion that Belgium's contribution to the settlement of America has been largely neglected by the standard historical surveys of American development.

53. *Reports of the Immigration Commission* (2 vols. Washington, D.C., 1911), *Abstracts of Reports of the Immigration Commission, 1,* 167 (called the Dillingham Report, after its chairman, Senator William Paul Dillingham of Vermont).

54. Albert Bernhard Faust, *The German Element in the United States* (2 vols. New York, 1909), 2, 11–12.

55. Carl Wittke, *We Who Built America* (Cleveland, Western Reserve University Press, 1939), p. 324.

the Scandinavian tide of settlement into Minnesota, the territorial legislature had explicitly recommended to Burnand an intensive campaign for Belgian settlers.[56] Similarly, when the Dominion of Canada opened its prairie provinces for settlement, it sent emigrant agents directly to Antwerp in the hope of gaining Belgian farmers for Saskatchewan, Manitoba, and Alberta.[57] Even the highly selective Dillingham Report, submitted to the Senate in 1907, presented the Belgian immigrants as promising candidates for American citizenship.[58]

The subsequent record of the Belgian-Americans has proved these early predictions correct.[59] Their success in this country as farmers and as skilled artisans is especially striking in view of their small numbers. For the student of immigration the modest proportions of the Belgian immigration, mostly settled in three or four major Belgian centers,[60] provide unusually clear materials for comparative studies in social history. This is particularly true of the settlements at Ghent and Minneota. Unfortunately, the Catholic colonies in Minnesota have most often been treated solely as part of the story of the Irish in America. In narrations of this type, the large Belgian settlements, for all their success, had no part

56. Livia Appel and Theodore C. Blegen, "Official Encouragement of Immigration to Minnesota during the Territorial Period," *Minnesota History Bulletin*, 5, 167–203. See also Wittke, *We Who Built America*, p. 106.

57. Dillingham Report, 2, 607.

58. At the time this report was prepared (1907), it represented the Belgian immigrants in America as having a literacy rate of 99.3 per cent. See the Dillingham Report, 1, 438, table 77. In its survey, "Immigrants as Charity Seekers," made in 43 major American cities, this report listed no Belgian families at all. See 2, 96–101.

59. On this topic very little documented history has been written. Among published materials the most helpful are: J. F. Stillman, *Belgium's Contribution to America's Making*, New York, 1921; W. E. Griffin, *The Story of the Walloons, at Home, in Lands of Exile and America*, Boston, 1923; and J. A. Griffin, "The Contribution of Belgium to the Catholic Church in America, 1523–1857," *Studies in American Church History*, 3d ser., Catholic University of America, 1932.

60. The largest of these Belgian centers are: Rochester, New York; Detroit, Michigan; Moline, Illinois; Lyon County, Minnesota; and South Bend, Indiana. The Catholic parish of St. Albert, on West 47th Street in New York City, has 30,000 registered Belgian-American members who live in New York City, Long Island, Hoboken, and Paterson. The present study is deeply indebted to Mr. Arthur Bulens, Vice Consul in the Belgian Consulate General, 333 North Michigan Avenue, Chicago, Illinois, for these data and for the interview granted to me on November 3, 1953.

simply because they were not Irish colonies.[61] The relative obscurity of this Belgian group might also be explained by the good fortune it seems to have enjoyed since its establishment in 1881.

In July 1879 Bishop Ireland opened his 45,000-acre tract of railroad land near Minneota to receive Irish and English settlers. Presumably, the several English families who then came to Minnesota were sent out by Father Nugent, Bishop Ireland's agent in Liverpool.[62] One indication that Ireland originally intended this to be largely an English colony is seen in his placing the new parish under the patronage of the English Saint, Edward the Confessor. English settlers in this colony, however, were always a minority. Those English families who did come in answer to Bishop Ireland's offer have for the most part stayed on the land; their descendants still farm this land.

Most of the open colony lands near Minneota were taken up in 1879 and 1880 by Irish settlers, many of them newly arrived from Ireland.[63] The first pastor of this colony was Father M. J. Hanley, who was appointed by Bishop Ireland in the spring of 1880. Hanley was a native of Ireland but had been ordained in 1866 for the Diocese of Chicago. During one of John Ireland's lectures in Chicago young Father Hanley was in the audience and was much impressed by the details of the Minnesota colonization plan. After this first meeting with the St. Paul prelate, Hanley returned to Ireland and recruited twenty Irish families. He brought them to Minneota in the spring of 1880, to form the nucleus of St. Edward's parish.[64] These Irishmen, however, were not subsidized

61. Egan, "Irish Immigration to Minnesota," in *Mid-America,* 12 (October 1929), 133–66; (January 1930), 223–45. These two articles, taken from a master's dissertation presented at the University of Minnesota, offer the most intensive published account of the Minnesota Catholic colonies but do not touch on the Belgian, French, German, and English elements in the program of Bishop John Ireland.

62. New York *Times* (October 9, 1880), p. 3.

63. Arthur P. Rose, *The History of Lyon County* (Marshall, Minn., 1912), pp. 177–88. See also Rose, "We the People," Marshall *Messenger,* March 19, 1953. I am indebted to Father Rudolph Neudecker of Marshall, Minnesota, for a copy of the six newspaper articles on Lyon County written by Mr. Rose, one of the oldest settlers of that county.

64. Based on the parish records of St. Edward's parish, Minneota, Minnesota. I am especially indebted to Father Vincent Hope, former pastor at Minneota, for permission to study and copy the carefully preserved journals and registers of

emigrants, as were the Connemara and Sweetman colonists. Rather
they were independent settlers, possessed of at least sufficient
means to pay their passage west and to make a down payment
on colony lands. In most other instances the Irish were in no position to pay for their entire farms immediately on arrival and they
were quite happy to accept the credit terms offered by Ireland's
contract with the Winona and St. Peter Railroad. In time even the
wealthier Irish in Minneota were destined to give up their lands
to the more agriculturally inclined Belgians from the neighboring colony of Ghent; but in the beginning and up until 1900, Irish
names predominated on the parish rolls.[65]

In the summer of 1880 Father Nugent came from Liverpool to
Minnesota to survey the work of the new colonies. He stopped off
to see the colonies in Nebraska also and even went into Manitoba
in search of some new lands for additional settlements. His complete satisfaction with all that he saw on this survey is reflected in
an interview he granted to a ship's reporter from the New York
Times.[66] Nugent must have been especially impressed with Bishop
Ireland's newest colony at Minneota, for he promised "as a result
of his mission that an increased immigration will flow to America." [67]

In the same interview the priest from Liverpool announced that
several bands of Belgian emigrants were then preparing to leave
their native land for Lyon County, Minnesota. Earlier in 1880
he had put the latest copies of Minnesota colonization publicity
in the hands of one Canon Peter Van Hee, a native of Belgium
who was at that time a priest of the Diocese of Liverpool. Canon
Van Hee had taken the publications back to Belgium and had per-

---

this pioneer parish. Among them is a copy of a sermon by one Father O'Donnell,
presumably a eulogy of Father Hanley's priesthood. This document supplies the
facts given above on Hanley's part in founding Minneota. A further source of
material that proved most enlightening is a collection of three large family
scrapbooks, kept by the James Boulton family of Minneota, covering the entire
history of that colony. The Boultons are one of the original English families.
Their farm, at which the scrapbooks are now kept, is on State Highway 68, just
north of Taunton, Lyon County, Minnesota.

65. See esp. the baptismal register and the parish census files for St. Edward's
parish, Minneota.

66. New York *Times* (October 9, 1880), p. 3.

67. Ibid.

suaded his brother, Angelus Van Hee, a wealthy farmer, to accompany him on a trip to investigate the farming opportunities in Minnesota. It is not recorded that Nugent and the Van Hees toured Minnesota together, but it is clear that they were all three in Minnesota during August 1880.[68] Bishop Ireland personally accompanied Father Van Hee and Angelus Van Hee on a tour of the western colonies.

The Belgian visitors were satisfied with the quality of the soil and the condition of the crops in and around the Minneota settlement. And since he was a man of means, Angelus Van Hee purchased outright a half section of land (320 acres), hired twenty teams and drivers, and ordered immediate breaking of 100 acres of land. After supervising the beginning of this project, he returned to Belgium for his wife and nine children. Many of his friends, who were also men of some means, inquired about the prospects in America. His account of the religious centers promised by Bishop Ireland for the fertile farming areas of western Minnesota convinced several of his Catholic neighbors of the desirability of emigration.

At that time Belgium was, as it is today, the most densely populated country in the world.[69] Its standards of education were high and it was not suffering from any political unrest. Historically, its people had been content to stay at home, probably because of the sound condition of their national economy, based on a careful

68. C. F. Case, *History and Description of Lyon County, Minnesota*, Marshall, Minn., 1884. One chapter, "The Catholic Colony of Ghent," was written by Father Jules Emile De Vos, the first resident pastor at Ghent. This chapter, together with his parochial journal book, written in longhand, are the most accurate sources for material on the early history of Ghent. The "History of the Parish of St. Eloi," prepared by Rev. John Pilger in June 1933 while he was pastor of the parish of St. Eloi at Ghent, relates that Canon Peter Van Hee, Angelus Van Hee, and the latter's son Aime visited Lyon County with Bishop Ireland during August 1880. The New York *Times* account of Father Nugent's trip, quoted above, indicates that Nugent was in Minnesota between August and October 1880.

69. De Vos, "The Catholic Colony of Ghent," in Case. Father De Vos records that in 1881, when the Belgian settlers first came to Minnesota, the population of their native land was nearly 6,000,000. This meant that there were 462 persons for each square mile of land, allowing each person slightly less than two acres of land. The *World Almanac* for 1953 records (p. 339) that "Belgium is the most densely populated country in Europe with a population of 710 to the square mile."

balance between industry and agriculture. Among European nations Belgium has always been an exception as one country in which immigration to it regularly exceeds emigration from it. And its people have been exceptionally prosperous. In fact, the only motive strong enough to impel the home-loving Belgians to migrate has been the fact that there were six million people living in an area of slightly less than 12,000 square miles. This very density of people (462 persons per square mile) forced the Belgians, especially the Flemish farmers, to cultivate their small farms most intensively and made them unusually capable farmers. Their tradition of successful farming inclined them to stay on the land if it was at all possible. However, with a rapidly rising population and a fixed land area it was inevitable that many Belgian farmers would be forced to migrate if they hoped to continue as farmers.

As far back as 1683, when the Belgian priest, Louis Hennepin, published the account of his wondrous voyage down the Mississippi Valley, Belgian farmers had read of the abundant open lands in America.[70] More recently they had heard from an English priest, Father Henry Formby, of the possibilities of sending organized Catholic colonies into the newly established western states. Hence when Angelus Van Hee, one of their own friends, returned from America and assured them that the publicity they had read was not exaggeration, fifty young families of his acquaintance prepared to join him in the new settlement.[71] These men were not indigent migrants; they were successful farmers, possessed of sufficient capital to transport their families to Minnesota and to buy outright not the railroad lands offered by Bishop Ireland but improved farms that had originally been claimed by the earlier Scandinavian homesteaders. In his interview with the *Times* reporter Father Nugent predicted that the Belgians would be competent farmers.[72] And if the judgment of history has been hard

70. Jean Delanglez, *Hennepin's Description of Louisiana*, Chicago, 1941.

71. This statement is taken from Father John Pilger's account of the founding of the Ghent parish, referred to in note 68 above. This manuscript account, in the record file of that parish today, is based exclusively on the parochial records and the testimony of the old settlers, many of whom were alive at the time the document was compiled. I am indebted to Father John Siebenand, present pastor at Ghent, for making the document available for study.

72. New York *Times* (October 9, 1880), p. 3.

on this zealous English priest for his sponsorship of the unfortunate Connemaras, it should be emphasized with equal vigor that
he was originally responsible for recruiting the long line of Belgian settlers who began arriving in Lyon County, Minnesota, in
the spring of 1881.

When they first saw Grandview station, the site selected by
Van Hee and later renamed Ghent in honor of the ancient Flemish
city, most of the original fifty families (350 persons), dismayed
by the reports of the great blizzard of 1880, gave up the notion
of settling in Minnesota and went back to live among the Belgian
communities already established near Chicago and Moline.[73] In
later years when members of this contingent heard favorable reports of the crops being harvested by their Minnesota cousins,
most of them returned to settle permanently in Lyon County, but
at the beginning Angelus Van Hee's little band had no more
than a dozen families.[74]

Van Hee set the pace for his fellow settlers by constructing on
his farm a large and comfortable home in the style of their Belgian homeland. The other settlers followed his lead and built spacious homes and large storage houses in the European style. All
of them "bought large tracts of land, and Messrs. Vandewoe-
styne, Decock, Vergote and Foulon bought improved farms of 160
acres." [75]

In accord with his usual practice, John Ireland had arranged
for a Belgian priest to accompany this emigrant group from its
native land to the new colony. Father L. Cornelius arrived in Lyon
County with Angelus Van Hee and the other Belgian families in
April 1881. Ireland then appointed Cornelius pastor in Minneota,
the colony center at that time, and transferred the Irish Father
Hanley to another post.[76] The bishop undoubtedly assumed that
Cornelius could learn English in his dealings with the English

73. Lyon County *Independent,* Marshall, Minn. (June 15, 1933), p. 1. This
statement was confirmed by several old settlers at Ghent, Minnesota, in an interview on June 20, 1953.

74. Ibid. See also Rose, "We the People," Marshall *Messenger,* March 19, 1953.

75. De Vos, "The Catholic Colony of Ghent," p. 1. This document is the typescript of the chapter referred to in n. 68 above and is part of the parish files at
Ghent, Minnesota.

76. Rose, *The History of Lyon County,* p. 184.

and Irish colonists more easily than Hanley could learn Flemish in ministering to the Belgian parishioners. Father Cornelius constructed a frame church at Minneota and then arranged to offer Mass at regular intervals in the railroad station at Ghent.[77] This schedule was not difficult, since the two settlements were only six miles apart, and both were on the railroad.

During the summer of 1882 the Lyon County settlements were visited by two French-Canadians named Letourneau and Regnier. These men were members of a French-Canadian Catholic settlement at Kankakee, Illinois. Their numbers in this settlement were then expanding so rapidly that the community leaders had sent Letourneau and Regnier on a tour of western lands to find a suitable site for a new farming community. They had traveled through most of the open land still available in western Iowa and in the eastern portion of the Dakota Territory, but they were especially impressed by the fact that the open lands in Lyon County were part of an organized Catholic parish, with a resident French-speaking pastor. They reported on these lands to the older settlement in Illinois, and within a few months fifty new French-Canadian farmers had bought and paid cash for more than 4,000 acres of railroad land within Bishop Ireland's Lyon County holdings. Possibly an equal amount of non-railroad land was purchased by the same group.[78] "The arrival of these people in the spring (1883) was very encouraging. They filled a whole train, several freight cars and a coach. There were [sic] furniture, horses and cattle enough to provide a whole township. There were about fifty persons and more than one Illinois horse for everyone." [79]

77. Lyon County *Independent* (June 15, 1933), p. 1.

78. De Vos, "The Catholic Colony at Ghent," p. 2. See also Lyon County *Independent*, June 15, 1933. These French farmers were definitely not poor men. One Mr. Paradis bought an improved farm of 240 acres for himself, another 240 acres for his two sons, Amilien and Cyrille, and a half section (320 acres) for his two nephews, Suprenant-Lord and Lord-Paradis. Messrs. Antony Paradis, Suprenant-Prairie, and Metty each purchased improved farms and buildings from earlier owners. The Mr. Regnier who had made the original tour of inspection bought an entire section (640 acres) for himself and his son. A Mr. Caron bought 400 acres; Le Beau, 320 acres; Caron, another 200 acres; Nevall, 160 acres; Duchene, 160 acres; Emilien Suprenant, 160 acres; and a Mr. Padnaud, a modest farm of 60 acres.

79. De Vos, p. 2.

At a time when oxen were still the most common type of draft animal on the frontier, such extensive ownership of the more expensive horses and dairy cattle indicates a high level of prosperity among these French-Canadian settlers.

The winters in this region were both long and severe. The roads were simply tracks on the prairie sod. In wet or cold weather the long trip to the county grist mill at Lynd was arduous in the extreme. The prairie was vast, the houses dotting its surface were far apart, and the sod huts of the less-endowed settlers did not mitigate its bleakness and solitude.[80] Hence the arrival of every new settler—presaging as it did more production, improved roads, and closer neighbors—was met with a degree of enthusiasm that has since been considered typical of frontier hospitality.

In January 1883 Father Cornelius returned to Belgium to recruit additional settlers for the young colony. He delivered a series of lectures in Belgium and Holland explaining the opportunities for settlement in Minnesota. In this tour the Belgian priest had the advantage of speaking to audiences which for the most part had already been favorably disposed by the "America Letters" they had received from friends and cousins in Minnesota. Within a few months he left Belgium for America, accompanied by another Belgian priest, Father Jules Emile De Vos, and seventeen families of settlers from Belgium and Holland.[81]

When this contingent arrived, Bishop Ireland named Father De Vos resident pastor of Ghent and gave the parish of St. Eloi independent status, separate from the parent parish of St. Edward in Minneota. Almost all the settlers who came with Father De Vos were able to buy large farms and build comfortable houses at once.[82] Those who were not able to purchase their own farms signed on as farm laborers during their first spring and summer in the colony. After the autumn harvest, these laborers left the colony to go to Moline, Illinois, to spend the winter months as

80. Ibid.
81. Ibid., p. 1.
82. Lyon County *Independent*, June 15, 1933. See also the Ghent parish journal, started by Father De Vos. On p. 3 his entries, written in French, begin with the events of the spring of 1883. This book is part of the Ireland Papers, St. Paul Seminary Archives.

Fig. 6. Interior of a passenger coach on the St. Paul and Pacific Railroad

factory workers in the John Deere farm machinery plant in that city.[83]

Previous to the Civil War, Rock Island and Moline in Illinois had attracted great numbers of immigrant settlers because of their rich lead mines. The presence of this valuable ore, strategically situated on the Mississippi River and far enough north to be safe from Confederate raiding forces, had made the twin cities of Rock Island and Moline prosperous arsenals during the Civil War. After the war the two cities managed to retain their industrial prominence by turning some of their idle factory space to the production of farm machinery. The Cyrus McCormick "Old Reliable" wire self-binder was then at the height of its popularity, and the rapid expansion of wheat planting in the western states was creating a ready market for new and improved planting and harvesting machines.[84] During this period these two cities established themselves as world centers for farm machinery production, and they have never lost this position of leadership.

How the personnel for these factories and mines was originally recruited is not clear, but it is known that by 1875 a sizable colony of Belgian skilled artisans had secured employment in the John Deere factory at Moline.[85] It was their practice to send money back to Belgium to enable other skilled laborers to come to America. The same factories also provided numerous unskilled jobs for such men as the farm laborers from the Lyon County settlements in Minnesota. These winter jobs enabled the young Belgian workers to save the income from their summer harvesting jobs and eventually provided enough additional capital for most

83. According to information given to me orally by several old settlers at Ghent, June 20, 1953.

84. Rogin, *The Introduction of Farm Machinery*, p. 112.

85. One of the old settlers still living at Ghent related to me his experiences in first coming to the United States. He arrived as a laborer, hoping to earn enough money to buy his own farm. His passage money, paid by a friend who had already secured a factory job in Moline, had come with a letter telling him to go to Rock Island, Illinois; hence "Rock Island, Illinois" were the only English words he knew. At New York, on the immigrant train, and at all points of transfer, he merely repeated these magic words. During the last lap of his journey, the train conductor came to him, indicated by sign language that he should gather up his luggage, and repeated "Rock Island, Illinois," as he pointed out the window to the city just ahead (interview, June 20, 1953).

of them to purchase their own land in the Minnesota colonies. One remarkable feature in this story of the enterprising Belgian immigrants is that when they came to America looking for good farm land, they seldom lost sight of this objective. They shuttled between farm labor and factory labor jobs until they had enough money to buy their own farms. In the meantime they did not become enamored of city life or factory occupations. In Belgium they had been farmers, and they had come to America specifically to find good land and to continue as farmers. If land was not immediately available, they would rent or lease a farm at some distance from their friends and relations, but only until such time as they could buy their own land near their friends.[86]

In 1880 the newly arrived Belgian farmers at Ghent were only a handful of prairie settlers in the vast distances of Lyon County. Today their children and grandchildren own and operate almost every farm in the vicinity of Ghent [87] and Minneota, and their descendants make up a great part of the neighboring settlements of Marshall, Green Valley, and Cottonwood.

If the work of John Ireland, Dillon O'Brien, and John Sweetman in settling western Minnesota demonstrates conclusively any single axiom for future colonizers, it is that contained in John Sweetman's discerning remark: "Men taken at haphazard will not succeed in Western farming." [88] Of all who came to the Catholic settlements in Minnesota between 1875 and 1881, the Belgians

86. This practice is still observed among the Belgian-American farmers at Ghent, Minneota, Green Valley, Cottonwood, and Marshall, Minnesota. All these rural communities, located in a circle around the original Belgian colony, now have a large Belgian-American population. If a young man from this area marries at a time when no farms nearby are for sale, he will rent a farm in a neighboring county until a farm near home comes up for sale; then and only then will he buy his own farm. It is almost unknown for any young man to want to leave the area or change to another vocation. Very rarely does any young person go to college. Farming is their life; and their farms are prosperous, with modern houses, large barns, colorful flower gardens, an abundance of modern machinery, and a late-model car or two in every garage. The Katholieke Digest for November 1950, published in Louvain, Belgium, in an article on Ghent, Minnesota, reproduces a photograph of a very modern set of farm buildings, taken at Ghent, with the caption: "een goede doeninge, met twee cars in de barn" (p. 63).

87. According to the most recent census (1950) there are 332 inhabitants of Ghent, Minnesota. Of these 316 are Catholics.

88. Sweetman, Farms for Sale, p. 64.

have been the most successful colonizers, because they were
farmers when they left home. They knew the science of agriculture, and they wanted to continue as farmers. The only reason
for their leaving home was a desire to find more and better land
than was then available to them in Belgium and Holland.

Conversely, the Irish settlers who were brought to Minnesota
by various forms of "assisted emigration" were almost universally
unsuccessful. These were men, to use Sweetman's term, "taken
at haphazard." Almost without exception they left the land as
soon as they could. This should not surprise anyone who will consider their previous training and qualification. Few of them had
ever farmed before; none had money at stake in the farming
venture and hence risked no loss by giving up the land. Probably
of even more significance, they had not been tested by the rigors
of independent farming on any earlier frontiers in states lying
east of Minnesota.

The Irish-American farmers who came to Minnesota by stages
are the ones who have persevered. These are the farmers with
Irish names who now farm the land at De Graff, Clontarf, Graceville, Avoca, Currie, Adrian, Lismore, and Iona. The stages of
their respective treks westward can be followed in the pages of
the unpublished state and federal census reports for the years the
colonies were getting started. These census schedules indicate the
place of birth for every child and adult listed. Such listings make
it possible to check the various stages in the movement of a family. For example, the Irish-American settlers who made up the bulk
of the De Graff and Clontarf settlements in 1876 had already
moved at least twice before coming to Minnesota. Often the head
of the family is listed as having been born in Ireland, his wife in
New York or Massachusetts, his first two children in Pennsylvania
or Ohio, and his last two or three in Indiana or Illinois.[89] The evi-

89. Complete files of these unpublished census schedules can be found today
only at the Minnesota Historical Society library in St. Paul; the files of the National Archives in Washington are incomplete for these counties for these years.
See esp. the Minnesota state census schedules for 1865, 1875, and 1885; and the
United States census schedules for 1870, 1880, and 1890. The overlapping of the
figures for the decennial federal census and the mid-decade decennial state
census gives unusually complete and reliable material for the historian of local
history.

dence is overwhelming that the actual process of migration, through various stages, conditioned the Irish-American farmer. At home he had not learned the science of agriculture, because that science was then neither widely known nor carefully practiced in Ireland.[90] Settlers coming from farms in Belgium or Germany or Quebec had a tremendous initial advantage over the Irish farmer brought directly from his native land to the American West. The European farmers knew the value and importance of fertilizer and the necessity for crop rotation, and they knew from experience the bountiful rewards the earth would yield to those who tended it wisely and with perseverance. These important truths the Irish-American farmer had to learn by trial and error on small farms in the East before he could succeed on a large farm in the West.

This interpretation does not imply or assume any kind of national genius on the part of either European settlers or native Americans. It is based simply upon a recognition of the vital importance of the cultural heritage and previous training brought to the western frontier by new settlers.[91] Free land did not make these settlers over; it merely challenged them to apply the talents and training they brought with them. By and large, the European settlers (from Belgium, Holland, and Germany) came with superior training and knowledge in agriculture. Other Europeans and many Irish immigrants who came to Minnesota by progressive stages had learned on various eastern "frontiers" the new skills necessary for western farming. And what is just as important, they had learned to appreciate the demands and the rewards of the farming life. The immigrant newly arrived from Galway, with his memories of farm life, its insecurity, its poverty, and its intolera-

90. Richard H. Shryock, "British versus German Traditions in Colonial Agriculture," *Mississippi Valley Historical Review*, 26 (June 1939), 39–54. Although Shryock here speaks primarily of the weakness of British agricultural training, his remarks can be applied with even greater force to Irish agricultural practices. For more evidence on "backward farming methods in Ireland" see William Forbes Adams, *Ireland and Irish Emigration to the New World, from 1815 to the Famine* (New Haven, 1932), pp. 42–6.

91. For additional documentation on this point see Shryock, pp. 39, 47. Here Shryock advances the opinion that immigrants "sought out the soils with which they were familiar" and the "tendency of (some) groups to select superior soils was in itself a cultural factor of considerable significance."

ble injustice did not plunge joyously into the life of a western farmer.

Ole Rolvaag's hero, Per Hansa, conversely, is very much a farmer in the European tradition. As he awoke at dawn on his first day on the Dakota prairie, he dressed quickly and hurried out to yoke his sleepy oxen. Long before breakfast he had plowed several furrows in the rich prairie loam. This was his own, his very own land; and it promised him wealth, social position, and honor. In Norway his father had labored a lifetime but had never been rich enough to own eighty acres of such soil as this.

Similarly, after Kirtland, Ohio, Nauvoo, Illinois, and Council Bluffs, Iowa, Brigham Young knew when he saw the Great Basin in Utah that this was "the place." European, French-Canadian, and Irish-American farmers who knew what they wanted when they left home recognized it when they found it in western Minnesota. Others who came and saw that vast prairie, stretching for miles to the western sky, were only repelled by its loneliness. They moved back to the cities in search of another kind of opportunity.

CHAPTER SEVEN

The Poor Men Failed

THE TWENTY-FOUR FAMILIES of destitute Connemara Irish peasants brought directly to Big Stone County, Minnesota, in the spring of 1880 by Bishop Ireland were complete failures on the land. Similarly, the earliest Sweetman colony settlers, recruited largely in County Meath, Ireland, in the spring of 1881 and brought directly to Murray County, Minnesota, proved to their benefactor, John Sweetman, that western lands should only be claimed by men who were already skilled in agriculture.[1] Sweetman learned that the best western farmers were those men who had had earlier successes on smaller farms in the East and who had been attracted to the West by the greater harvests and cheaper lands. After years of experience he felt that western colonizers should never try to pick their settlers; a kind of process of natural selection would bring to their colonies the settlers best qualified to succeed there. After failing in his initial proposal to aid indigent Irish cottiers, Sweetman saved his colony in Minnesota by selling his lands "to the sons of farmers in the Eastern States who were anxious to obtain cheap lands."[2] Writing thirty years after the opening of this colony, he summarized his experience in recruiting colonists: "There is a great difficulty in making a selection of persons who have these qualities [i.e. traits qualifying them to be successful in the West], and perhaps it is wise to make use of natural selection, by choosing those who have laid by something themselves which proves them to have been more thrifty than their neighbors."[3]

Unfortunately, the dramatic overtones of the Connemara and Sweetman failures have proved too great a temptation to many

1. Sweetman, "The Sweetman Colony," p. 64.
2. Ibid., p. 65.
3. Ibid., p. 64.

154

popular historians. There is something peculiarly attractive about
the narration of misfortune. When it is used in the writing of
history, this human fascination for calamity has often produced
dramatic but distorted and inaccurate portrayals. One recent speci-
men of this type of history cites the Connemara incident as typical of the "failure" which marked the Minnesota colonies, but it
does not indicate that the twenty-four families from Connemara
and the handful of early Sweetman settlers were only a tiny fraction of the larger numbers who came to the Catholic colonies of
Minnesota and stayed to become successful farmers. The work dis-
misses the entire Minnesota project of Bishop Ireland in three sentences. "John Ireland . . . did not get very far [in the work of
colonization], because by then it was too late. . . . In 1880 . . .
he induced three hundred fishermen from Donegal to migrate to
Minnesota . . . [and] it is hardly surprising that they proved
failures as farmers. What should have been done was not to bring
over more immigrants from Ireland but to induce those already in
the great cities to settle on the land." [4]

The facts of the Connemara incident are pertinent to the present study of why certain Minnesota colonists failed while others,
given the same opportunities, succeeded. Early in 1880, when
the effects of the bad harvest of 1879 were beginning to be felt in
the poorer districts of Ireland, one pastor in a western county there
wrote to Father Nugent in Liverpool: "This locality is not fit for
human habitation. Not more than a third of the present population can live in any sort of comfort on the land." [5] In answer to this

4. Maynard, *The Catholic Church and the American Idea*, pp. 121–2. Maynard
compresses five major errors within these three sentences. (1) The record shows
that John Ireland did not begin colonizing in Minnesota "too late." He began
just after the time when the cheap railroad lands were first opened. (2) It is not
at all clear that "he did not get very far": see above, Chap. 3. (3) Bishop Ireland did not "induce" the Connemara settlers to migrate to Minnesota; he
yielded, against his better judgment, to the importunate pleas of Father Nugent,
who implored some help for the starving famine sufferers of 1879–80. (4) These
settlers did not come from Donegal, as Maynard says, but from Connemara in
Galway. (5) John Ireland also realized, even in 1880, that emigration from
Ireland was not to be encouraged and that eastern urban dwellers should be
solicited to move west. Maynard's assumption that Ireland did not understand
this truth is in conflict with Ireland's own statement in *NWC* (January 22, 1876),
p. 5, col. 3.
5. Moynihan, "Archbishop Ireland's Colonies," p. 221.

and similar pleas, Nugent solicited contributions from his friends in Liverpool and crossed over to the West of Ireland to distribute the alms thus collected. Unfortunately, his resources were not sufficient to relieve the distress he found among the stricken Irish, and "He decided that something radical was needed, that the country was growing less able year by year to support its population." [6]

He found some Irish families paying an annual rent of five pounds for three- or five-acre plots of soil so wretched that it afforded its tenants nothing more than a place to live.[7] He reasoned that if means could be found to evacuate one hundred of these families, the remaining residents in that district would be able to survive by dividing the meager land holdings of those who had emigrated. He wrote to Bishop Ireland and Bishop O'Connor to ask if fifty such Irish families could be sponsored in Minnesota and fifty in Nebraska. Bishop O'Connor and Onahan replied that they could not accept such destitute families in their Nebraska colonies. On the other hand, although it was contrary to all the fundamentals of good colonization previously laid down by John Ireland, that Minnesota prelate appealed to the people of Minnesota, through the columns of the *Northwestern Chronicle*, to help him meet this plea.[8] His appeal brought in $5,000. A similar one published in Chicago, however, brought in nothing.[9] Since the Irish Land League in Liverpool had denounced the plan of Father Nugent and had labeled him and Bishop Ireland "Minnesota enemies of Ireland"—and since Parnell was in the United States at this very time soliciting funds for the Irish Land League—it is not surprising that the Chicago Catholics, led by Onahan, denied John Ireland's appeal out of loyalty to the voices from home.

With more courage than his $5,000 warranted, and assured by several railroads that his "Connemaras" would be transported without charge from Boston to St. Paul, Ireland cabled Nugent to send the fifty families to Boston. The Bishop instructed Major Ben Thompson, his agent in Big Stone County, to reserve fifty

6. Bennett, *Father Nugent of Liverpool*, p. 101.
7. *NWC* (March 20, 1880), p. 1.
8. Ibid.
9. *Catholic Review* (April 10, 1880), p. 10.

farms of 160 acres each for these settlers, to construct a small frame house on each farm, and to break five acres of prairie sod for immediate tillage on each farm.[10] "On June 11, 1880, the 'Connemaras,' three hundred and nine in number, not one of whom probably had ever put his hand to a plough, embarked on board the 'Austrian' at the port of Galway, and landed at Boston on June 22." [11] Dillon O'Brien met the ship in Boston and escorted the group to Minnesota. At the sight of the destitute emigrant band, his worst fears must have been confirmed.

"The kindly but visionary Father Nugent . . . . [had chosen] from the most congested districts not the competent but the incompetent; not the industrious but the shiftless; a group composed of mendicants who knew nothing of farming, and were entirely unfitted to cope with life upon the American prairie." [12] O'Brien was careful, however, not to express his fears about their future and confidently predicted to a newspaper reporter, "It does look bad, but I'll wager a new hat that before twenty years some of these same people will come to Boston dressed in broadcloth; that they put up at your best hotel and eat at the best table in the house." [13] It is not recorded that any of the little band ever saw Boston again, but within twenty months, not twenty years, the reporter could have collected his new hat.

In Chicago, O'Brien and his charges were met by Onahan, whose St. Patrick's Society provided them with warm meals and additional articles of clothing. Onahan was appalled at the poverty and suffering which were evident in these people. "The famine

10. Henthorne, *The Irish Catholic Colonization Association*, pp. 109, 111. Sister Mary Evangela's account of the Connemara settlers in Graceville is by far the best study of this group. She is too modest when she asserts that Egan's account (above, Chap. 3, n. 38) is superior to hers. The Egan account of the Connemara settlers is considerably weakened by its error in assuming that the people sent from Connemara to Minnesota in 1883, financed by the Quaker philanthropist James Hack Tuke, are the same "Connemaras" as those who settled at Graceville in 1880. The group sponsored by Tuke settled in Murray County, at Avoca, Minnesota.

11. Moynihan, "Archbishop Ireland's Colonies," p. 221.

12. O'Brien, "Dillon O'Brien," p. 50. This account, written by Dillon O'Brien's son, is based on family reminiscences of the older man's private remarks on the settlers from Connemara.

13. *Catholic Review*, July 3, 1880, quoting a reporter for the New York *Herald*, recorded in Henthorne, *The Irish Catholic Colonization Association*, p. 110.

was visible in their pinched and emaciated faces, and in the shriveled limbs—they could scarcely be called legs and arms—of the children. Their features were quaint, and the entire company was squalid and wretched. It was a painful revelation to all who witnessed it." [14]

Delegations of citizens met the immigrants in St. Paul, and Bishop Ireland secured employment in the city for forty-five young men and thirty-five young women.[15] Very likely the latter were mostly employed as domestics. But even in these positions they were able to send some money on to their families in the colony. When the main body of the settlers arrived in Graceville, Big Stone County, Bishop Ireland instructed each of the families already established in the colony to take one immigrant family into its home until all the new homes were completed. Here the friction started. Several of the earlier colonists objected to the dirty clothes, rough speech, and offensive manners of the newcomers. One prominent lady in Graceville announced that she would not receive such persons in her home.[16] Fortunately, most of the new houses were soon ready, and the Connemaras moved into their own quarters.

In a private letter to Bishop O'Connor, Onahan promptly voiced his fears about the unfitness of the Connemara group for western settlement, and warned the bishop to be prepared for further pleas from Father Nugent on behalf of other such contingents from Ireland:

14. *Catholic Review,* January 1, 1881, quoting a statement by Onahan in the Chicago *Tribune,* recorded in Henthorne, p. 110.

15. Ibid., p. 111.

16. Mrs. Maurice Greene was so disturbed by the sight of the Connemara people "fighting like animals" that she refused them admission to her home. This statement is taken from an interview granted me by Sister Grace Aurelia, C.S.J., at the Provincial House of the Sisters of St. Joseph, St. Paul, Minnesota, September 5, 1953. Sister Grace was the daughter of Mrs. Maurice Greene. Her family moved to Graceville in 1880 from Marlboro, Massachusetts, when she was nine years old. She was the first girl from this colony to enter the religious life, and took the name Grace Aurelia out of deference to Bishop Ireland's request that she take some form of the name of Graceville. As will be evident in subsequent pages, I am greatly indebted to Sister Grace Aurelia for her willing contribution of a wealth of interesting details on the early life of the Graceville colonists.

Father Nugent is not content to rest with the one experiment of fifty families of the Connemara people he lately sent over. He is eager to send the other 50 to Nebraska and he writes me pressing strongly for cooperation. I had my share of trouble with the Minnesota contingent, nearly 300 in number, last week, and though I would not shirk any duty in regard to aiding my poor countrymen I most sincerely hope I shall have no such task again. A more wretched lot of people I never saw, and their condition at home must have been deplorable. I would not care to say publicly but I am convinced they would ruin the prospects of any colony into which they would find an entrance. I do not wish to give the reasons for this opinion—they would not be to the credit of the Connemara Emigrants. Despite these convictions I applaud Fr. Nugent for his work and Bp. Ireland for his cooperation. For these people any change is a boon and a blessing and it is God's work to help them. If land can be obtained for them apart from the colonies and aid given them as in the late experiment, well and good. I write this as likely Fr. Nugent will address you on the subject.

We can get plenty of emigrants from Ireland for Greeley Co. who, besides possessing means, will also have the other necessary qualities—which I am sorry to say the late emigrants seem to be wholly lacking.[17]

At Bishop Ireland's expense, each of the new families was given a supply of clothing, the necessary articles of house furnishings, farming implements, a year's supply of seed, and credit at Graceville for a year's supply of food.[18] Their arrival on the farms coincided with the time for spring planting, and the prospects for a heavy grain crop were good. There was also at this time ample opportunity for the men in the new families to secure employment as day laborers. Prosperous farmers among the earlier arrivals were paying hired men wages of $1.50 to $2.00 a day.[19] The west-

17. Onahan to O'Connor, July 1, 1880, Omaha Chancery Archives, Colonization File.

18. Henthorne, *The Irish Catholic Colonization Association*, p. 111.

19. *NWC* (September 11, 1880), p. 1.

ern extension of the Saint Cloud and Lake Traverse Railroad from Morris, Minnesota, was coming closer each day. The farmers had the assurance of a rail terminal and grain elevator in their colony before harvest time of that year. Moreover, construction on the new line offered additional opportunities for employment for those new settlers who needed ready cash.[20] Nearly every family among the newcomers had at least one member working in the city of St. Paul and earning enough to be able to send home additional money each month. All in all, the prospects for the little band looked very good.

As might have been expected, Bishop Ireland was not at all disposed to hear any criticism of these Irish settlers or pessimism about their prospects as farmers. He urged O'Brien and Major Thompson to do all they could to make adjustment easier for the settlers and promised the people that he would be most patient with them in any difficulties they might experience in their new positions.[21] The Bishop looked on this particular band of Irish settlers as a test case in his grand plan. He knew that their background as fishermen and garden farmers handicapped them for large-scale farming in the West. Nonetheless he fondly hoped that they might, with his extensive aid, become successful farmers and thus silence any nativist critics who held that foreign-born settlers made second-rate citizens or third-rate farmers.

During the first summer no signs of trouble appeared among the Connemaras. Day laboring jobs were plentiful, and a good growing season promised an abundant harvest. In September of 1880 Bishops Ireland and Spalding toured the Minnesota colonies and inspected the Graceville settlement with particular care. Ireland recalled later that he personally visited more than 100 of the 400 colony homes. He found no evidence of any want or suffering, but he did sense an uneasy atmosphere of discontent in the conversation of some of the Connemara people. He was displeased to discover that some members of this group did not look forward to a life of farming but were content to take their place as day laborers in the community. What was worse, several of them indicated to him that they were not satisfied with the treatment they

20. Ibid. See also Henthorne, pp. 112–13.
21. Henthorne, p. 113.

were receiving from their employers, particularly with the "low"
pay scale of $1.50 to $2.00 a day. Ireland's answer was prompt
and effective. He immediately inaugurated at Graceville a system of public works, financed by the diocese, offering day laboring jobs to all comers at a wage of $1.00 a day! He also announced
that any man who could not find employment to suit him in the
public works program or on colony farms, would have his credit
for provisions cut off in Graceville.[22]

It was obvious to the bishop, if not to his protégés, that day
laboring jobs would never bring in enough money to enable the
colonists to pay for their farms. At the basis of the entire colonization program lay the assumption that it was individual ownership
of land that gave a man status and security. For Ireland it was
unthinkable that any colonists could seriously consider staying on
farms without farming the land. The earlier settlers, displaying the
energy and industry characteristic of frontier areas, were at this
time quickly paying off their debts to the railroad. The average
price of hard Minnesota wheat during these years was $1.00 a
bushel, and it was not unusual for the Graceville lands to yield
twenty bushels of wheat to the acre. This meant that in an average
year the yield from an acre of wheat sold for nearly five times the
original cost of the land. The arrival of the railroad and the erection of a grain elevator in Graceville assured the farmers that this
same happy state of affairs would likely continue in the future.

The unfortunate Connemaras, however, had never learned to
think in terms of future crop prospects. During the summer of
1880 they were content to hire themselves out to other farmers,
satisfied with a small cash income at the end of each week and possibly reassured by the underlying conviction that if they came on
hard times Bishop Ireland would support them. It was this readiness on their part to receive relief that alarmed the bishop. Other
colonists noticed the same traits and "the improvidence of the
Connemaras quickly aroused the ire and indignation of the Graceville colony and alienated sympathy from the newcomers." [23]

In partial explanation of the failure of this group it should be

22. *NWC* (September 11, 1880), p. 1.
23. Moynihan, "Archbishop Ireland's Colonies," p. 221. See also Reardon,
Diocese of St. Paul, p. 242.

observed that no farmer showed a profit during his first or second year in these colonies, because it took at least this long for him to break up a reasonably extensive portion of the unusually hard and tough prairie sod. Breaking was a most arduous process. Sometimes it was done by huge breaking plows, drawn by four oxen.[24] Less fortunate settlers had to devise heavy "stone boats," equipped with steel prongs to break up the sod. Several trips with these implements were required before a given patch of sod turned over. It was then necessary to leave the upturned sod exposed to the elements for a whole year before it would rot and break up. If a man could turn and break ten acres a year, he was doing well. But time, of course, was working for the settlers. Minneapolis had already become an important milling center. It had also been discovered by this time that Minnesota hard wheat, a particular species grown most successfully in western and southern Minnesota, produced a superior grade of white flour. Wheat buyers as early as 1876 had announced that premium prices would be paid for all Minnesota hard wheat delivered at the Minneapolis mills.[25] This rising market, the arrival of the railroad, the increased export of American grain, and the improvement of bonanza farming equipment all augured well for the future. In the meantime, however, it took years of patient labor to get the western soil in condition for intensive farming operations. But even when this important qualification has been taken into account, the performance of the Connemaras as farmers still left much to be desired.

Some of them sold the seed given them by Bishop Ireland; others kept the seed but did not plant it; still others picked up additional cash by selling the farming tools he had given them. It is small wonder that they were totally unprepared for the unusually early and severe winter of 1880. On their arrival in the spring they had been warned by Dillon O'Brien of the severity of Minnesota winters and had been instructed by Major Thompson on the necessity of sodding the exterior foundations of their frame

24. Benson *Times* (June 5, 1876), p. 4.
25. Taken from a letter by Dillon O'Brien, originally published in Ignatius Donnelly's *Anti-Monopolist* and later reprinted in the Benson *Times* (February 23, 1876), p. 4.

houses as a protection against the cold. This many of them neglected to do. Once winter was upon them it was not long before
reports of great suffering began to emanate from the Connemara
section of the Graceville colony. Bishop Ireland appealed to his
people in St. Paul and managed to send the Connemaras about
$600 each month during their period of greatest need. He also sent
Dillon O'Brien to Graceville to administer these funds and advise
the unfortunate settlers. O'Brien publicly expressed his disappointment with the Connemaras in an article published the next
spring in the New York *Sun:*

> Last winter when the snow was too deep for horses and
> sleighs, the other farmers in the colony bought flour at the
> Society's station and drew it by hand on sleds over the snow
> to their homes. The Connemara men would not take the flour
> away, although to them it was a free gift. Some of the farm-
> ers, when a sum was offered them to carry the flour to the
> homes of the Connemara men, said they were willing enough
> to make a dollar, but that they would not turn their hands to
> benefit such a lazy people.[26]

Writing on the same topic in the Chicago *Tribune*, William J.
Onahan shared O'Brien's shame at the improvidence and laziness
of the Connemara crowd: "If their shanties were cold, it was because they neglected to sod them as they were advised to do. If
their potatoes were frozen, they had plainly omitted to dig cellars
for their protection. If, perhaps, they suffered from the lack of
fuel, it must be remembered that they suffered in common with
the prairie population of the extreme northwest generally." [27]

When officials of the colony chided these settlers for spurning
the means of existence offered by Bishop Ireland, the offenders
replied, "the Bishop brought us here and he must care for us." [28]
Reports of the suffering within the colony began to multiply and
soon a printed account of the disaster was published by the
Board of Trade at Morris, Minnesota, a small town twenty-five

26. New York *Sun*, quoted in the *Catholic Review*, March 26, 1881. See also
Henthorne, p. 113.
27. Chicago *Tribune*, quoted in the *Catholic Review*, January 1, 1881, and in
Henthorne, p. 114.
28. Moynihan, "Archbishop Ireland's Colonies," p. 222.

miles east of Graceville. Charges of neglect were made against Ireland and O'Brien. Public sympathy for the settlers increased when the same reports were reprinted by the St. Paul *Pioneer-Press*. It was especially painful to Dillon O'Brien, whose death was to occur within a year and who had given his life to the cause of Irish immigrant aid, to realize that his countrymen could display such ingratitude for the favors they had received. And "although it was mid-winter and he was well over sixty years of age, Mr. O'Brien went at once to the scene (i.e. to Graceville), and taking with him non-Catholic citizens from Morris, proved these charges to have been unfounded, and refuted them in newspapers, some as distant as the New York *Sun*, for even that far had slander traveled." [29]

Investigation showed that some of the complaining settlers had even hidden extra food and clothing in a vain attempt to prove to the investigators that they were suffering acutely.[30] The *Northwestern Chronicle* for December 1880 and January 1881 carried extensive reports on the true conditions at Graceville and cleared the colony sponsors of any responsibility for the hardships suffered by these few families. The evidence thus presented was impressive enough to convince the editor of the St. Paul *Pioneer-Press* that his earlier credence of the Morris reports was not justified. He agreed to print an explanatory letter on the colony written by Bishop Ireland, and printed in the same issue his own carefully worded editorial on the whole affair.

Bishop Ireland's letter on the subject of the Connemara colony will be read with great interest. He freely admits that he has got an elephant on his hands in these twenty-four families. In transporting them as an act of charity, from the wild mountains of Galway to homes on the prairies of Minnesota he supposed they were, like most of the Irish emigrants to this state, an industrious and thrifty, though in this case, a poverty-stricken people. He found that they were mostly paupers and beggars. He had a tough problem before him. . . . A little reflection on the nature of the materials the

29. O'Brien, "Dillon O'Brien," p. 51.
30. Moynihan, "Archbishop Ireland's Colonies," p. 222.

bishop has to deal with, and on the methods absolutely necessary to convert them from incorrigible beggars into industrious, self-supporting men and women, will enable their American neighbors at Morris to understand that they have not
been so cruelly dealt with as was imagined.[31]

At least in this instance cheap and fertile lands, with their promise of good harvests to come, did not remake all comers into sturdy
western yeomen.

Having cleared his name with the general public, Ireland turned
to the task of providing further help for the Connemara settlers.
Since these unfortunate people had shown some eagerness to work
for daily wages, and since the city of St. Paul was growing very
rapidly, it was agreed that they would give up their farms and seek
employment in the city. The bishop paid for their transportation to St. Paul and secured jobs for them with the railroad companies, which were then hiring many new workers. Most of these
settlers took up residence "in what came to be known as the 'Connemara Patch' in St. Mary's parish under Dayton's Bluff." [32] Back
in Graceville, "Bishop Ireland finally arranged to distribute among
neighbors the cattle assigned to the Galway immigrants. . . .
The final scene in the Connemara drama was their last moment
effort to recover their cattle and return to their cabins." [33]

In spite of the small numbers involved, the adverse effect of
this failure on the entire colonization movement was nationwide.
In a letter to Bishop O'Connor in Nebraska a Mrs. E. A. Quinn
of Rochester, New York, remarked, "I see the Connemara colonists have badly repaid the trouble taken to provide them comfortable homes. Bishop Ireland must feel a good deal disheartened
about the work." [34] At the same time one Father H. A. O'Kelly
was touring the parishes of New York City in search of settlers for
Bishop O'Connor's colonies in Nebraska. On January 8, 1881, he
wrote to the bishop from New York:

    31. St. Paul *Pioneer-Press*, reprinted in the *Catholic Review* for January 8,
1881, and quoted by Henthorne, p. 116.
    32. Reardon, *Diocese of St. Paul*, p. 242.
    33. Moynihan, "Archbishop Ireland's Colonies," p. 222.
    34. Mrs. E. A. Quinn, Rochester, N.Y., to Bishop James O'Connor, January
12, 1881, Omaha Chancery Archives, Colonization File.

Since my coming I have secured about nine or ten families and I feel confident I would have double the number were it not for that unfortunate Connemara affair. It completely demoralized many who were contemplating emigrating to the West. I have spoken in most of the Churches of New York [City]. I am inclined to think my labors will bear more fruit a year hence than at present. People require some time to think the matter over before they resolve to make a change of such importance.[35]

In a letter to Bishop O'Connor, William J. Onahan also spoke of the bad press which had been caused by the Connemara affair: "I was last week in Minnesota. . . . I saw Bishop Ireland. He has recovered from the Connemara events and thinks that cries will be heard no more. It was a bad business here and elsewhere for colonization—though I think the effect will not be permanent, except possibly as affecting immigration to Minnesota."[36]

In his biography of Dillon O'Brien, his son, Judge Thomas D. O'Brien of St. Paul, related that the strain and disappointment resulting from the Connemara incident contributed greatly to the sudden death of this zealous Catholic layman. Monsignor Humphrey Moynihan, who in later years served as Archbishop Ireland's secretary, summarized the effect of the affair on Ireland himself:

In the undesirable prominence attained by this insignificant group of born beggars the public at large seemed to overlook the existence of hundreds of happy homes dotting the prairies for miles around Graceville. That the disastrous record of the Connemaras caused untold pain and humiliation to the best benefactor Catholic colonists had in America, need not be emphasized. Indeed, Archbishop Ireland confided to Mr. William O'Neill, one of the most prominent members of the Graceville community, that the incident was the greatest grief of his life.[37]

35. Rev. H. A. O'Kelly, New York City, to Bishop James O'Connor, January 8, 1881, Omaha Chancery Archives, Colonization File.
36. Onahan to O'Connor, February 24, 1881, Omaha Chancery Archives, Colonization File.
37. Moynihan, "Archbishop Ireland's Colonies," p. 222.

Less spectacular, hence less publicized, was the initial failure of the Irish emigrants brought by John Sweetman to Currie, Murray County, Minnesota, in the spring of 1881.[38] By this time Sweetman certainly knew of the recent trouble in Graceville. He probably reasoned, however, that since most of his forty-one families of Irish settlers had been farmers in County Meath, they would stand a better chance in Minnesota than the Connemara fishermen. But within a year he found that his colony was heir to the same shocks that had upset the Graceville settlement. He had agreed to pay the passage to Minnesota for all Irish settlers who joined his colony, just as Father Nugent and Bishop Ireland had arranged for the Connemaras. The danger in this practice quickly became apparent when he discovered that "people would profess to be anxious to settle on farms for the sake of obtaining a passage to that paradise of an Irish labourer's imagination—the United States. But having arrived there, they would not remain on their farms, but would go to the cities for the sake of escaping the debt incurred for their passage." [39]

In Ireland men on the land had been saddled with debts and rents too high to be paid in one lifetime. Blighted crops came with such increasing frequency that farmers were demoralized. No one dared contract a debt on the strength of future crop yields. The very idea of debt became repugnant to such persons, and of course the notion that debt could be, under favorable circumstances, a necessary and promising means of credit was totally foreign to their mode of thought. Hence, even though Sweetman's settlers were recruited from the farming districts of Ireland, they proved bad risks on American farms. "Many of them were so poor in Ireland, earning a shilling a day, that when they heard of eight shillings a day for common labourers in the Western cities, it completely turned their heads, and they were unwilling to wait for the slow returns of a farmer's life." [40] Sweetman also learned the folly of extending large credit to untried colonists. "Unless a settler has something of his own invested, he will in too large a per-

38. The high points of the origin of the Sweetman colony at Currie, Murray County, Minnesota, have been recounted above, pp. 67–72.
39. Sweetman, "The Sweetman Colony," p. 62.
40. Ibid., p. 63.

centage of cases lose heart in facing the difficulties of the first few years, and he will find it hard to resist the temptation to leave with the proceeds of his first harvest, for which he has paid nothing himself." [41]

Sweetman's original purchase of 10,000 acres from the Winona and St. Peter Railroad was increased by his later purchase of 7700 acres from the same company. All this land was in the northeastern quarter of Murray County, Minnesota. On each of sixty farms he built a small frame house and announced his intention of building similar small homes on another 30,000-acre tract for which he was negotiating. His initial optimism was soon checked by the great exodus of his first band of settlers. "Of the forty-one settlers who came to Currie [from Ireland] in the spring of 1881, only sixteen were left by 1883." [42]

Among the Sweetman Papers there are countless copies of the land contract which his Irish American Colonization Company negotiated with its settlers. Extended examination of these contracts reveals that in most instances title to the land was held first by someone with an Irish name. With the passing of years, German, French, and Scandinavian names gradually increase, to outnumber the Irish.[43] Among the same papers is an interesting letter sent

41. Ibid.
42. Egan, "Irish Immigration to Minnesota," p. 231.
43. The gradual shift away from Irish names in these colonies is reflected in a variety of records. The manuscript census schedules for 1875, 1880, 1885, and 1890, on file at the Minnesota Historical Society, offer some data on the change within Swift, Lyon, and Murray counties. In the parish baptismal register at Minneota, the first several pages (covering the years 1880–82) contain Irish names almost exclusively. In the same series, the baptismal register for 1900 and the years since rarely lists an Irish name. The shift away from Irish names is more gradual but none the less real in the parish registers for St. Bridget's parish at De Graff: see esp. the baptismal, marriage, and funeral registers on file in the parish office. See also Rose, "We the People": "The Irish arrivals were, as a rule, unskilled in agriculture pursuits and were not successful, and many engaged in other pursuits." See also the lists of homesteads officially declared abandoned by the U.S. Land Office, Swift County *Advocate* (October 12, 1877), p. 4. Most of the names listed are Irish, whereas Irish names are much less common in the lists of those who sought to reclaim these same lands: see Swift County *Advocate* (September 28, 1877), p. 4; (October 5, 1877), p. 4; (October 26, 1877), p. 4; (November 2, 1877), p. 4; (November 28, 1877), p. 4; (March 8, 1878), p. 4; (March 22, 1878), p. 4; and esp. the long summary list (April 12, 1878), p. 4.

to Sweetman by one William Geraghty, an Irish emigrant, who, writing in September 1882, complained that he was not able to meet expenses on his farm and indicated that he had accepted an offer of employment in the city of St. Paul.[44] His story is typical of the "assisted emigrants" from Cavan and Meath who came to Currie in 1881.

John Sweetman lost a great portion of his investment during the first year this colony was in operation. He was, however, a man of great wealth, and also a man of unusual integrity. He was so concerned at the thought that some of his friends in Ireland would lose money in an undertaking directed by him that he returned to Ireland in 1882 and bought up 90 per cent of the stock in the Irish-American Company.[45]

In 1882 he tried again, this time bringing forty more Irish families to Currie. He hoped that by making these emigrants pay their own passage to America he might secure a more reliable type of settler. He was still prepared to finance the purchase of their land, implements, seeds, and food for one year. Even these new precautions and revised credit terms, however, were not enough to make the new settlers successful. Within a year most of this second wave of colonists had also abandoned Currie for the social and economic opportunities of St. Paul.[46]

The venture had cost Sweetman more than 30,000 pounds sterling, but after a decade he was able to recoup most of his loss by selling the colony lands to German Catholics and to French Catholics who came to Minnesota from Kankakee, Illinois.[47] The original plan of transporting colonists directly from Ireland to the West simply did not work. In the end the colony site became a successful Catholic parish. Today it has a Catholic school, a large and beautiful new church, and about 900 registered parishioners. The success which it has achieved as a Catholic center in western Minnesota, however, is not precisely the kind envisioned by

44. William Geraghty, Currie, September 16, 1882, to John Sweetman, among the Sweetman Papers.

45. This statement is based on the oral testimony of Walter Sweetman, nephew of John Sweetman, and on the record of Egan, "Irish Immigration to Minnesota," p. 232.

46. Egan, p. 233.

47. Ibid.

its founder and patron. Writing in 1911, long after he had retired in Ireland, Sweetman observed, "As a scheme for helping Irish emigrants to settle on land in America, my work thirty years ago was a failure, but as establishing a Catholic colony on the prairies, it seems to have been a success." [48]

Strictly speaking, the Sweetman colony was not one of Bishop Ireland's Minnesota settlement projects. In several ways Sweetman's policies differed from those of the bishop. Except in the case of the Connemara group, Ireland accepted no destitute people; Sweetman's colonists were almost entirely from this class. Ireland left the land under railroad title and only transmitted payments from the settlers to the railroad; Sweetman became the actual owner of the land and for several years was in danger of losing heavily through owning land he could not sell. Ireland, while always solicitous for the welfare of his charges, never favored the overwhelming paternalism that characterized Sweetman's project.

In spite of these dissimilarities, Ireland always maintained an abiding interest in the Currie settlement. It was he who first encouraged Sweetman to settle in Minnesota. Also, he sent Dillon O'Brien into western Minnesota with Sweetman, prospecting for a colony site. And once the Sweetman colony began to operate, Ireland immediately sent one of his priests to be the resident pastor. There is strong evidence to indicate that Ireland hoped Sweetman would eventually be so successful as a colonizer that Ireland could entrust all the Minnesota colonies to the Irish philanthropist and thus free himself for the increasingly heavy duties of his episcopacy. Early in 1881 he wrote to Sweetman, "With the present year I will conclude with my colonies to make way for your work and to co-operate more freely with you to the best of my ability." [49] The initial reverses of the Sweetman venture probably prevented Ireland's proposed retirement from active leadership in the colonization movement at the time specified.

In November 1882 the weekly newspaper at Currie printed John Sweetman's first public advertisement of lands for sale. From

48. Sweetman, "The Sweetman Colony," p. 65.

49. NWC (May 7, 1881), p. 4. Bishop Ireland's letter to Sweetman is reprinted entirely in this issue of the NWC.

that date his settlement was no longer an "Irish immigrant colony," and from that date its fortunes began to rise. The same
tide of land-seeking American farmers which was then filling up
the other Minnesota lands began to pour into Murray County.
"It was made the invariable rule that no passage fares would
henceforth be paid by the company, and that one-tenth of the
price of the land must be paid upon the date of purchase. The
company [also] refused to advance any live stock, fuel, food, or
any other perishable articles." [50] The evidence presented by this
shift of policy in the Sweetman colony, coupled with the record
of the Connemaras in Graceville, is at least partial proof of the
general tenet held by John Ireland and disputed by Father
Thomas Butler: successful settlement of the West could not be
financed as a benevolent project. Other Catholic settlements in
Minnesota at this time offered overwhelming evidence in support
of Sweetman's own conclusion on this matter: "A man's interests
are where his money is invested and . . . the hope of making
over human nature by a change of environment is futile, indeed." [51]

It is significant that both the Connemara settlers in Graceville
and the Sweetman colonists in Currie came to Minnesota not
primarily because of any particular good foreseen there but rather
in order to escape an evil at home—in this instance famine. And
since they did not come in search of a particular advantage to
be found in Minnesota, its advantages made no appeal to them
on their arrival. They were in no way prepared to appreciate the
opportunities which this western region then offered. The same
possibilities awaited them that had already enriched many enterprising farmers, but the Irish settlers in these two groups were
unable to respond to the challenge of the almost free land on the
frontier. Their conduct would seem to confirm the opinion that
the frontier does not have the same effect on all persons indis-
criminately but that its much emphasized influence depends upon
the specific conditioning and the receptivity of the settlers who
are brought within its environment.

50. Smith, "The Sweetman Irish Colony," p. 343. This article, based on the
Sweetman Papers at the Minnesota Historical Society, is the best narrative
account in print of the history of the Sweetman colony.
51. Ibid., p. 343.

CHAPTER EIGHT

Life on the Prairie

WHATEVER social, intellectual, or cultural life existed in the western colonies centered around the parish church. Usually it was possible to make only one trip to town each week, the journey to Sunday Mass. Travel by ox cart was tedious and the distances between neighbors so great that families were limited during the week to the social life within their own household. Occasionally the men met their neighbors as they plowed adjoining fields at the limits of their respective farms, but the women were denied even these brief and infrequent social contacts. One extant account by a traveler through this region describes "the stay-at-home woman's view of the prairie as a vastness unrelieved; its utter silence, its appalling rigidity, as of an enormous thing long dead." [1] For all of its inconvenience and the careful planning it required, the weekly trip to Sunday Mass must have been a significant event eagerly anticipated by the isolated settlers. A partial description of one such Sunday gathering is preserved in the biography of James J. Hill.

When Hill decided in June 1876 to take over the insolvent St. Paul and Pacific Railroad, he appealed to George Stephen (later Lord Mountstephen), one of the directors of the Bank of Montreal, for financial backing. The total indebtedness of the road then amounted to $44,000,000. Hill hoped that Stephen would be able to solicit a great part of this sum from his influential friends in Montreal, London, and New York. In order to impress the Canadian banker with the potential of the western rail line, Hill chartered a special train in the spring of 1877 and invited Stephen to inspect the farms and resources along the St. Paul and Pacific. [2] As the train rolled into the West, Stephen was seen to shake his

1. Seth K. Humphrey, *Following the Prairie Frontier* (Minneapolis, 1931), p. 131.
2. Pyle, *The Life of James J. Hill, 1,* 204.

head ominously. On every side he saw "nothing but wild, un-
tenanted prairie." He could not understand how such a barren
region could ever attract settlers or support a railroad. However,
it was a Sunday morning; and as the train pulled into De Graff,
the town was filled with "crowds of people" moving into a "good-
sized structure" near the center of the town. "The trails leading
toward it were covered with conveyances, most of them drawn
by oxen." Turning to Hill, Stephen inquired, "What is all this?"
Hill replied, "This is a colony opened by Bishop Ireland one
single year ago. Already the settlers brought in by the Bishop are
counted by hundreds, and hundreds of others are coming to join
them from different parts of America and Europe. This is Sunday
morning, and the settlers are going to mass." [3] In later years Lord
Strathcona told Archbishop Ireland that the sight of so many settlers gathering at the village church for Sunday Mass had convinced Stephen that the refinancing of a rail line through these
lands was feasible. "From that moment he was won over to the
enterprise." [4]

This graphic incident symbolizes in a way the dual motives
which prompted many of the settlers who moved into the Minnesota colonies. In general they had decided to go west for economic
reasons; but they were moved to settle in this particular portion of
the West because here they were assured the ministrations of a
priest and the consolations of their religion. As farmers these men
wanted better lands, bigger fields, and larger crops. As devout
Catholics they wanted the assurance that they would be able to
assist at Mass, receive the sacraments, and rear their children in
the traditions of Catholic piety. Among such people the Church
definitely acted as a factor of selection. The pioneer parishes
of western Minnesota began with nuclei of Catholics who thought
enough of their religion to make some sacrifices for its preservation and extension.

German settlers who had fled the religious tyranny of Bismarck's May Laws, Irishmen whose filial piety toward the Church
and the priest went back to the "hedge schools" of penal times,
and French-Canadians who had been rated as second-class citi-

3. Ibid., p. 206.
4. Ibid.

zens in the Anglo-Saxon provinces of eastern Canada were prepared to make sacrifices in their new homes in order to foster the
religion for which they had already endured much. Moreover,
the relationship existing between these settlers and the Church
was significantly different from that which had obtained in the
land of their birth. In the Old World the Church, for the most part,
had been "established" in the sense that it continued to exist without seeking regular contributions from the faithful. "At home the
peasants had never to consider the means of paying the expenses.
The Church supported itself by grants either from the State or
from the income of its own lands. [But] all such revenues disappeared with immigration." [5] In the New World there were no
churches to begin with, and the immigrants soon learned that
houses of worship would arise only in those places where residents were willing to sacrifice generously for their erection. "Here
the pious had to create afresh, and at once, what in Europe had
always been at hand, the product of centuries of growth. [And]
the magnitude of the task was multiplied by the circumstance that
it was executed without the support of the kind of authority that
had familiarly operated on the peasants at home." [6]

Although such limitations were serious handicaps for American
Catholics in an earlier day, it is obvious that these trials have in
time worked to the great advantage of the Church in America. In
the transatlantic crossing and in the westward passage, indifferent Catholics found little difficulty in giving up the religion of
their fathers.[7] As a result, the formal efforts at Catholic colonization in the West attracted settlers of more than average zeal and
piety. In his letters to the *Pilot* and the *Northwestern Chronicle*,
Father Martin Mahoney cited the sacrifices the colonists were
willing to make in order to erect new parish churches in western

5. Handlin, *The Uprooted*, p. 126.
6. Ibid., p. 127.
7. However, it has now been demonstrated that "leakage" from the Church
was not so great during the years of the great migration as had once been charged
by such men as Peter Paul Cahensly, Jules Tardivel, editor of *La Vérité* (Quebec),
and Dr. Anton Gisler, professor of Dogma at the University of Fribourg in
Switzerland. For an extensive and conclusive study of both sides of this important question, see Barry, *The Catholic Church and German Americans*, pp. 96,
260–3.

Minnesota.[8] In America, and especially in the West, it required some effort to remain a Catholic. Financial demands—such as substantial contributions for the erection of churches and schools, together with physical efforts—such as building the very churches of the West or of bringing one's family many miles each Sunday in an ox-drawn wagon, assured the Church in the West that its parish lists would seldom carry "nominal" Catholics.

Working on the land, these people acquired a deep appreciation for the role of Divine Providence in their lives. As they said the prayers for a good harvest at Vespers each Sunday,[9] as they followed Bishop Ireland in the procession of the Blessed Sacrament through the streets of De Graff during the grasshopper plague of 1876,[10] and as they sang their jubilant *Te Deums* after a successful harvest season, these pioneers gave evidence of their faith in God. The Minnesota colonists were not a random group of individuals who had merely been born and reared as Catholics. They were persons who had deliberately elected to make an extraordinary effort to live in a community in which their religious life could be fulfilled.

Undoubtedly the privations of frontier life gave new meaning to the settlers' beliefs in the promise of another life to come and deeper conviction about the spiritual value of suffering sustained in this life. In blizzards which piled snow to the eaves of their shanties and forced members of every family to stay awake in relays through the night twisting flax straw and slough hay into figure eight faggots of fuel,[11] after the devastating flight of the

8. *Farms for Sale*, pp. 12–14. See also the memorial pamphlet *Dedication of St. Francis Xavier School*, p. 15.

9. Thomas Jefferson Jenkins, *Six Seasons on Our Prairies and Six Weeks in Our Rockies* (Louisville, 1884), p. 64. This book is a travel journal kept by Father Jenkins, a priest from Louisville, Kentucky, who spent several weeks observing the Minnesota Catholic colonies in 1882 and 1883. In May 1882 Father Jenkins left Louisville to visit "the Northwestern Catholic Colonies." He was accompanied by a Kentucky farmer and the farmer's son. Jenkins wrote that they went to seek "new homes for some families who were wearing out both patience and good Irish and American muscle on Middle-Kentucky farms lying back from the Ohio, and cut off from railroad lines" (p. 7). This journal is one of the best published accounts of life within the colonies during this period.

10. *Dedication of St. Francis Xavier School*, p. 14.

11. Humphrey Moynihan, "Archbishop Ireland's Colonies," p. 228.

ravenous grasshoppers cut the harvest of 1876 by as much as 66 per cent,[12] and amid the general sense of isolation and loneliness which reduced even the strongest women to tears of anguish and regret,[13] there were daily occasions for thoughtful settlers to ponder the significance of this hard life. It would be an injustice, however, to conclude that such external physical sufferings explained their attachment to religion or to imply that in their lives the Church stood *merely* as a refuge from loneliness and pain.[14] The Catholics who came to the Minnesota colonies after 1876 had demonstrated some attachment to religion even before they experienced the trials of frontier life. And by the same token, the subsequent material prosperity they have enjoyed has, so far at least, not weakened their original religious devotion.

When one prospective settler wrote to Bishop Ireland, inquiring about the social organization of the Minnesota Catholic colonies, he received the reply, "Our colonies have no by-laws." [15] For the most part this answer was accurate, but it did not advert to the fact that Ireland expected all his priests and settlers to take and observe the total abstinence pledge. In his mind, "the total abstinence movement . . . was closely interwoven with the work of systematic colonization," [16] and by the fiat of the bishop there were no grog shops allowed in any of his colonies.[17] In an era of militant teetotalism, press notices—especially those in Catholic and Irish papers—praised the Minnesota colonies highly for this regu-

12. Swift County *Advocate* (September 7, 1877), p. 1.

13. Anonsen, *A History of Swift County*, p. 17. In this passage Anonsen cites a letter written to the Swift County *Advocate* by a Mrs. M. E. Mathews on December 29, 1899, recounting the hardships of prairie life in 1870. Swamps, mosquitoes, sod huts, and the vast treeless area presented the pioneer women with a singularly cheerless prospect for settlement. Sister Grace Aurelia, C.S.J., told me that she had never seen her mother cry till their first day in the Graceville settlement. After that she cried every day for two weeks, until she adjusted to the demands of frontier life. Relative to this feminine reaction to the rigors of western life, Ole Rolvaag's *Giants in the Earth* is an unusually accurate fictional account of the way the West affected many women.

14. Handlin, *The Uprooted*, pp. 122, 129.

15. J. P. O'Connor, St. Paul, to Mr. B. M. McGalley, Pittsburgh, Pennsylvania, March 22, 1889, St. Paul Chancery Archives, Diocesan Letters, 1888–89, p. 98.

16. Reardon, *Diocese of St. Paul*, p. 237.

17. *Catholic Colonization in Minnesota*, p. 44. See also Spalding, *The Religious Mission of the Irish People*, p. 175.

lation.[18] It will be recalled that when Ireland and Spalding toured the East lecturing to Catholic audiences, Spalding usually spoke on colonization and Ireland on temperance. The ultimate goal of the Minnesota bishop, however, was not only temperance in the use of alcohol, but total abstinence. In one of his brochures he warned all prospective colonists, "There is no hope for those who love whiskey in our colonies, and as we have built no poor-houses they will starve on the prairies. We do not want them." [19] All of the men closely associated with John Ireland shared this same devotion to the total abstinence movement. Dillon O'Brien, Father Nugent, Martin Griffin, and John Sweetman were loyal followers of Father Theobald Mathew, the "Apostle of Temperance."

Most of the settlers in these colonies were also convinced total abstinence men. Press reports in both secular and religious publications generally support this conclusion.[20] In his journal on life in the Minnesota colonies, Father Thomas Jenkins concluded that "the best colonizers are unanimous in declaring abuse of drink to be the greatest enemy of their projects. And we find those most engaged in planting Catholic settlements taking a firm stand against intemperance and holding up, in general, for total abstinence as the surest means to cut off even remote temptations from the unwary." [21]

After the initial reverses at his Currie colony, John Sweetman, in outlining his revised qualifications for new settlers, advised all those who were fond of drinking to stay off the prairies. "They cannot succeed. They will surely find their way to the nearest village, where the vilest drink is always to be found, no matter how much it may pretend to be a temperance town with saloons strictly prohibited." [22] In the colony towns the sale of any alcoholic beverage was illegal for almost two decades after the founding of

18. Martin Griffin's *ICBU Journal* was especially articulate in promoting the abstinence movement.

19. John Ireland, quoted by Jenkins, *Six Seasons on Our Prairies*, p. 74.

20. Benson *Times* (May 1, 1876), p. 4; (May 26, 1877), p. 4. See also the *ICBU Journal* and *NWC* press notices on these settlements for the years 1877–81.

21. Jenkins, pp. 73–4.

22. Taken from a letter by John Sweetman, December 15, 1883, quoted by Jenkins, p. 74.

the settlements; [23] but Sweetman's remarks and those of other observers indicate that there were ways in every settlement for thirsty colonists to evade both the law and the pledge. In speaking of some unspecified Catholic settlement near Fulda, after the July 4th celebration of 1883, Father Thomas Jenkins recorded his displeasure at the "unscrupulous fun of a small clique of half-grown boys and fellows, whose proof of asserted manhood lay only in the exhibition of the quantity of beer they could gulp in an out-of-the-way grove, and the racket they could raise, what with crackers and pistols, what with their brazen-muzzled throats." [24]

It is especially interesting to speculate on the degree of faithfulness with which the many German, Belgian, and French Catholic settlers observed the total abstinence pledge. Even within the ranks of the American hierarchy and among the clergy there was frequent criticism of the total abstinence movement and a tendency to look on it as the "Hibernian Crusade." [25] It is not surprising, therefore, to discover that among the laity in John Ireland's settlements there would be many who were prepared to give lip service to the prohibitions against drink and were ready at the same time to retain their old custom of a cheering glass of friendly schnapps whenever the occasion presented itself.[26]

With the exception of the regulation on drinking, the Minnesota colonies had none of the detailed social legislation which had characterized earlier utopian or religious settlements. In those few instances at Graceville, Currie, and Adrian where colonists were

23. Anonsen, *A History of Swift County*, p. 22.

24. Jenkins, p. 73.

25. Barry, *The Catholic Church and German Americans*, pp. 192–3. Father Barry's judicious discussion of this controversial topic is especially enlightening for its many citations from the private correspondence of leading non-Irish members of the American hierarchy. For example, Bishop Francis S. Chatard, in a letter to the Reverend Hermann J. Heuser, in praise of a series of articles just written by Heuser on the temperance question, observed, "You can hardly find a Catholic Temperance Society which is not more or less extreme. I do not want to offend them and I do not want to compromise myself." Father Barry's own comment on the more prominent crusaders is that "their wild defenses of abstinence from drink did little to convince Catholics from the European continent of the validity of this campaign." See also Sister Joan Bland, S.N.D., *Hibernian Crusade,* Washington, 1951.

26. This statement is based primarily on several interviews granted to me by original members of the Belgian colony at Ghent.

sponsored by the diocese, by John Sweetman, or by Onahan's association, improvident settlers or bad farmers were always in danger of having their credit cut off at the general store in the colony, but these were the exceptional cases. Relatively few of the Minnesota settlers were in the category of assisted immigrants; hence few of them were in any danger from this regulation. It should be mentioned, along with the total abstinence pledge, however, as qualifying slightly Ireland's general statement on the absence of by-laws or social regulation in his colonies.

Ultimately the only sanctions which Bishop Ireland and his priests exercised over the settlers were the same as those held by any bishop or priest in his diocese or parish. True, in their dual role as spiritual shepherds and land agents, the colony priests were expected in the early years of western settlement to perform many functions in the temporal realm. In a sense these extrinsic activities gave them a kind of power not essentially related to their role as priests. The final intention, however, was that in time such extraneous responsibilities would be gradually passed on to other persons in the community and that thus the priests would again become exclusively concerned with their primary duty of guiding the religious life of the settlers.

Within the Minnesota colonies responsibility was definitely fixed for the various jobs in the Colonization Bureau's chain of command. Ireland personally selected and contracted for the various colony sites, and after this continued to visit the western lands with a frequency which seems surprising, considering the distances involved and the slow means of transportation then available.[27] In spite of this continuing interest in the affairs of each colony, however, he delegated to his subordinates all the responsibility he could in the daily affairs of administering the colonization program. Hence, although the various settlements lacked rigid social controls and elaborate organization, the bureau itself was highly organized and carefully supervised. The value of this kind of planning can best be appreciated by studying the history of those colonization efforts which were attempted without it—at Pink

27. On one occasion, while visiting the Graceville colony, Ireland and Bishop Spalding became lost on the prairie and were forced to spend the night in a convenient, if not comfortable, haystack. *NWC* (September 11, 1880), p. 1.

Beds, North Carolina; Keileyville, Virginia; Blaine, Kansas; Fort Smith, Arkansas; and Spalding and O'Connor, Nebraska.[28]

The absence of by-laws or of regimentation of the settlers, however, definitely weakened the colonies in the early years of settlement. If a colonist did not like the weather, the land, or the neighbors, he was perfectly free to leave, and neither Ireland nor his priests could force him to stay. Often the colony leaders tried to discourage settlers from going back to the "bright lights and glitter" of the cities,[29] but none could maintain that Catholics had any specifically religious obligation to remain on the land. Dillon O'Brien's famous lecture, "Home," was most eloquent in its description of the beauties and virtues of life on the land,[30] but if such rhetoric failed to sway the discouraged farmer, O'Brien had no more powerful alternative argument. Consequently, each colony had an appreciable number of defections. The largest and most noteworthy exodus to the city was that from John Sweetman's Currie colony,[31] but in every settlement a similar pattern of action was repeated on a more modest scale.[32] When neighbors were few and distances great, the departure of every disillusioned colonist dampened the spirits of those who stayed behind on colony farms. In the long run, however, this process of natural selection brought into the western colonies a body of settlers who were convinced that the region offered the kind of homes and security they sought. After many discouraging shifts of population, Ireland's method of democratic settlement assured his western towns a stable rural population of families who understood and appreciated the values of life on the land. Unlike the earlier closely ruled communal settlements and religious Utopias which secured social agreement by the fiat of the leaders, the Minnesota colonies recruited a body of like-

28. See below, Chap. 9, for details of the North Carolina, Virginia, and Kansas settlements. See also Kelly, *Catholic Immigrant Colonization Projects*, pp. 187-9.

29. Letter of J. P. O'Connor, St. Paul, to the editor of the Philadelphia *Catholic Standard*, January 10, 1884, reproduced in *Farms for Sale*, p. 6.

30. Benson *Times* (March 29, 1876), p. 1.

31. See the discussion of the Sweetman colony given above, pp. 67-72. See also the letters of discouraged settlers, among the Sweetman Papers, Minnesota Historical Society, St. Paul.

32. Moynihan, "Archbishop Ireland's Colonies," p. 228.

minded farmers who shared in general the same background and ambitions.

In his discourses on the spiritual advantages of moving west, the Minnesota bishop often stressed his conviction that a modicum of economic security is necessary for man to lead a virtuous life. "Until their material condition is improved, it is futile to speak to them [the underprivileged] of super-natural life and duties." [33] At the opening of the De Graff colony he had announced, "In laboring to form Catholic settlements in Minnesota, my whole motive has been the temporal and spiritual welfare of the immigrant." [34] Acting on this principle, he selected as pastors in the new colonies men who were qualified by experience and a wide variety of talents to instruct the people in the ways of God and to train them in the habits of good farming. "He [Bishop Ireland] chooses a priest, with a special view to his knowledge of farming and farm life, to preside over the new colony." [35] The pastor of each frontier community was already a man of some years in the priesthood but still young enough to endure the physical hardships and privations of life on the prairie. Since life in these settlements during the first years was at best a trial, the bishop could hardly afford to jeopardize the success of his project by entrusting it to weak or inexperienced priests.

The language barrier was one factor to be considered in assigning the colony pastors. In Clontarf, mostly an Irish settlement, a large number of families spoke only French. To this post Ireland sent Father Anatole Oster,[36] who had come to St. Paul as a French seminarian in the days of Bishop Cretin. In Adrian and Avoca, where the congregations were about two-thirds Irish and one-third German,[37] Ireland needed two multilingual priests. He had them in the persons of Father C. J. Knauf, a German priest from Cologne,[38] and Father Charles Koeberl, who had been trained in the seminary in his native Austria, but who had learned English

---

33. Moynihan, *The Life of Archbishop John Ireland*, p. 233.
34. *NWC* (June 22, 1876), p. 5.
35. Spalding, *The Religious Mission of the Irish People*, p. 175.
36. Swift County *Advocate* (April 19, 1878), p. 4.
37. Jenkins, *Six Seasons on Our Prairies*, p. 43.
38. Onahan, "A Chapter on Catholic Colonization," p. 71.

during his years "on the mission" in England.[39] To the Belgian settlers at Ghent and Minneota, Ireland assigned the two Belgian priests, Father Cornelius and Father Jules Emile De Vos.[40] To the Irish settlements of De Graff, Graceville, Minneota, Avoca, and Iona he appointed Fathers F. J. Swift, T. Ryan, M. J. Hanley, Martin Mahoney, and M. McDonnell respectively.[41]

The parish records kept by these men demonstrate the particular talents which each of them brought to the frontier. Today the most exact and extensive records on any Minnesota colony are those which the meticulous Father Knauf kept for the Adrian colony. When this German immigrant priest first stepped from the train in the village of Adrian on September 20, 1877, "he found that it consisted of a wayside station and three houses." [42] Five years later he had sold 70,000 acres of colony land, had built a Catholic church and rectory, and could name 250 Catholic families in his parish.[43] Among other transactions Knauf arranged to sell 8,000 acres of railroad land to Onahan's Irish Catholic Colonization Association [44] and agreed to serve as the Adrian agent for that ill-fated federation—a decision he was later to regret. The extant records of this settlement tell very little about the success of the 200 families who settled on the 62,000 acres of railroad land provided by Bishop Ireland but reveal rather a chain of lawsuits, eviction actions, claim jumping, and disputed titles among the "assisted" immigrants sponsored by Onahan. Many of these settlers had been recruited for Onahan by Father J. P. Bodfish, vicar general of the Archdiocese of Boston. There were at least thirty and possibly fifty such families, mostly Irish and mostly from the environs of Boston.[45] These sponsored colonists, protégés of the

39. William Gorman, "The History of the Parish of St. Rose of Lima" (unpublished typescript, parish archives, Avoca), p. 5.

40. Pilger, "History of the Parish of St. Eloi," p. 1.

41. NWC (July 19, 1879), p. 1; Reardon, Diocese of St. Paul, pp. 628, 631, 633; Sweetman, Farms for Sale, p. 5; Jenkins, Six Seasons on Our Prairies, pp. 40–1.

42. Moynihan, "Archbishop Ireland's Colonies," p. 223.

43. Reardon, Diocese of St. Paul, pp. 241–2; Henthorne, The Irish Catholic Colonization Association, p. 107, quoting the Association reports for 1880 and 1882, as given in William J. Onahan's private scrapbook.

44. Henthorne, p. 105.

45. Ibid., p. 106; see also Moynihan, "Archbishop Ireland's Colonies," p. 223.

benevolent association, were for the most part unsuited to farming life, and the record of their litigation and dissatisfaction is
recorded in the voluminous correspondence which passed between
Father Knauf and Onahan.[46] It was a source of great displeasure to
the German priest that he was forced on occasion to issue eviction
notices or press the association colonists for land payments. More
than once he complained to Onahan that the association colonists
were a "bad sett" and he reaped nothing but abuses.[47] He would
have preferred to pass his days as the pastor of the other 200
Catholic families sponsored by Bishop Ireland; but each year,
during the month of October, he would arrange for two Jesuit
fathers to conduct a mission in his parish, in order that he might
have a week free "to take a team and visit everyone of the Assoc.
colonists to collect the amount due for last year." [48]

In England, Father Charles Koeberl had acquired a reputation
as an accomplished horseman, and it would appear from the no-
tations in his parish journal that only an enthusiastic horseman
could have maintained the schedule he kept in ministering to the
numerous settlers in his extensive parish of Avoca. In 1878 his
jurisdiction included twenty towns, ranging from Fairmont, Minnesota, to Flandrau, Dakota Territory, a distance of 140 miles. On
June 2, 1878, he baptized a baby at Heron Lake, Minnesota; on
June 9, another child at Flandrau, eighty miles west; and on June
14 he registered still another baptism at Windom, Minnesota,
eighty-five miles east of Flandrau.[49] True, the land was flat and
the going was relatively easy in the dry months; but there were
still no roads and all travel was by horseback or buggy. Traveling
by buggy, however, was far more tiring, and most of the priests preferred to go by horseback when visiting those stations beyond or
between rail lines.[50] For official church functions, such as Sunday
mass, Sunday afternoon vespers, benediction, and eucharistic
processions, the priests could expect the settlers to come to the

46. See the Adrian Colony Papers and William J. Onahan Papers, St. Paul Seminary Archives.
47. C. J. Knauf, Adrian, Minnesota, April 30, 1884, to William J. Onahan,
Onahan Papers, St. Paul Seminary Archives.
48. Idem, October 4, 1882; October 6, 1884; Onahan Papers.
49. Gorman, "The History of the Parish of St. Rose of Lima," pp. 2, 5.
50. Jenkins, Six Seasons on Our Prairies, p. 44.

church; but such trips were far too arduous for newborn babies and their mothers. Hence the colony priests reserved some days in each week for moving about their parishes baptizing the latest arrivals in Catholic families already distinguished for their large numbers [51] and bringing Holy Communion to those too aged or infirm to come to the church.

As each new group of settlers arrived in a colony, it was the duty of the local pastor—in the absence of Major Thompson—to supervise the erection of a frame house and the breaking of five acres of land for every family.[52] The priest was also expected to know the quality of the various parcels of land in his colony, so that he might advise newcomers on the best sites still open. It was presumed that he would know the best type of seed for that region, the most propitious time for planting, the intricacies of real-estate and tax laws, and the most reliable interpretation of the provisions of the homestead and tree-culture statutes. When the grasshoppers visited De Graff for a second time in 1877, a Father McDermot, who was then helping Father Swift, made the first move to stem their ravages. He went to Willmar, the nearest division point on the St. Paul and Pacific, to buy one of the recently patented "hopperdozers." These large steel, scooplike machines were to be filled with tar and drawn along the fields behind two horses. It was hoped that they would trap the grasshoppers without injuring the crops. McDermot demonstrated the contraption to the farmers and reported that he had arranged with the St. Paul and Pacific to transport free of charge from St. Paul all the coal tar that would be needed to replenish the "dozers." [53]

As the colonization program expanded and demands on the local clergy increased, it was necessary for Bishop Ireland to recruit additional priests. On one occasion early in 1881 William J. Onahan, who knew of the shortage of priests in St. Paul, procured a railroad pass for one Father O'Dwyer and sent him to St. Paul for an interview with Bishop Ireland. A few days later, in a crisp postscript on a letter to Onahan, Ireland summarized his policy

51. See the parish baptismal registers in the respective parishes. For example, at St. Bridget's parish in De Graff, between 1877 and 1883, there were an average of 43 baptisms each year.
52. Moynihan, "Archbishop Ireland's Colonies," p. 226.
53. Benson *Times* (May 26, 1877), p. 4.

on the subject of "unattached priests": "I shipped back to Chicago
Father O'Dwyer. Do me the favor of not procuring any more free
passes for unattached priests to come to St. Paul. We never receive such priests into the diocese, and they simply lose time and
money in coming to see us. Refer them to Peoria or Omaha."[54]
Ireland must have thought that Bishops Spalding (Peoria) and
O'Connor (Omaha) expected less of their priests than he did of
his. At all events he staffed his diocese on the assumption that his
projects would move forward only under the direction of better
—not simply more numerous—priests.

After exercising such care in the selection of his subordinates,
he did not hesitate to delegate authority to them in conducting the
affairs of the Colonization Bureau. The local priests in the western colonies of Minnesota, in contrast to those of the association
colonies in Nebraska, could sign contracts, purchase equipment,
sell lands, and contract debts in the name of the St. Paul office.
The colonization effort in Minnesota was too extensive for one
man to regulate all its details, and with the passing of time Ireland relied more and more on the assistance of the pastors and
his two lay helpers, Dillon O'Brien and Major Ben Thompson.

O'Brien was executive secretary of the Colonization Bureau,
giving lectures in the East, serving on the Minnesota Board of Immigration, and bearing the responsibility for the daily administration of the over-all colonization project. Under him Major
Thompson was the man in charge of land distribution. O'Brien
had his office in the Cathedral building,[55] but Thompson had his
in the Union Station, where he could meet the immigrants arriving by train and could more conveniently settle his daily land
transactions with the railroad.[56] Although these two men ranked
just below Bishop Ireland and just above the colony pastors in
the bureau's table of organization, both of them functioned in
daily affairs rather as advisors to the local pastors. O'Brien was
usually consulted on problems involving personal affairs, whereas
Thompson was the man who supervised the locating of new fam-

54. John Ireland, St. Paul, to William J. Onahan, March 13, 1881, Adrian Colony Papers.
55. O'Brien, "Dillon O'Brien," p. 45.
56. NWC (January 13, 1877), p. 4.

ilies, breaking of the land, erection of houses, and procurement of half-fare immigrant tickets on the railroad. And because both of them followed Ireland's principle of extending confidence and authority to the local pastors, the Minnesota colonies had a minimum of jurisdictional disputes. To appreciate what an advantage this was for the colonies one need only consider the unhappy record of the Irish Catholic Colonization Association under William J. Onahan, who refused to delegate any authority to the agents on the local level. In Spalding and O'Connor, Nebraska, both the pastors and the tradesmen pleaded with him and with Bishop O'Connor to appoint local agents with effective powers. These petitioners charged that every day opportunities arose and passed away simply because there was no person on the local scene who could act in the name of the association.[57] In the end their bitter predictions came true when the railroad by-passed both settlements, in spite of Onahan's confident assurance to Bishop O'Connor that this could never happen.[58]

Similarly, in Adrian, Minnesota, where Father Knauf had agreed to act as local agent for the association, difficulties multiplied because he was never able to give questioners a final answer on association affairs without first writing to Onahan in Chicago. This unfortunate situation has assured all subsequent historians of an ample fund of letters covering the tiniest details of colony business; but it was also responsible for gradually draining the life from the association portion of the Adrian settlement. In a letter dated January 16, 1884, Father Knauf wrote to Onahan, "I think it also necessary that the Assoc. gives [sic] me a legal power of attorney (in writing) to act as their agent."[59] When the letter was later shown to Bishop Spalding, president of the association,

57. For a summary of this situation see the two letters written by T. C. Phelan, president of the Brayton Commercial Bank, Brayton, Nebraska, to Bishop James O'Connor, September 19 and October 21, 1889, Omaha Chancery Archives, Colonization File: "I wrote to Mr. Onahan twice asking him to send me or some person at O'Connor a plat and price list of O'Connor City, as there were several persons wishing to purchase lots, but I have received no answer from him." "We are here with our hands tied, practically, in this matter, and you would confer a great favor by attending to it."

58. See above, pp. 79–80.

59. Adrian Colony Papers, St. Paul Seminary Archives, folder for 1884.

he scrawled across the bottom of its last page "I think it would be well to give Father Knauf power of atty., J. L. Spalding, Bp. of Peoria." For reasons best known to himself, Onahan failed to do so; and on April 30, 1884, Father Knauf in his serviceable, if imperfect, English, referred to the matter again. "As I wrote to you sometimes ago, I do not intent to act for the Assoc. as agent any more. . . . The Assoc. better either deals directly with them [the settlers] or appoints a lawyer as agent. I am not inclined to do so any longer and I wish you to inform the Assoc. of this, my resignation." [60]

When it became clear to Onahan that Bishops O'Connor and Spalding were not entirely satisfied with his administration of the association colonies, he was genuinely puzzled that they should have any reservations about his accomplishments. "Are we to wind up affairs and declare that our work is finished—that with the little colony, or nucleus of a colony in Nebraska, and the still smaller fraction of a settlement in Minnesota, we have sufficiently tested and tried the experiment of Catholic colonization? Or is the work to go on and widen out entering into new fields and enlarging in those already pioneered?" [61] The coolness of Bishop O'Connor to such plans for expansion would have been more intelligible to Onahan if he had compared the achievement of his colonies with that of the Minnesota settlements. O'Connor must certainly have been aware of what was being done in John Ireland's diocese, at least in a general way from news reports. And he already knew in great detail the story of thwarted progress in his own Nebraska settlements.

It has often been asserted, and with good reason, that settlers on the western frontier sacrificed many of the cultural advantages which had graced their lives in the more populous eastern centers. A distinction should be made, however, in assessing the effects of this cultural loss in the West. There is no reason for assuming that the Catholic colonists in Minnesota after 1875 were initially any less educated or refined than the national population at

60. Ibid., p. 2.
61. Onahan, Chicago, to Bishop James O'Connor, February 24, 1881, Omaha Chancery Archives, Colonization File.

large.[62] Quite the contrary, there is impressive evidence to show that many of them were persons of means who had been able in the East to procure for themselves and their families reasonably complete instruction in the standard academic curriculum.[63] Once they arrived in the West and took up an isolated farmstead, of course, opportunities for literary and intellectual activities were severely reduced. When the American poetess Eliza Allen Starr sent Bishop O'Connor a copy of one of her recent books and suggested that the Nebraska prelate should organize some kind of library in his colonies, he replied: "Our people are so wholly absorbed in building up homes for themselves in this new country, that it is exceedingly difficult to interest them in anything else. Besides, it is very hard for book agents to reach them scattered as they are over such a vast extent of country. The experiment [of founding a library] has been made twice since I came here, but with such little success that others seem to be deterred, for the time being, from repeating it." [64]

The limitations placed on literary activities by the frontier, however, could neither stifle nor replace the original interest in books which the settlers brought with them. In Nobles County, Minnesota, just one year before the establishment of the Catholic colony at Adrian, the county paper boasted, "The educational interests of the . . . county are in the hands of advanced men, who appreciate the importance of superior educational facilities and who will have them whatever the cost. . . . There are now about fifty school districts organized in the county." [65] One writer who settled in western Minnesota in 1870 recounts that his entire early education was received from his father at reading sessions in his frontier home every evening:

62. For an illustration of the general literary taste of one such settlement, see the column "Literary Notices," Worthington *Advance* (November 15, 1877), p. 3.

63. See the evidence presented above, pp. 125 f., to establish the economic position of these settlers. See also the Worthington *Advance* (March 21, 1878), p. 3, and the Benson *Times* (April 28, 1877), p. 1.

64. Bishop O'Connor to Eliza Starr, May 12, 1881, Omaha Papers, Notre Dame University Archives. It may be that Bishop O'Connor did not care to become involved in further correspondence with Miss Starr. Nonetheless his comments on the failure of two earlier efforts to establish libraries are significant for the present study.

65. Worthington *Advance* (January 4, 1877), p. 1.

The greatest single factor in our education was father's reading aloud during the long winter evenings. After the supper things had been cleared away, the family gathered around the dining-room table under the hanging-lamp. . . . Then we had read to us the best things in the language, from Shakespeare to Lincoln. . . . We never saw an English grammar and never analyzed a sentence; instead we listened by the hour to the music of good English. Thus did we skip the horrors and garner the beauties of the mother tongue.[66]

There is considerable evidence to indicate that among many families who settled in the Minnesota Catholic colonies the parents were themselves sufficiently well instructed to act as tutors for their children. By and large the extant correspondence from these colonists reveals that they wrote well and expressed themselves in the fashion of educated persons. In both De Graff and Adrian plans were proposed shortly after the opening of the colonies for the erection of a small college and normal school for the training of teachers.[67] The caliber of the lecturers invited to the colony halls in the early years also argues a reasonably cultivated audience.[68] One lecture, delivered to the people of De Graff in July 1877, recommended that teachers in the schools should have special training for their jobs and should be "classified and paid accordingly." [69] In the same colony, one year after its foundation, a night school was organized for the benefit of those adults who wanted further education.[70] Among the records of the parish in Clontarf is a library account book which reveals that in this colony a parish circulating library was set up in 1878, the second year the colony was in operation.[71] In the neighboring settlement of Appleton, as early as 1875, "a few public spirited men organized the Appleton Library Association." One year later this association could announce that "150 volumes [are now available], a lyceum has been

66. Humphrey, *Following the Prairie Frontier*, pp. 62–3.
67. Worthington *Advance* (January 4, 1877), p. 1; Benson *Times* (June 19, 1876), p. 1.
68. Benson *Times* (June 19, 1876), p. 1.
69. Ibid. (July 7, 1877), p. 4.
70. Ibid. (September 29, 1877), p. 4.
71. See the Parish Cash Book, St. Malachy's rectory, Clontarf, Minnesota.

maintained, and a lecture course has been established." [72] Wherever the Catholic colonists did not know the English language, John Ireland had instructed his priests to inaugurate classes in English reading and speaking. In Ghent, for example, "The first school taught in the village was under the direction of Father De Vos. He established a free [sic] school for the education of the children and to teach the many foreign born residents the English language," and proceeded to record the event in French: "Comme il n'y a pas d'école plus près du village que 2 milles, M. le Curé prend sur lui d'ériger une école catholique, pour laquelle chaque famille paiera ce qu'elle pourra, au moins $1 par mois." [73]

After 1865 the number of children of Catholic immigrant families in the United States grew so large that the American bishops were unable to provide parochial schools for all of them. In 1875 Rome informed the hard-pressed American hierarchy that Catholic children might attend the public schools as long as additional religious instruction was given them by their parish priest or under his direction.[74] This relaxation of the traditional insistence on Catholic schools for all Catholic children came just at the time John Ireland was named a bishop. And in view of the extensive public school system already organized in Minnesota,[75] he might have been expected to take advantage of the Roman decree by enrolling the children of his diocese in the public schools. Yet in spite of his frequent statements in praise of the free, state-supported schools and his insistence on the need for such schools in a democracy, Ireland felt that "they made no provision for instruction in religion, but rather tended to eliminate it from the minds and hearts of the youth of the country." [76]

Accordingly he instructed his priests and people that wherever it was financially possible, parochial schools should be established.

72. Benson *Times* (July 7, 1876), p. 4.

73. *The History of Lyon County,* chap. 15, quoted in Pilger, "History of the Parish of St. Eloi," p. 2. See also the parish journal kept by Father Jules Emile De Vos, "Mission de Ghent, 1883, Colonie Flamande et Canadienne de Monseigneur Ireland," pp. 5, 6, 8. This record, written by Father De Vos in French, is part of the Archbishop Ireland Papers which are now housed in the St. Paul Seminary Archives.

74. *NWC* (December 25, 1891), p. 8.

75. Folwell, *A History of Minnesota,* 4, 142, 147, 162.

76. Moynihan, *The Life of Archbishop John Ireland,* p. 80.

On the western frontier this decision, which may have been considered divisive in other regions, met no noticeable opposition.[77] The expansion of the general population in the West at this time was so rapid that county officials were finding it difficult, even with the liberal educational funds provided by the Minnesota legislature, to build and staff sufficient schools.[78] Hence the Catholic effort to build parochial schools was a decided benefit to many western counties. In fact this amicable relationship between Catholics and their neighbors of other religions on the school question can be considered typical of the absence of religious friction on the frontier.[79] In that region, where every new settler was a vital asset eagerly welcomed by the entire community, questions were seldom asked about a man's religious convictions. In social gatherings when national or religious differences did arise, it was expected that the host or sponsor of the event would apologize to his guests for the note of disharmony.[80]

77. For conclusive proof of the good will enjoyed by the new Catholic settlers in all the western communities, see the Benson *Times* (February 16, 1876), p. 4; (March 29, 1876), p. 1; (May 1, 1876), p. 1; (May 26, 1877), p. 4; the Swift County *Advocate* (September 28, 1877), p. 1; (November 16, 1877), p. 4; (January 11, 1878), p. 2 (including also a recommendation from Governor John S. Pillsbury's annual message, urging further inducements to immigrants to settle in Minnesota, in view of recent competition and also in view of publicity from other states "South and West of Minnesota"); (January 25, 1878), p. 1; (March 1, 1878), p. 1; (May 24, 1878), p. 4; Worthington *Advance* (September 13, 1877), p. 3.

78. Folwell, *A History of Minnesota, 4*, 135, 147–8.

79. Several decades later (1917), the Minnesota Commission of Public Safety investigated the extent to which foreign languages were being used in private and parochial schools in the state and found that a considerable number of them were "using a foreign language wholly or in part as a medium of instruction, and that some 10,000 children receiving their education in these schools were brought up as aliens and foreigners." Folwell, *A History of Minnesota, 4*, 166. Undoubtedly this criticism referred primarily to Catholic schools, and quite probably to German-Catholic schools. And it is reasonable to suppose that in the early years of the western colonies there was similar criticism of the German language used in Fulda, the Flemish spoken in Ghent, and the French used at Clontarf. However, the most articulate opponent of foreign language in America was John Ireland himself. If his colonists were labeled as foreigners, he was doing all in his power to teach them the English language and thus relieve them of the stigma of being called "aliens." For an extended consideration of his crusade for English among American Catholics, see Moynihan, *The Life of Archbishop John Ireland*, chap. 4, "Resisting Nationalism in the Church," pp. 54–78.

80. Benson *Times* (March 17, 1877), p. 1.

Moreover, the Catholic settlers, having taken up new land, were for the most part separated from the established school districts [81] and hence not likely to arouse antagonism by erecting their own schools in townships settled mostly by their coreligionists. In Clontarf, Graceville, Iona, and Avoca, Catholic boarding academies were opened under the direction of religious orders of sisters or brothers. In Ghent and De Graff short-lived attempts were made to conduct parochial schools. In Fulda, Minneota, De Graff, and Currie the Catholic children attended the public schools. Considering the financial burden under which the colonists then labored, and the contrastingly liberal school fund allowance then being made by the state of Minnesota for its public school system,[82] the attempt to open Catholic schools in this portion of the West was definitely premature.

During the period 1875–95 the young state of Minnesota passed several laws organizing new school districts, voting increased educational taxes, establishing standards of competency for teachers, and providing free text books for state schools.[83] In these two decades the state authorities were clearly conscious of their responsibility to organize a good school system. But at the same time there is every evidence that whether the children of the western colonists were enrolled in rural public or parochial schools, their curriculum still left much to be desired. For the public schools in Swift County the school term in 1880 averaged only four months.[84] "The state superintendent of public instruction, in his biennial report for 1883–84, called attention to the large numbers of children out of school and recommended remedial legislation." [85] A com-

81. De Vos, "Mission de Ghent," p. 5.

82. At the time the territory of Minnesota was organized, the Congress of the United States, acting on the impression that land in Minnesota was not suited to agriculture, doubled the ordinary land grant (one full section of 640 acres in every township) for the school fund in the new territory. From the beginning the citizens of the territory appreciated the advantages that would flow from this generous allowance. However, it took time to set up well regulated public schools, especially in the rural regions. Reporting on the status of such schools for the last decade of the century, Folwell complained: "The inspection of the rural schools was left to busy county superintendents, who were often incompetent and indifferent" (A History of Minnesota, 4, 135, 186).

83. Folwell, 4, pp. 135–89; Holmes, Minnesota in Three Centuries, 3, 519.

84. Anonsen, A History of Swift County, Appendix XII, p. 74.

85. Folwell, 4, 163, quoting the Superintendent of Public Instruction, Reports, 1883–84, p. 32; Minnesota General Laws (1885), p. 261.

pulsory education statute was enacted by the Legislature in 1885, threatening negligent parents with fines or imprisonment for failing to send their children to school. For two more decades, however, this law and similar ones continued to have little effect on rural parents who needed their older children to help with chores and farm work and who had no means for taking their younger children to daily instructions in the local village. Reports of the commissioner of education continued to complain "that large numbers of rural and village children were out of school more than half the time." [86] School attendance during the winter months was the exception. In most districts classes were "in session for but two or three months during the spring and summer, and then with very irregular attendance." [87] One county historian has said of the rural Minnesota schools in this period that they were "little more than reading, 'riting and 'rithmetic schools." [88]

County officials often found it hard to convince rural parents of the need for increasing taxes to provide better school equipment and larger salaries for professionally trained teachers.[89] Graduates of the state university and the three state normal schools [90] were filling the need for more teachers in the larger cities of the state, but very few of them sought employment in the isolated western settlements. There it was still a question of finding a reasonably qualified member of the community who was willing to accept the modest pay offered for conducting the local school.[91] Classes were sometimes held in the local railroad station, in private homes, or in the community churches. For many years after the founding of the colonies pastors and public school superintendents alike found it difficult to interest competent teachers in work in the

86. Folwell, 4, 164, quoting the same Reports: 1903–04, p. 22; 1905–06, p. 15; 1907–08, p. 22.

87. Anonsen, p. 34.

88. Ibid.

89. Ibid.

90. At Winona, St. Cloud, and Mankato. See Minnesota in Three Centuries, 3, 521.

91. Anonsen, Appendix XII, p. 74. According to this table, the average monthly pay scale in the rural districts of Swift County in 1880 was $32.00 for male teachers and $26.00 for female teachers. At the same time farmers at Graceville offered wages of $2.00 a day for farm laborers. The St. Paul and Pacific, then engaged in laying the rails of its Glyndon cut-off, was offering $1.50 a day for laborers. And Bishop Ireland had announced his system of public works in Graceville, with wages of $1.00 a day.

West.[92] Moreover, the duties of the local school boards and commissioners were not then clearly defined; and as a result educational administration above the level of the classroom was badly neglected. As late as 1909 it was necessary for the state legislature to enact a law threatening negligent truant officers and county school superintendents with fines and imprisonment if they were found guilty of not enforcing the compulsory education statutes.[93] Hence although a sound program of public education had been inaugurated, its fruits became apparent in the western settlements very slowly.

Attendance at parochial schools may have been slightly higher than in the public schools because of the encouragement given to it each Sunday from the pulpit; but even in the Catholic schools classes were small and tuition fees, often paid in farm produce, were not enough to meet the expenses of conducting them. In Avoca, at the Academy of St. Rose, five teaching sisters engaged by Bishop Ireland had a total enrollment of 21 pupils.[94] The journal of their convent life reveals that their years in the West were spent in constant poverty.[95] At Ghent the parish account book kept by Father De Vos records similar trials encountered in his attempt to maintain a parochial school. From time to time it was necessary for "Les demoiselles organis [er] un petite loterie." [96] Occasional lotteries were not enough, however, and within two years of its establishment the parochial school was closed and the townspeople at Ghent asked the county officials to organize a public school district for them. Not until after 1900, when parish debts for churches and rectories were paid, did parochial schools reappear in the western colonies.[97]

In the western counties of Minnesota and in Dakota Territory clumps of cottonwood, willow, and box elder trees follow the

92. Ibid. The same table reveals that in Swift County in 1880, out of a total of 49 teachers (22 male, 27 female), only three were normal school graduates.
93. Folwell, 4, 164–5.
94. Gorman, "The History of the Parish of St. Rose of Lima," pp. 13–14.
95. Ibid., pp. 14–15.
96. De Vos, "Mission de Ghent," p. 4.
97. Almost all the present day parochial schools in these western towns were opened after 1900: Graceville (1900); Ghent (1901); Currie (1907); Adrian (1895); Fulda (1901); Iona (1901); Minneota (1938). De Graff, Clontarf, and Avoca have no Catholic schools today. See also James P. Shannon, "Catholic Boarding Schools on the Western Frontier," *Minnesota History*, 35 (1956), 133–9.

water courses and lake shores; but the soft pulpy wood from these trees cannot be used for building timbers or lumber. Before the coming of the railroad, firewood was precious and lumber was almost unknown. Some notion of prairie life under this limitation can be gleaned, as we have seen, from the unfortunate experience of Bishop O'Connor's colony at Spalding, Nebraska. Because this colony site had no railroad service it retained the physical features of a frontier settlement long after the contemporaneous Minnesota colonies—thanks to the rail lines—had entered upon a building boom.

Even after 1880, the Nebraska colonists continued to build sod houses, for lack of lumber and building materials.[98]

> The cost of bringing timber in was at first prohibitive. If there were none on the spot, home would be of another material. Some would burrow dugouts into the slopes, return unknowingly to the life of the caves. Many cut the sunbaked surface of the earth, piled the sod in a double wall with dirt between, and in these huts spent a long period of trial. [These pioneers] felt the wind of winter through the cracks, heard the sides settle in the spring thaw, saw surprised snakes or gophers penetrate the floor.[99]

Prairie sod, native clay, and willow bushes were all that a pioneer settler needed to fashion such a home for his family. The sods, cut by a plow, were used as bricks, and were piled to a height of seven feet to make the walls. Cottonwood, poplar, or willow saplings served as ridge poles and rafters. On these, bundles of prairie hay were laid; and on top of the hay, long thin prairie sods were fitted together. Two or three inches of clay subsoil, tamped down on top of the sods, provided an outside waterproof layer. A door and one or more windows were fitted into the walls; and the interior was plastered with a mixture of hay and clay or sand and clay.[100] "This made a house that was warm and dry in winter and cool and dry in summer. Weeds and even flowers sometimes grew on the roof. The house did service for about five years, when it

98. Henthorne, *The Irish Catholic Colonization Association*, pp. 165–7.
99. Handlin, *The Uprooted*, p. 166. Handlin is not here speaking explicitly about the Nebraska settlers, but about frontier sod house dwellers in general.
100. Henthorne, p. 166.

would begin to crumble; but in the meantime the industrious farmer would have been able to build a frame dwelling to take its place." [101]

There were a few such "soddies," as they were called, in the Minnesota colonies; but their number was not large, for none of these settlements were opened until each was assured its own rail line. Hence even the first Minnesota colonists enjoyed the benefits of frame houses and permanent churches. Before a railroad was completed to Graceville, Bishop Ireland shipped five carloads of lumber overland by ox cart from the rail terminal in Morris to the building site of his proposed church in Graceville.[102] In almost every colony a frame church was available for worship soon after the foundation of the colony. In each settlement these structures were later replaced by brick churches, but even at the opening of the colonies each settlement had a comfortable house of worship.[103]

The modest three-room frame houses built by the bureau on the colony lands were not very imposing. It was not intended that they should be permanent dwellings, but only that they should provide decent shelter and moderate comfort until the farmers could secure sufficient money and leisure to erect better homes. One such colony house was built on each tract of 160 acres. Major Thompson, who supervised the physical details of settling newcomers, arranged for construction in advance of the arrival of new colonists. A settler usually found his house finished and five acres of land broken and ready for seeding when he arrived. This arrangement assured the farmer an ample vegetable garden for his family and at least a few acres of a cash crop during his first season on the land.

Extant photographs of these frontier homes would never persuade the reluctant urban dweller to come west; and yet these modest dwellings represented, for their time, a distinct advance in home construction on the frontier. Some of them were even prefabricated and could be assembled without nails or screws. One

101. *Catholic Review,* August 7, 1880, quoted in Henthorne, p. 166.

102. Moynihan, "Archbishop Ireland's Colonies," p. 219.

103. With the exception of Avoca and Iona, where new frame churches have been built more recently.

Fig. 7. A typical sod house

such model measured 14 × 20 feet and contained a living room,
kitchen, and bedroom. Although it was made in Chicago, it could
be bought in the colony for $200. An extravagant advertisement
issued by the association for Greeley County, Nebraska, guaran-
teed this marvelous dwelling to be "rain, wind and waterproof"
and assured all potential buyers that such houses "do not need
plastering inside, a hurricane can make no impression on them,
and, if painted regularly, will last for a century." [104]

In reality, hurricanes or tornadoes made lasting impressions on
these fragile shanties, as the Nebraska colonists had reason to
know after the disastrous wind storm in that region on June 19,
1881,[105] in which the parish church, the largest structure in the
O'Connor settlement, was totally demolished. The settlers also
learned that paint was not enough to make such frame dwellings
"last for a century." Since there were no basements or foundations under them, it was necessary to pile sod and earth to a thick-
ness of two feet along the outside walls to insulate the interior
against the winter cold. As a result the lower portions of the
wooden walls, packed in damp earth, often rotted through within
a few years and left the whole house untenable. However, with
care and effort this rotting could be arrested or prevented, and in
most instances the settlers were financially able to build larger
conventional farm houses by the time their colony cabin showed
signs of wear. "The cabin, no doubt, had its defects as a residence.
. . . But the people who settled in such quarters had only to
compare situations with those who found no wood nearby, to
count their blessings." [106]

During the decade following the opening of the colonies, western farmers continued to prosper economically, although the market value of their basic crop, wheat, continued to fall each year.
In time this trend would build up sufficient agrarian discontent
to organize the western farmers behind the People's party; but
until the bad effects of lower prices were demonstrated to the
grain producers, many of them felt confident that their increas-

104. Henthorne, p. 148. See Fig. 8.
105. See letter of Father P. F. McCarthy, O'Connor, Nebraska, to Bishop
O'Connor, June 19, 1881, Omaha Chancery Archives, Colonization File.
106. Handlin, *The Uprooted,* p. 166.

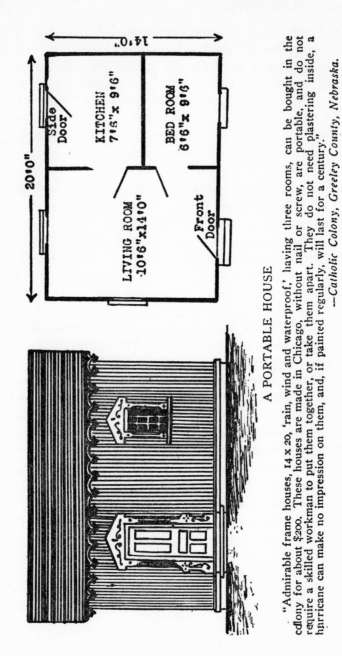

A PORTABLE HOUSE

"Admirable frame houses, 14 x 20, 'rain, wind and waterproof,' having three rooms, can be bought in the colony for about $200. These houses are made in Chicago, without nail or screw, are portable, and do not require a skilled workman to put them together, or take them apart. They do not need plastering inside, a hurricane can make no impression on them, and, if painted regularly, will last for a century."

—*Catholic Colony, Greeley County, Nebraska.*

Fig. 8

ing acreage and mounting production assured future security. With the profit realized from their first few crops it was possible to build the comfortable and spacious homes which have become characteristic of midwestern farms in America.[107] Labor was not expensive, neighbors gladly helped in home building or "barn raising," and the farmers themselves did much of their own construction work. The railroads made available in the western colonies any building materials obtainable in the eastern cities.

The present rectory at St. Malachy's parish in Clontarf, built in 1878 just after that colony opened, is an illustration of the costs of construction on the frontier. It has five bedrooms upstairs, large, high-ceilinged rooms, and a kitchen 24 × 22 feet. It was obviously intended as a halfway house for priests traveling between the western missions and St. Paul. Among the earliest records of this parish is the builder's contract, listing the specifications for the rectory and stipulating that the construction cost would be $325.[108] This astounding figure does not include all the building materials, but it provides a graphic example of the modest cost of housing in the West in 1878. Once a man's land was paid for, the income from a single crop would build as fine a home as he could desire.

At Willmar, De Graff, Benson, and Morris the St. Paul and Pacific built large emigrant houses as temporary dwellings for new settlers. As soon as the newcomers moved into their own houses, these railroad hostels were taken down and moved farther west.[109] In Avoca, the parent colony of the Catholic settlements in Nobles and Murray counties, the railroad did not provide an emigrant house; hence Ireland built his own and called it the Colony House. It was a two-story frame structure 30 × 60 feet. One large room 26 × 30 feet served as the parish chapel until the colony church was ready for occupancy.[110]

107. *Dedication of St. Francis Xavier School*, p. 14. See also Jenkins, *Six Seasons on Our Prairies*, p. 53; and Father Martin Mahoney's letter to *NWC*, December 15, 1884, reproduced in Sweetman, *Farms for Sale*, p. 14.

108. This table of specifications, written by Father Anatole Oster, is now part of the parish records at St. Malachy's rectory, Clontarf, Minnesota. It was made available to me by Father Richard King, present pastor at Clontarf.

109. Benson *Times* (February 16, 1876), p. 1.

110. Gorman, "The History of the Parish of St. Rose of Lima," p. 6. Father Gorman graciously supplied me with a typescript of his forthcoming history of the Avoca parish. This manuscript has since been published in booklet form; but the material quoted above is taken from the original copy.

The colony house or emigrant house in each community was never allowed to compete with the local hotels. Once the settlement was established, these temporary dwellings were either taken down and moved west along the line of settlement or were converted into community centers. Neither the railroad nor the diocese had any desire to get into the hotel business, and both welcomed the arrival of businessmen and hotel keepers who were anxious to provide bed and board for travelers and visitors in the colony towns.

West of the Mississippi, townsites were often platted by railroad engineers who were, understandably, more interested in organizing centers for the efficient distribution of freight than in town planning or community beautification. As a result, the depot is still the most important structure in many such towns today. During the 1870's, construction men, anxious to push on with the important task of laying rails, paced off village sites—usually all on one side of the tracks—in uniform rectangular patterns, and named all the north-south streets after trees and all the east-west avenues after famous Americans, with little concern for aesthetic considerations. In an earlier day settlers in colonial New England had reserved a large open village green, surrounding the parish church, in the heart of their town sites; and in time this center of their religious life became also the focus of their civic and social activities. Farther west the towns in Ohio, Indiana, and Illinois, founded by New England settlers, still reflect their New England origins in the town plans, with gracious village greens or town squares in the center of each community. Not so in the West. Efficiency, stark simplicity, and uniformity characterized the cheerless little towns which sprang up in the wake of advancing rail lines. Leaders might appear later who would have an eye for beauty; but in the beginning the empire builders had no time for such nonessentials.

John Ireland was aware that the lonely open prairie stretches in themselves offered the eastern settler a new environment, so different from his green and wooded acres farther east as to make the shock of readjustment a serious threat to the stability of the new colonies. Moreover, the plain, monotonous features of the railroad towns did nothing to soften the harshness of the western landscape. In this region there are no mountains or natural wonders to impress the new arrival with the grandeur of creation— simply rich land, well watered, lying flat, swept by hot winds in summer and buried beneath drifted snow in winter. Part of John Ireland's plan to relieve this western plainness is revealed in his search for imposing church sites and in his orders to construct large and beautiful houses of worship. At least in the house of God his new colonists would be surrounded by the beauty and splendor which they had once known in other homes and which after their migration west was so often lacking in their daily lives.

In Graceville, Currie, Avoca, and Fulda he ordered the parish churches to be built on the shores of natural lakes lying adjacent to the village sites. In the days of Bishop Cretin, General James Shields had brought a band of Catholic settlers to Minnesota, and its first official act had been the erection of a parish church on a high hill overlooking beautiful Lake Mazaska. Whether John Ireland was using the first Minnesota colony site as a model or not is uncertain, but all through his years as a western colonizer he regularly urged his priests and people to take pains to enhance the beauty of their new homes. In Fulda he donated "to the public lots 1, 2, 3 and 4 of the Davis Addition" to serve as a public park.[111] The City Park in Currie was also a gift to that village from the bishop.[112]

On his frequent trips to Graceville, Ireland often suggested to the Irish and Irish-American colonists that they should spend more time and money in the beautification of their homes and lawns. He was particularly anxious that these new settlers, whose homes in Ireland had most often been stone cottages, should learn the economic and psychological value of a new coat of paint.[113]

111. Murray County, Minnesota, Abstract Title Book (1883): Book B, p. 265; Book C, p. 342. The references given above are taken from the photostat copy referred to in Chap. 5, n. 153, above.

112. J. P. O'Connor to W. D. Sheehan, Madison, Dakota Territory, April 26, 1889, St. Paul Chancery Archives, Diocesan Letters, 1889. When this letter was written, O'Connor had succeeded Dillon O'Brien as lay director of the Catholic Colonization Bureau and Sheehan was a western land agent who represented the Bureau in southwestern Minnesota.

113. Based on an interview with Sister Grace Aurelia, St. Paul, September 10, 1953.

It is not likely that he gave the same message to the Belgian settlers in Ghent or the German settlers in Fulda. The latter had
come from European communities which placed a high premium
on pleasantly landscaped lawns and attractive houses.

It will be recalled that Angelus Van Hee and his fellow Belgian
colonists on arriving in Ghent, Minnesota, set about buying or
building large comfortable homes at once. In one way this action
can be explained economically: the newly arrived Belgians had
money, whereas the recent Irish immigrants and Irish-Americans
were less fortunate. But in addition to the economic factor, or
possibly as a result of it, the Belgian settlers brought with them
certain cultural traditions which inclined them to put great value
on the construction and ornamentation of imposing houses. Seldom has any member of the Belgian community from that day
to this sought any other life save that on the land.[114] It is the custom among these model farmers to present their grown sons with
160-acre farms, stocked and paid for, on their wedding day. The
children are not encouraged to consider the desirability of higher
education after finishing high school. It is generally accepted
among these people that higher education, with all its admitted
values, hardly fits a man for life on the farm. Hence within the
rich and well-kept farms of Lyon County there can seldom be
found a college graduate or professional man who came originally
from the colony. And amid the growing wealth of American farmers in general these Belgian-American settlers have had their
share. Meanwhile, their exceptional religious zeal, their family
solidarity, and their unquestioning loyalty to the values of agrarian
life go on unabated. Values which they brought with them from
Belgium—devotion to the Catholic Church, loyalty to the land,
and the bourgeois values of capitalistic enterprise—have been
deepened and reinforced by the opportunities they found in the
American West.

If in the course of time the Belgian and German colonies have
demonstrated a superior skill in the creation of large and fruitful
farms, the various Irish communities within the colonization pro-

114. Several interviews with old settlers at Ghent revealed that most of the
local settlers who have gone away from Ghent stayed away only briefly and returned to the group as soon as they could.

gram can lay claim to having sponsored an unusually full and
varied program of social and recreational activities as their contribution to the good life in the West. Considering the Irish birth
and previous American residence of many of these colonists, it is
difficult to explain their leisure time activities solely in terms of
Irish or purely in terms of American traditions; but it is abundantly
evident that the Irish settlements were distinguished by an unusually active social life, with great emphasis placed on sporting
events. Such extracurricular activities in the life of a farming
community probably meant that routine agricultural chores were
occasionally neglected. At all events one searches in vain through
the local papers of other colony groups for a similar variety and
frequency of athletic contests, races, and games of chance.

As soon as the frost was out of the ground in 1877 the De Graff
settlers organized a town baseball team [115] and notified other
settlements along the St. Paul and Pacific that they were ready
for competition. Within a month there were three such teams in
the same town of De Graff,[116] and it was a matter of some civic
disappointment in August of that year when the sponsors of a
proposed "fat man's team" had to announce that there were not
enough fat men in town to put a decent team on the field.[117] However, community pride must have been bolstered when it was
learned that one John Boyle, who had originally come to the colony as a carpenter, felt that he was ready for the major leagues
by midseason. In late June 1877 he announced that he was moving
east (to Wisconsin) with the intention of becoming a full-time
professional ball player.[118]

The obliging manager of the St. Paul and Pacific agreed to furnish the various ball clubs with low-fare excursion tickets to other
towns on days that games were played away from home.[119] In this
and in many similar instances the management of this railroad
showed remarkable astuteness in its readiness to grant concessions
to win the good will of the settlers. As a result, at a time when the
western press was unanimous in its denunciation of Cornelius

115. Benson *Times* (June 23, 1877), p. 4.
116. Ibid. (July 7, 1877), p. 4.
117. Ibid. (August 4, 1877), p. 4.
118. Ibid. (June 23, 1877), p. 4.
119. Ibid.

Vanderbilt's personal wealth and his "big" railroad,[120] local editors spoke as one voice in their praise and admiration for the good service and fair treatment they were receiving from the St. Paul and Pacific.[121]

Monthly fairs quickly became standard economic and social events in the Swift County colony. In Ireland each hamlet had its weekly fair day, on which neighboring farmers brought livestock and produce into the village streets and there enjoyed themselves in an elaborate trading ritual which lasted throughout the day and which satisfied both an economic and a social need among the participants. In America, where distances were greater, the fairs were held only once a month.[122] On these occasions necessary business was transacted early and with dispatch in order to leave the greater part of the day for the even more necessary sporting events.

There were always two or more contestants ready to try their prize trotting mares against all comers.[123] And without the benefit of parimutuel windows, the neighbors from miles around were welcome to place a small wager on the contest. This was not the desperate last chance kind of gambling that flourished among the saddened indigent immigrants in tenement slums.[124] At the

120. Swift County *Advocate* (April 26, 1878), p. 2; Benson *Times* (June 5, 1876), p. 4.
121. Swift County *Advocate* (February 15, 1878), p. 1.
122. Ibid. (May 10, 1878), p. 4.
123. Benson *Times* (November 18, 1876), p. 1; (January 29, 1878), p. 4.
124. See Handlin, *The Uprooted,* p. 160. In this excellent study of the urban immigrant, Handlin presents a moving account of the suffering and hopelessness which often characterized the life of first generation immigrants. His account of immigrant life on farms shows it to have been almost as cheerless and forlorn (see pp. 165–9). In general, research done for the present study does not support Handlin in his description of the hopeless odds against which rural immigrants labored. See *NWC* (June 7, 1879), p. 5; (June 14, 1879), p. 1. In spite of the admitted hazards of grasshopper plagues, winter blizzards, summer heat, and monotonous diets—all cited by Handlin and all endured by the Minnesota colonists— their lot was by and large not a bad one. Their own spokesman could say, "The colonists are in the very best of spirits" three years after De Graff was established (*NWC,* June 14, 1879), p. 1. In the same year M. J. McDonnell, the colony land agent in Graceville, reported: "The farmers here in the Colony are contented and happy. They have their small grain nearly sown and anticipate great results and a big return from the soil" (*NWC,* May 3, 1879), p. 4. See *NWC* (September

western fairs and trotting days a friendly bet was merely part of the sport, one way of adding excitement to an already enjoyable occasion.

The Irish fondness for sport even triumphed over an equally warm antipathy toward the English when it was discovered that the English colony settlers at Fairmont, in Martin County, Minnesota, had brought with them several hunters and jumpers of thoroughbred stock; and the Irish colonists planned an excursion by rail to see the "exhibitions of English field sports, genuine hunting with a full pack of hounds, cross-country riding, hurdle racing, etc." [125] On less festive occasions or for indoor entertainment on rainy days, trained badgers were pitted against local coon hounds in a frontier equivalent of the more traditional cock fighting.[126]

After sundown, at the close of the trading and racing day, the wives of the settlement summoned their children and menfolk to one of the "oyster suppers" which they sponsored for the building fund of the parish church and which in time came to be the social highlights of the fall and winter months.[127] Following such suppers in De Graff, the settlers repaired to Moore's Hall for an evening of dancing and community singing.[128] On special occasions the De Graff Minstrel Troupe, which had been organized with home talent to tour the neighboring colony settlements, performed its repertoire of humor, song, and melodrama.[129] Amid the evening gaiety there may have been an occasional dram passed among the boys in violation of their colony total abstinence pledge, but the local press, always quick to report such lapses—with comment—most often praised the sobriety and refinement of these evening programs.[130] And while it was on occasion necessary for the editors in Irish settlements to inform their readers of the

---

29, 1877), p. 7; (December 14, 1878), p. 11, for similarly encouraging reports of the Adrian and Clontarf colonies.

125. Swift County *Advocate* (August 23, 1878), p. 2.

126. Benson *Times* (June 23, 1877), p. 4.

127. Ibid. (November 28, 1876), p. 1.

128. Swift County *Advocate* (November 16, 1877), p. 4.

129. Benson *Times* (February 15, 1877), p. 4.

130. Swift County *Advocate* (November 16, 1877), p. 4.

"frequent pugilistic encounters" which took place at De Graff, the news writers were equally quick to assure the public that the offenders had not been drinking—just fighting.[131] At one time the editor of the Swift County *Advocate,* disturbed by the large number of Irish settlers being jailed for fighting, suggested that such offenders be boarded on bread and water during their stay in the county jail.[132]

It is not perfectly clear whether the Irish enthusiasm for cele- brating such American holidays as July 4th and Washington's Birthday arose entirely out of loyalty to their new land or through a natural desire to multiply the occasions for public celebrations. At least the editor of the Benson *Times* thought that the vigor with which the colonists at De Graff celebrated these patriotic days demonstrated their loyalty to American ideals and indicated the rapidity with which they had become assimilated to the American mode of life.[133] On such occasions it was customary to invite Bishop Ireland to address civic gatherings on his favorite topic, "Christian patriotism." [134] It is difficult for the reader of today to appreciate the fact that the settlers looked on such ora- tions, "occupying something over an hour," [135] as entertainment of the finest kind. In those days, however, trips to the community center were seldom made, except on Sundays. In fact Ireland branded as a loafer any man who would make two or three trips to town in one week.[136] Hence any celebration which attracted outside speakers was considered a social event of some importance. On these occasions there was always a village elocutionist who was prepared to recite "in an oratorical and emphasized manner" the full text of the Declaration of Independence. After the official civic portion of the program the rest of the day was given over to "desultory sports, and bicycle races, winding up with a dance

131. Ibid. (February 15, 1878), p. 4. It will be recalled that Sister Grace Au- relia's comments on life in Graceville during the Connemara period further docu- ment this point. One of the criticisms made by the Irish-American farmers against the incoming Connemaras was that the latter fought too much among themselves and with their neighbors.

132. Swift County *Advocate* (February 15, 1878), p. 4.

133. Benson *Times* (June 23, 1877), p. 4.

134. Jenkins, *Six Seasons on Our Prairies,* p. 72.

135. Ibid.

136. Ibid., p. 74.

at 8 P.M., and thereafter into the 'wee sma' hours.'" [137] On March 17th the Irish on the prairies prepared even more elaborate celebrations. Although the Irish in America seldom spoke with a single voice on issues pertaining to their life in this country, they were unanimous in their demonstration of affection for "the old land" on the feast day of their patron saint. The parade in New York City was undoubtedly longer than those in the western towns, but it was organized and executed with no more enthusiasm than those which enlivened the patronal feast in the Catholic colonies.

The lakes surrounding the various colonies offered several forms of sport and recreation to the colonists. The journal of one traveler who stopped at the Avoca colony in summer recounts that Sundays and holidays were often spent sailing on Lime Lake.[138] Maurice Farrar, the English emigration agent for the North Western System, recommended the pleasures of boating in southwestern Minnesota most enthusiastically when he returned to London in 1880, after five years "on the prairie." [139] In the heat of summer the lakes were especially inviting for swimming and fishing. Bass, pickerel, pike, sunfish, crappie, and perch abounded in the virgin waters of Minnesota.[140] The normal mode of entertaining colony visitors during the spring and summer months was to take them fishing or hunting for the day. One such visitor recorded after his visit to Murray County that "the innumerable lakes teem with varieties of the sweetest fish that ever swam." [141] In the spring, when the buffalo fish were "running," a favorite night sport was that of spearing them as they swam into the range of a powerful lantern fixed to the bow of a boat.[142] One visitor to the prairie colonies was amazed to find the winter sport of ice fishing popular among the settlers. "Fishing in winter through a hole in the ice, over which is built a little wooden house, is, even to the angler wrapped up in buffalo-robes, rather a questionable amusement, with the glass generally

137. Ibid., p. 73.
138. Ibid., pp. 75, 95, 102.
139. Ibid., p. 78.
140. Ibid., p. 59; McClung, *Minnesota as It Is in 1870*, p. 180; Farrar, *Five Years in Minnesota*, p. 164.
141. Jenkins, *Six Seasons on Our Prairies*, p. 59.
142. Farrar, *Five Years in Minnesota*, p. 165.

a long way below zero." [143] Another traveler was pleasantly surprised to find that the huge mud turtles, "found in all the lakes, make capital soup." [144]

In this era, before the enactment of conservation laws and the creation of wildlife preserves, a man's only guide in despoiling nature was his conscience and the "code of the hills." It was considered improper to kill game wantonly or to take more fish than one's family could eat. However, it was not unknown for commercial hunters and fishermen to take ducks, geese, and fish by the hundred pounds, to be shipped in barrels to eastern markets.[145] "Fish by the wagon-load . . . are caught in about every county in the state . . . winter and summer." [146] And "deer are so abundant as to sell lower than beef in the St. Paul market." [147] By selling venison at six cents per pound a commercial hunter could market an average sized deer for ten dollars.[148]

Wild ducks, geese, prairie chickens, partridges, curlews, plovers, and great white cranes supplied the frontiersman's table with delicacies which few of the settlers had ever tasted before going west. It was a matter of some pride to a priest visiting the Avoca colony that within a span of one hour he "dropped five game birds and a mallard," to supply "the ecclesiastical supper for three priests and the Rt. Rev. Bishop [Ireland]." [149] In fact, the ease with which the western settlers bagged their game often threatened to make the sport a bore. Maurice Farrar, recalling the stringent game laws, the gun tax of three guineas a year, and the rent of one shilling an acre on hunting preserves in his native England, contrasted the abundance of game and leisureliness which characterized the field sports in western Minnesota.

> All over the western prairies the prairie chicken . . . is found in great abundance. Americans are, as a rule, luxurious sportsmen, and seldom think of tramping many weary miles after their birds. In the "chicken season" you see them "hunting"

143. Ibid.
144. Jenkins, p. 102.
145. Ibid., p. 66; Farrar, p. 59.
146. McClung, p. 180.
147. Ibid., p. 181. See also Farrar, p. 59.
148. Jenkins, pp. 42, 44; McClung, p. 181.
149. Jenkins, p. 27.

(as they call it) in pairs, in a light-top buggy, with a hamper and a bottle of whiskey under the seat, and plenty of cigars. When the dog points, one descends from the buggy and takes a leisurely shot. The same dog is usually trained to retrieve and to take to water.[150]

Prairie wolves were still common and they were especially feared by the stock farmers for their raids on sheep folds during the cold winter months. The western farmers were always glad to join the hunt whenever a wolf was sighted. Sometimes such a chase covered twenty miles. A bounty of three dollars was paid for every wolf that was killed; and the hunters were generously praised by the local press.[151]

Nearly every settler had his own trap line in winter. Muskrat and otter pelts were then the most lucrative items in the Minnesota fur trade.[152] But "black bear, grey wolf, fox, raccoon, mink . . . and wild-cat [abounded] on the [Minnesota] frontier."[153] The income realized from trapping and hunting offered the settler a supplement to his finances in his early years on the land, but it was always a very minor part of his income. Most men hunted and fished and trapped as a means of providing food for their families. "The field, forest and lake are not only useful for the sportsman, but a never failing resource to the frontier settler, who can *live* by them, with a small amount of labor to secure his bread, potatoes, and the products of the dairy." [154]

After their first harvest season, even the poorest of the western residents could supply their families with a variety of wholesome and tasty food. Shortly after the Avoca colony was established, a visitor from Kentucky recorded in his journal that the western gardens produced "lettuce, greens, onions, radishes, corn, potatoes, strawberries, peas, beans, cabbage, beets, rhubarb, currants, gooseberries, turnips, and carrots." [155] Wild cranberries, wild rice, and several varieties of melons also supplied the tables of new settlers

150. Farrar, pp. 157–8.
151. Ibid., pp. 162–3; Worthington *Advance* (December 20, 1877), p. 3.
152. Farrar, p. 159.
153. McClung, p. 181.
154. Ibid.
155. Jenkins, pp. 54, 81, 83, 85.

with additional delicacies.[156] "Far-seeing people who are industrious will raise all the vegetables they can; and the enormous quantities they can produce from even an ordinary garden plot in this soil will keep them jumping to clear the fast growing weeds and wild grasses; but in the end yield them all they can house for the longer winter one may expect. This is the paradise of gardeners and root raisers." [157]

Beef remained a rare item on the settlers' menus for a long time after their arrival in the West. In the beginning their herds were mostly dairy, not beef cattle. In later years James J. Hill was to supply the settlers along his Great Northern route with imported Shorthorn "dual-purpose" stock cattle, which could be milked as dairy stock or fattened as beef cattle; [158] but for their first years on the land few of the pioneer settlers could afford the extravagance of butchering their foundation stock. Moreover, the difficulty of preserving fresh meat during the summer heat gave them additional reason for not laying in a quarter or a side of beef very often.

Pork, on the other hand, was easier to obtain and could be preserved in more than one way. Pigs were more prolific and more expendable than beef cattle. Nearly every family could afford to fatten and butcher a few of its own hogs each year. The bacons and hams could be smoked, or pickled in salt brine. On the days immediately following butchering day the family might enjoy fresh pork sausages for breakfast and pork chops for dinner, but for the greater part of the year salt pork appeared as the main dish all too many times. However, an occasional mess of fresh fish, a roast wild duck, or a bowl of turtle soup must have helped to relieve this necessary monotony of frontier diets.

In every county, if not in every colony, there was a grist mill to which the farmers could haul their wheat to be cracked or ground and their oats to be rolled. Whole-wheat cereals, bread, and muffins may have been coarse fare, according to modern standards of

156. Farrar, p. 127.

157. Jenkins, pp. 81-2. Jenkins is here writing about Avoca and Murray County in particular.

158. Pyle, *The Life of James J. Hill*, 2, 358.

milling and baking, but it can hardly be inferred that these farmers lacked nourishing baked goods. Although it was undoubtedly true of less fortunate settlers, of these Minnesota colonists one could not say that "On a limited monotonous diet the immigrants sickened, from the sudden shifts in climate the ague got them, from the prevalence of dirt, the itch." [159]

It will be recalled that the white settlers entering Minnesota in the 1870's most often had their own small dairy herds and poultry flocks with them on arrival. In Bishop Ireland's colonies Major Ben Thompson was charged with procuring a milk cow for every family which settled on colony lands.[160] Although the frontier housewife had no refrigeration to help her in the preservation of food and preparation of meals, she could usually count on having fresh milk, eggs, butter, cream, and cottage cheese during most of the year.

Lacking modern refrigeration, the settlers resorted to a variety of means for preserving perishable foods. Those fortunate enough to have a live or bubbling spring near their homesite were assured both a fresh supply of clear water and the cool, flowing stream necessary to chill a spring house. This was usually a small, one-room building, separate from the farm house. It was constructed over the flowing stream and had in the center of the floor a large, scooped-out tank lined with bricks or stones. This tank, filled with constantly moving cold water, offered the frontier housewife the best kind of refrigeration then available.

Root cellars, which required no flowing stream or spring, were more common in the frontier colonies. These cold storage rooms were usually small closets dug into the side of a hill or down into the moist earth. In this well-watered region the subsoil water level was usually close to the surface of the land and relatively little labor was involved in excavating a satisfactory root cellar or digging a clear water "boxed well." In most of the colony sites the soil was so soft that two men, using a hand auger, could bore wells as deep as forty feet. In the Avoca colony, Father Jenkins reported in 1883,

159. Handlin, *The Uprooted*, p. 167.
160. Moynihan, "Archbishop Ireland's Colonies," p. 222.

There have been several wells dug in our township lately. It is a very simple process. The borers erect a three-legged derrick, with block and tackle, whence a windlass lets down an auger a foot or two in diameter. Two men turn the auger with hand spikes, boring down thro' the soft loam sand, and sometimes gravel, then blue and black clay, for say, fifteen or sixteen feet, and meet veins of water in abundance. . . . Wells are dug and "curbed," that is, planked down the sides, for eighty or ninety cents a foot.[161]

To counterbalance these modest advantages of western life there were countless hardships which no settler could have imagined before experiencing them. Long winters delayed his spring planting and early frosts killed whatever grain was not mature. In 1876 and 1877, the very years the colonies were starting, the worst grasshopper invasions ever recorded swept over Minnesota. On alternate years withering hail storms ravaged the crops in mid-summer. In winters such as that of 1880 drifted snow kept every settler locked within his own farm lands for weeks at a time. In spring, the muddy tracks which were prairie roads mired plodding ox teams and killed the more excitable bronco mustangs used by the settlers as draft horses. And in the long lonely days that passed without benefit of visitors or new faces, many farmers, and more especially their wives, resolved to give up the steady round of labor, modest returns, and monotony of life which characterized the western settlements. But in the end an even greater number stuck it out and learned that John Ireland had spoken cautiously and truthfully in announcing his first colony:

I am not inviting anyone to a terrestrial paradise, to a land where without effort or sacrifice, they are to be suddenly lifted into opulence. There are hardships to be endured; patience and labor will be in demand more especially for the first two years. But this much I say to them—if they have

161. Jenkins, pp. 93, 97. By this time settlers living on the shores of lakes in western Minnesota must have had some means of cutting lake ice in winter and storing it in summer. Sawdust and straw packing, which still serve to store ice in isolated western farms, were then available to the settlers. However, I have not found any specific reference to such ice houses or ice storage in the early years of these colonies.

courage and perseverance for a while, they will have homes; they will be the owners of the soil, their own landlords; they will have for themselves and families comfort and ease which they never could have attained in large cities. . . . And their children will grow up good and virtuous Catholics.[162]

162. *NWC* (January 22, 1876), p. 5.

CHAPTER NINE

Competition and Opposition

AT THE OPENING of John Ireland's first colony in Minnesota he had announced that these settlements were to be made for the benefit of the indigent immigrant. For many years he continued to hope that this plan might still be realized, but in the end he was forced to admit that it was not possible. Long before they finished their eastern speaking tour in 1879, Bishops Spalding and Ireland knew, as Daniel O'Connell and D'Arcy McGee had learned before them, that great financial drives for resettling the poor on the land must seek their support from the poor. The crusading bishops also knew that the only agency which could possibly have secured the backing of the rank and file American Catholics for a colonization scheme at that time was the Irish Catholic Benevolent Union. And this federation failed at the critical moment because of its poor leadership. Far from measuring up to its original promise of coordinating Irish Catholic activity in the United States, it eventually became itself an instrument of discord, thereby destroying its own colonization settlements and compromising irreparably those undertaken by Bishops O'Connor, Spalding, and Ireland in Minnesota and Nebraska. Paradoxically, the man most responsible for the creation of the ICBU colonization committee was in the end the one most responsible for its destruction. This man was Father Thomas Ambrose Butler of St. Louis, Missouri.

The activities of this Irish-born priest in directing the colonization of the ICBU in Virginia and Kansas not only discouraged many prospective settlers from going to Minnesota but ultimately succeeded in discrediting the entire colonization movement in America. John Ireland's decision to found no new settlements in Minnesota after 1881 and his failure to carry through a plan for additional colonies in Dakota Territory can only be appreciated in the light of Father Butler's attempt to undermine the Minnesota colonies and discredit the motives of their episcopal sponsor. Several reasons have already been presented to explain why the Minnesota colonies advanced as far as they did. It remains to be seen what forces, acting against them, arrested their further development. The greatest of these was the opposition created by Father Butler.

Thomas Ambrose Butler was born in Dublin, Ireland, on May 21, 1837. He was trained at Maynooth Seminary and was ordained a priest on March 17, 1864. Since Maynooth graduates are regularly retained in Ireland to serve the home missions, it is reasonable to suppose that at the time of his ordination Father Butler and his superiors expected that he would spend his priestly years on Irish soil. His biographer does not relate the details of the young priest's decision to transfer the field of his labors to the United States but tells us only that, "The flame of patriotism lit his poet-soul from early childhood, and as a young priest in his native land he plunged into radical reforms to help the poor and oppressed around him. His zeal, however, brought him into conflict with the authorities, and, having friends in Kansas, he came to America." [1] It was not to be the last time that Father Butler's enthusiasm outdistanced his prudence.

On his arrival in the United States in 1867 he was accepted into the Diocese of Leavenworth, Kansas, by Bishop John B. Miege, S.J., and was named a curate in the cathedral parish in Leavenworth.[2] From this residence he often went west on missionary journeys to minister to the spiritual needs of the few Catholics then to be found in western Kansas. The vastness of the open land oppressed him and made him long for the tidy fields of home. His book of poems, *The Irish on the Prairies*, was written during this period and might have been more appropriately called "Thoughts of Home." Most often the poems are lamentations for the green fields, thatched cottages, and cheering hearths of Ireland or melancholy meditations on his lot in the West.[3]

It has often been remarked that the Irishman newly arrived in

1. John Rothensteiner, *History of the Archdiocese of St. Louis* (2 vols. St. Louis, 1928), 2, 208.
2. Donohoe, *The Irish Catholic Benevolent Union*, pp. 42–3.
3. Thomas Ambrose Butler, *The Irish on the Prairies*, New York, 1874.

America finds little difficulty in establishing immediate contact with fellow exiles from the Emerald Isle, and Father Butler was no exception. Undoubtedly the publicity given his poems by the *ICBU Journal* introduced the young priest to many Irish-Americans who often felt the same nostalgia for home that he wrote of so feelingly.[4] By 1873 he had gained sufficient prominence among the Irish in America to be elected to the executive committee of the ICBU at its third annual meeting in Richmond, Virginia.[5]

In 1874 Father Butler became the resident pastor of Big Stranger, Kansas.[6] Although in later years he often spoke with pride about these months on the frontier, it would seem that during his two years at Big Stranger he regarded the assignment as exile. The solitude of frontier life he found especially depressing, and when he was offered the chance in 1875 to be incardinated into the Archdiocese of St. Louis and to serve as a curate in the cathedral parish, he readily accepted. It is a curious thing that this lonely priest who found the prairies of Kansas so uncongenial was to spend at least ten years of his life promoting a Catholic colony in that state and urging upon Irish immigrants in America the great spiritual and material gains to be found in the West.

At its annual convention in St. Louis in October 1873 the ICBU had created a National Board of Immigration and had directed its member societies to organize similar boards on the parochial level,[7] but within a year the leaders of these boards realized that their modest program was little more than first aid. At the annual convention in 1875 Butler endorsed a motion to replace the old immigration board with a new colonization board and was named the first president of the new bureau.

The very month Butler was elected to this position John Ireland was consecrated Coadjutor Bishop of St. Paul. Within a month the young bishop in Minnesota announced the opening of his first colony in Swift County, and Father Butler joined Martin Griffin in promising the full support of the ICBU for the Minnesota pro-

4. *ICBU Journal* (June 1874), p. 1.
5. Donohoe, p. 37.
6. Ibid., p. 43.
7. *ICBU Journal* (June 1874), p. 1.

gram.[8] This assurance, coming as it did from the only organization that could claim to speak representatively for the Irish in America, must have been encouraging to Bishop Ireland. In May 1876 Father Butler wrote an article for the *ICBU Journal,* commending the Minnesota colonies warmly. "Of all the states mentioned [for colony sites] it seems to me that Minnesota presents the best opportunity for poor men to commence farming. . . . The climate is said to be very like Ireland in Spring and Summer. The Winter is sometimes severe, but the farmers are not seriously impeded in the necessary work around their farms during this time." [9] Butler later reversed this position and did all that he could to defeat the Minnesota venture; but Griffin remained the firm friend of Bishop Ireland to the end. In fact, when Griffin's son decided to study for the priesthood, his father induced him to enter the seminary in St. Paul in order that he might be ordained to work under John Ireland in Minnesota.

In preparing the agenda for the ICBU convention of 1876 Father Butler wrote to Bishop Ireland asking for a summary of the colonization program in Minnesota and requesting, for the deliberations of the convention, "a few suggestions on the matter [of colonization] in general." [10] In the same letter Butler asked Ireland to reserve a portion of the Swift County lands for settlers to be recruited later by the various local boards of the ICBU. Ireland promptly marked off the lands requested and warmly confided to Butler that he expected great things to come from the union's colonization program: "I heartily congratulate the delegates of the I.C.B.U. upon their resolve to make colonization one of the chief works of their powerful organization. With nearly four hundred societies acting in obedience to their legislation, they can wield an influence for good among the Irish Catholic people, which has heretofore been seldom met with in the history of our race in America." [11]

In this letter Ireland urged upon Butler the importance of solic-

8. Ibid. (April 1876), pp. 1, 4; (May 1876), p. 4.
9. Ibid. (May 1876), p. 1.
10. Ireland to Butler, September 16, 1876, quoted in *NWC* (October 21, 1876), p. 1.
11. Ibid.

iting the 30,000 members of the ICBU to organize joint-stock companies in order that the union might underwrite the purchase of western lands for the urban poor who lacked the means of going west unaided:

> The crowning stone in the work of colonization would be the formation of joint stock colonization societies. I do hope that your convention will give some thought to this matter. . . . By no other means can the poor among our people—those most in need of homes—be colonized. However successful our Minnesota plan may seem to have been, it does not reach the poor. We have received hundreds of letters from most deserving persons, to whom we were obliged to answer that we had no place for them in our colony.[12]

It may have been this revelation that so far the Minnesota colonies had not been able to receive the really poor, or it may have been the realistic financial structure outlined by Ireland for making his settlement plan pay its way, that frightened Father Butler, who always favored "benevolent" plans. In any event, this letter marks the turning point in Butler's attitude toward Minnesota. After asking and receiving a reserved portion of Minnesota lands for the ICBU, he deliberately refrained from recommending Ireland's colonies to the delegates in Cleveland in October.[13] The dissipation of energy and internecine conflict that had plagued all previous efforts at Irish unity in America were beginning to affect the ICBU.

At the conclusion of the convention Butler announced that he had "been urged to name one particular state" for colonization. His report to the delegates stated that he had refused to do this for two reasons: (1) because such precipitate action might arouse suspicion that he was favoring one state over another; and (2) because "the same district of country might not please all."[14] Obviously the reference here is to the Minnesota colonies: they were the only ones in the field at the time. In the same report Butler outlined the course of action he thought proper for the ICBU

12. Ibid., p. 7.
13. Donohoe, p. 14.
14. *ICBU Journal* (December 1876), p. 1.

colonization program. He felt that it should be the responsibility of every local board (there were then 304) to form a joint-stock company, buy its own lands, solicit its own settlers (only poor people), and organize its own colony or colonies. The national board was henceforth to serve only as a clearing house for information.

At this critical time, the colonization movement needed, above all else, positive, direct leadership. It needed a director capable of commanding the allegiance of the numerous member groups and of focusing their energies on a common project. It may be that this was too great an assignment for any one man, considering the individualism of the Irish. This much is clear, however: Father Butler was not the man. He had been chosen to lead the national movement toward unification, but with his announcement that colonization was the concern of the numerous local boards, he shattered whatever possibility there may have been for concerted action in this field. For all his zeal, Butler was never a leader. Nowhere is this more apparent than in his life-long habits of avoiding serious decisions and of blaming others for the failure of his plans.

Many delegates had come to the Cleveland convention with instructions to vote in favor of a concerted national colonization plan. Since we have Father Butler's own word for it,[15] it is extremely difficult to appreciate the reasoning behind his decision to dissipate this energy and pass the responsibility back to the local societies. If earlier efforts in the field—from Daniel O'Connell to D'Arcy McGee—had demonstrated anything, it was the absolute necessity of unity and cooperation among great numbers of sponsors. Among the 304 member societies represented in Cleveland, there probably were not five that could have had any chance to found a successful independent colony. Only two of the member societies even tried: the Philadelphia unit and Father Butler's own St. Louis group.

ICBU members in Philadelphia had been encouraged by the reports brought back from the Minnesota colonies by Thomas

15. Butler's explanatory letter was printed in the *ICBU Journal* (December 1876), p. 1.

Green and M. J. Gorman, as well as by the favorable press Martin Griffin always gave the Minnesota venture.[16] At this time, however, Father Butler's influence within the ICBU was considerable, and when he backed away from the Minnesota colonies, the Philadelphia unit did the same. Led by the energetic Thomas F. Hannon, this group followed Father Butler's advice and organized its own stock company. It decided to open a colony at a place called Pink Beds, in western North Carolina. The decision to found a colony in the South ran counter to the advice generally given to the immigrants by their Church leaders. Bishop John Lancaster Spalding specifically warned the Irish that they should avoid settling in the South, where they might find the labor competition of the emancipated Negroes too much for them. "Since emancipation the presence of the negro population is almost as effective as slavery itself as a preventive of immigration." [17] Another economic factor against southern settlement was that usually lands in the South were improved and hence more expensive than virgin lands in the West.

A working party of thirteen men went out from Philadelphia in the summer of 1877 to open a road, build a chapel, and erect an immigrant depot at Pink Beds, North Carolina.[18] Within two weeks the party was back in Philadelphia with the report that the North Carolina site was unsuited for colonization because of its distance (45 miles) from the nearest railroad and because of its mountainous character. It would seem that such obvious defects could have been discovered at a much earlier time and by a much smaller scouting party. Within a few months, however, the Philadelphia members were ready for another try at colonizing. At the September meeting they resolved "that another location be selected as near as possible to the one previously agreed upon." [19]

At this time a southern plantation owner, one Samuel Barnes, proprietor of a great 7,000-acre estate, "Barnesville," in Charlotte County, Virginia, was considering how he might recoup the for-

16. Ibid. (February 1877), p. 1, wherein Secretary Thomas F. Hannon announced that within the year the ICBU would sponsor further colonization in the West.
17. Spalding, *The Religious Mission of the Irish People*, p. 108.
18. *ICBU Journal* (July 1877), p. 1.
19. Donohoe, p. 112.

tune he had lost in the late war and replace the crew of slaves taken from him by emancipation. Before the war Barnes had engaged in an extensive and lucrative slave trade.[20] Throughout his estate there were still standing some forty small cabins that had once served as slave quarters.[21] It was natural for an enterprising planter in these straits to consider the possibility of substituting poor immigrants, recruited in the port cities of the North, for the Negro slaves he had lost through emancipation. It is still not clear whether Barnes, secretly trying merely to replace Negro slaves with Irish laborers, at this point intentionally deceived the colonizers from Philadelphia, or whether he was genuinely interested in promoting the Irish settlement. In any event Barnes began negotiations with Thomas Hannon, through one Narcisse Plumadore, a land agent and member of the ICBU local of Raleigh, North Carolina.[22] Plumadore was also the man who had made preliminary arrangements for the short-lived settlement at Pink Beds in his native state.

The Barnes estate included the usual improvements to be found on many large plantations: a steam saw mill, grist mill, post office, store, distillery, and tannery.[23] The presence of these, together with the "forty frame houses" (i.e. slave cabins), gave Barnes a strong bargaining position in his negotiations with Hannon. It was finally agreed that the Philadelphia ICBU local would purchase the entire Barnes estate at an average price of about $10 per acre. This would enable the society to sell land to its settlers for about $11 per acre.[24] (In spite of the sanguine hopes of its founders, the Virginia settlement was never to be a haven for the poor man.) In February 1877 Bishop Ireland had told his Phila-

20. On August 31, 1953, the material given here as background for the Barnes story was supplied me in an interview with Daniel Murray Howerton and F. S. Howerton, who now occupy and farm the land in Charlotte County, Virginia, which once comprised the Barnes estate.

21. *ICBU Journal* (October 1877), p. 5.

22. Donohoe, p. 111. Plumadore was the man whom Griffin later accused of "speculating" in land at the expense of the colonists. Convinced that the project was tainted, Griffin resigned as vice-president of the Philadelphia ICBU unit. Thus far I have not found any evidence sufficiently convincing to exculpate Plumadore from the charges made against him by Griffin.

23. *ICBU Journal* (October 1877), p. 5.

24. Ibid. (December 1877), p. 5.

delphia readers that lands in his Swift County colony could be purchased with railroad bonds, at prices ranging from $1.30 to $3.25 per acre, depending on the proximity of the land to the railroad and the particular bond issue exchanged for it,[25] and even then the Minnesota Bishop had warned, "I regret to be obliged to say that I cannot advise very poor people to come to our colony." [26] Hence there must have been factors other than the price of the lands which influenced the Philadelphia leaders to prefer the more expensive Virginia land to that in Minnesota. The deliberations of the society, reprinted in their *Journal*, do not, however, make clear what these other factors were. In time, the costliness of the land and buildings at Barnesville was to be a prime element in the failure of the colony; but in the beginning Hannon and his faithful followers, encouraged by Father Butler, had high hopes for the settlement, which they named "Keileyville" in honor of Anthony M. Keiley, a former mayor of Richmond, Virginia, and then president of the ICBU.

On October 19, 1877, Bishop James Gibbons had departed from his Diocese of Richmond, Virginia, to become the new Archbishop of Baltimore.[27] His successor in Richmond, Bishop John J. Keane, was not appointed until August 1, 1878.[28] During the interregnum the Virginia diocese was administered by Father Francis Janssens, the vicar general. In the private journal which Gibbons had begun, Janssens' entry for July 1, 1878, chronicled the foundation of the Keileyville colony in that diocese:

> Colony, Keileyville, Charlotte County, Va., November 1877 a Catholic Colony was started under the auspices of the Philadelphia Catholic Colonization Association, at a place called Barnesville, which has been christened Keileyville in honor of the President of the I.C.B.U. A tract of 7000 acres of good land has been bought on easy terms, which are to be sold in farms from 50 to 100 acres to Catholic families. The colonists up to date [July 1, 1878], to the number of about

25. Ibid. (February 1877), p. 1.
26. *NWC*, quoted in *ICBU Journal* (March 1877), p. 7.
27. John Tracy Ellis, *The Life of James Cardinal Gibbons* (2 vols. Milwaukee, 1952), *1*, 162.
28. Ibid., p. 186.

120 are a sober and industrious class of people, and the colony bids fair to succeed. The colony is attended to once a month by a priest from Richmond.[29]

In the Minnesota colonies the pastor acted as the leader of the settlement. However, Keileyville, lacking the patronage of a bishop, had no resident pastor. Hence Thomas Hannon left Philadelphia to live among the settlers and direct their colony organization. In the first year fifty-two families settled on the colony lands.[30] Very few, if any, were recent arrivals in the United States. Hannon reported that most of them came to Virginia from "Pennsylvania, Massachusetts, Michigan, Maine, North and South Carolina." [31] He was also somewhat distressed to discover that very few of the colonists knew anything about farming. This initial handicap was intensified by the severe drouth that during their first year in the colony plagued the area and seriously injured the crops.

It was also a matter of great concern to these settlers, who had joined the colony in order to lead a more completely religious life, that they had no resident pastor. A priest from Richmond, 90 miles away, came to offer mass only once a month. This was the kind of religious isolation against which Archbishop Hughes had warned Catholic immigrants. On March 3, 1879, while cutting timber, a settler named Peter Clark was crushed by a falling tree. There was no priest sufficiently close to administer the last sacraments before Clark died, and the funeral service consisted of prayers read by a layman, without any Requiem Mass.[32] In a settlement founded in part to establish a Catholic center for community worship, this lack of spiritual direction was a serious deficiency.

The news articles published in the *ICBU Journal* were regularly optimistic about life in the Keileyville settlement. To encourage

29. Richmond Chancery Archives, Records: Diocese of Richmond, No. 6, p. 68. This journal book is really the diary kept by Bishop Gibbons while he was Bishop of Richmond. Father Janssens merely kept up the entries between the time Gibbons' entries stopped and those of Bishop Keane began.

30. *ICBU Journal* (April 1879), p. 1.

31. Ibid. (July 1878), p. 6.

32. Ibid. (April 1879), p. 1.

his followers, Hannon reprinted in this paper the rather cryptic remark made by a writer on the Philadelphia *Ledger:* "Land in Virginia at $10.00 an acre is cheaper than land out West for nothing." [33] Enthusiastic letters from several settlers revealed that in many ways the colony was making adequate progress. It was discovered that the soil at Keileyville, though it was not really very heavy, had produced an admirable crop of potatoes in 1877. For those who had read of or experienced the famine years in Ireland, this was no inconsiderable blessing. In the same year a Mr. Buckley, who operated the colony store, secured an order from a New York grocery merchant for 500 barrels of dried blackberries. Buckley hired all the men, women, and children who wanted work to harvest the crop of wild berries so abundant in that region.[34]

It would also appear that in spite of their distance from a railroad (eight miles), the colonists by and large were satisfied with transportation facilities and the local markets, which they found ready to take their grain and farm products.[35] The short crop of 1877, however, left many of the farmers with very little produce to market, and most of them had counted on a cash crop each year to meet the payments on their land. At the time each settler had picked out his land he had been required to make an initial payment of $1 per acre. The day he took residence on the farm, he was to pay in cash 10 per cent of his remaining debt. After that, the principal was to be liquidated by ten annual payments of equal amount, plus 6 per cent interest.[36] Even though most of the settlers had come to the colony with some cash reserves, many of them began to feel the pinch of economic distress in the spring of their second year.

One of these, a colony farmer named Robert Humphreys, wrote to Griffin in May 1879 to complain about conditions in the colony. He observed that for years before the arrival of the colony the Barnesville land had been overworked and abused. Better land could have offset some of the evil effects of the previous year's

33. Ibid. (July 1878), p. 4.
34. Ibid.
35. Ibid. (March 1879), p. 1.
36. Hannon's report in a letter to Griffin, published in *ICBU Journal* (July 1878), p. 6.

drouth. Humphreys also remarked that the cash reserve of $500 suggested by the colony officials as a minimum for every settler should be raised to $1,000. His experience—on a relatively small farm of fifty acres—had convinced him that a reserve of at least $1,000 was necessary to ensure the settler against the possibility of losing his initial investment in the year of a bad crop.[37]

Another handicap under which the colony labored was the large portion of unsold land for which the Colonization Board had to make regular payments. The board was not acting as a land agent for Barnes, as John Ireland was doing for the Minnesota railroads. Barnes had to be paid in cash each time a payment was due; and the board had to do its best to scrape up the money. Of the eighty-eight farms laid out in the colony, there were never more than sixty occupied at one time.[38] The columns of the *ICBU Journal* regularly carried financial appeals that grew more distressed with the passage of time.

In this matter, the ICBU local in Philadelphia was in a paradoxical position. It had undertaken the colonization venture as a local board. It had hoped to finance the settlement by organizing its own joint-stock company. This had been the essence of Butler's advice after the Cleveland convention. But once the colony was in the field and local contributions were not measuring up to the level of running expenses, the *ICBU Journal*, controlled for the most part by the members of the Philadelphia unit, began to remind its readers across the nation that the Virginia settlement was a responsibility of the national organization.[39] An attempt was made to assess every member in the ICBU ten dollars, to pay for the colonization work.[40] After this failed, a proposal was made at the national convention in Worcester in 1878 to levy a ten-cent *per capita* tax on all members in the union. This motion "received only grudging approval," and by February of the following year only eleven of the fifty-four societies represented at Worcester had paid the tax. By June the total contributions from all societies amounted to only $600.[41]

37. Ibid. (May 1879), p. 1.
38. Ibid. (April 1879), p. 6; (August 1879), p. 1.
39. Ibid. (April 1879), p. 6.
40. Donohoe, p. 118.
41. Ibid.

In April 1879 Hannon appealed to the members of the union to come to the rescue of the colony: "You must recollect we are under contract to pay for this land at stated times, and we have no means to meet these payments except from the installments paid by [the] colonists. As not quite one-half of the land has been sold . . . the burden of the other half is upon us now, together with the accruing interest. . . . If we fail, Catholic Colonization will be seriously injured." [42] This appeal stirred some members to pay their dues but did not beget any substantial contributions. Griffin did what he could to encourage additional contributions by writing a few editorials in the *Journal*, but the results were not at all encouraging.

With a shrewdness greater than most of his associates Griffin began to realize that the radical defect in the Keileyville colony was really its bad financial basis. If this was so, it was futile for its leaders to blame its weakened condition on their fellow members in the ICBU. In his editorial column for June 1879 he expressed this opinion publicly for the first time.

> If we understand Bishop Ireland's system, it is preferable to the plan upon which both the St. Louis and Philadelphia Colonization Societies are formed, and if we should ever be so unfortunate as to get into any more colonization schemes it will be those that have less responsibility than is imposed upon the management by the system we are now aiding to operate. . . . Bishop Ireland secured the control of large tracts, and without the burden of stated payments to be met filled up these lands as well as though he had been their absolute owner. We like that better than to buy up a large tract of land and obligate yourself to regular payments, and to have that responsibility and annoyance of the people you settle besides.[43]

After the foundation of the colony more than two years passed before the Bishop of Richmond was able to send a priest to Keileyville as resident pastor. On October 1, 1879, Bishop Keane appointed Father Adolph Habets (an elderly priest who had come

42. *ICBU Journal* (April 1879), quoted in Donohoe, p. 119.
43. *ICBU Journal* (June 1879), p. 1.

to America from Holland) to establish a parish in the colony settlement.[44] From this point Father Habets was also to attend the Catholics at Danville, Virginia, as well as any others residing along the route of the Richmond and Danville Railroad. The bishop noted in his journal that he had accompanied the new pastor to Keileyville on his first day and that "the colonists [were] greatly cheered by the appointment of Father Habets to reside among them." [45] While this gentle priest from Holland remained in the midst of the Irish settlers, he did all in his power to protect and extend the life of the struggling settlement. Within fifteen months of his appointment, however, it was necessary for him to be relieved of this arduous assignment, since he was "unable to continue visiting his missions during the winter, owing to deafness and ill health." [46] After his departure there was never again a resident pastor in Keileyville.

In spite of all such disappointments and hardships, the spirit manifested by the colonists in their letters to Griffin and the *Journal* remained remarkably high. Confidence was widespread that the land was good enough, the location satisfactory, and the prospects for the future encouraging. There was a general tendency among the settlers to regard their initial reverses merely as afflictions customary among pioneers. It is entirely possible that the Keileyville settlers were merely experiencing the "first two years of seemingly fruitless labor" of which John Ireland had warned his settlers. And it is equally possible that the tiny settlement might have grown to maturity, preserving its identity as a religious colony, if it had not been for Martin Griffin's denunciation of the colony leaders, Thomas Hannon and Narcisse Plumadore, in the summer of 1879.

During a visit to the Virginia colony on July 4 of that year Griffin discovered in casual conversation with Anthony M. Keiley, who was then the city attorney of Richmond, that Samuel Barnes had not been the sole owner of Barnesville at the time the colonization board purchased these lands, a Mr. Swepsin having been part owner of the estate. Further questioning revealed that the

44. Richmond Chancery Archives, Records: Diocese of Richmond, No. 6, p. 94.
45. Ibid.
46. Ibid., p. 107.

same Swepsin had been the owner of the tract in Pink Beds, North Carolina, which had been proposed as the first site for the colony. Griffin knew that the Philadelphia board had first heard about Pink Beds from Narcisse Plumadore, the Carolina land agent. He also knew that it was Plumadore who had selected Barnesville as an alternative site after Pink Beds had been rejected by the colonists. Griffin had always thought that Plumadore, a member of the Raleigh ICBU, had been motivated solely by a charitable interest in the welfare of the colonizing program. It came as quite a surprise, therefore, when he learned that Plumadore had been acting as an agent for Swepsin, both at Pink Beds and at Barnesville. Barnes, down on his luck after the war, had become indebted to Swepsin. Through this debt Swepsin acquired a part interest in the Barnesville estate. When Swepsin's agent, Plumadore, persuaded the Philadelphia colonists to purchase Barnesville, Barnes had signed an agreement with Swepsin that if the colonists bought the land, Plumadore, acting as Swepsin's agent, would receive a fee of $1 per acre, or a total of more than $6,000. Before Griffin's Fourth of July visit none of the colonists or colony directors, with the exception of Hannon, knew about the true relationship of Swepsin, Plumadore, and Barnes. Griffin questioned Hannon about these matters and discovered that Hannon, though he knew about the Barnes-Swepsin agreement, had felt it was none of his business, hence had never bothered to reveal it to Griffin or the other board members. Griffin insisted that the entire project, publicized as a benevolent aid program, had been tainted by speculation.[47]

In the next issue and several succeeding issues of the *ICBU Journal*, Griffin ran a curtly phrased notice of his resignation from the Colonization Board. It occupied a prominent position on the editorial page, in the same place where his commendations of the colony had previously appeared: "I have resigned the Vice-Presidency of the Philadelphia Colonization Society of the Irish Catholic Benevolent Union, and have henceforth no connection with that organization or its colony at Keileyville, Virginia." [48]

47. *ICBU Journal* (October 1879), p. 4. See also Donohoe, pp. 120–1, for a good summary of the story of Keileyville.
48. *ICBU Journal* (August 1879), p. 4; (September 1879), p. 4; (November 1879), p. 4.

Readers of the *Journal* were perplexed by this sudden and mysterious shift in the editor's allegiance. Since no explanation for his conduct was offered, inquiries poured in, asking for some kind of clarification. In the October issue, apparently after some consideration, Griffin wrote an extensive article, revealing to the public the financial facts behind the purchase of the Barnesville estate. He did not directly accuse Hannon of fraud or of an intention to deceive, but he implied that Hannon had been guilty of mismanagement. Neither Griffin nor anyone else could show that Hannon had received any profit from Plumadore or Swepsin. As soon as Griffin's article appeared in print, he received several letters from interested persons. Chief among these were letters from Father Habets,[49] who had just been appointed pastor of Keileyville; Anthony M. Keiley, president of the national ICBU; [50] and John J. Nolan,[51] who was then secretary of the Philadelphia Colonization Board. All of these men agreed that Hannon was completely innocent of fraud and felt that Griffin had done him serious injury by implying that he had in some way cheated the colonists. The writers did agree, however, that Hannon should have told the Philadelphia Board about the Plumadore-Swepsin arrangement. In a letter to Griffin, Hannon himself even admitted that it might have been a mistake for him not to confide these matters to the leaders in Philadelphia. Father Habets' letter defending Hannon is especially touching in its revelation of how Griffin's charges had shaken the confidence and the security of the colonists. "I feel sorry that you have separated altogether from working for this colony: the more so because I know your disinterested intention in promoting its progress. Though somewhat gloomy seems its aspect for the present yet I hope it will be a success, which I am sure it will be if the people can pay their installments and make a living. This will be hard if not impossible for a couple of years more, but by that time I think they ought to be able to get along better." [52]

In spite of the almost universal support given Hannon by his

49. See letter of Father Adolph Habets to Griffin, Keileyville, October 15, 1879, Griffin Papers.
50. Anthony M. Keiley to Griffin, Richmond, October 19, 1879, Griffin Papers.
51. John J. Nolan to Griffin, Philadelphia, October 23, 1879, Griffin Papers.
52. Habets to Griffin, October 15, 1879, Griffin Papers.

associates, Griffin remained adamant and would have nothing more to do with the Keileyville project.[53] Whether he was completely justified in his unqualified denunciation cannot be determined. It is beyond doubt, however, that his resignation from colony affairs was the greatest blow that could have befallen the settlement enterprise. At best the organization was in a precarious financial condition. Its only hope of meeting the payments due Samuel Barnes lay in soliciting funds from the readers of the *ICBU Journal,* and this avenue Griffin sealed off against them. In one letter Hannon reminded the fiery Griffin that the stinging editorials in the *Journal* had had their effect: "I consider that you have carried out your threat to the very letter to do me all the injury you could." [54] Of all the colony promoters Hannon had given himself most generously to the project, even to the extent of resigning his position in Philadelphia to take up residence among the settlers in Keileyville. It must also be observed that Hannon showed himself well disposed to effect a reconciliation; but Griffin was not. In his November editorial Griffin reiterated the charge of "speculation" and remarked rather sharply, "We have had our dose of colonization." [55]

The end was in sight, but the Keileyville residents valiantly

53. There is some circumstantial evidence to indicate that there may have been more known to Griffin than was brought to light in his column. A persistent legend among the residents of Charlotte County today relates that in all these negotiations Barnes was actually the double dealer whose machinations eventually brought downfall to the colony. According to this curiously durable legend, "when the settlers came [to Keileyville] they thought that they had bought the land; [but] after a year or two at Keileyville they realized that they did not own the land but had paid for no more than a ten year option on it. This shock helped bring about the end of Keileyville." For this information I am indebted to the Very Reverend Justin D. McClunn, Chancellor of the Diocese of Richmond. Father McClunn's letter of September 22, 1953, quotes this statement from information supplied to him by the Reverend Vernon J. Bowers, present pastor of the Sacred Heart parish, Danville, Virginia. The baptismal records and parish journals for the Keileyville parish are now kept in the Danville rectory. Substantially the same legend as that mentioned by Father Bowers was related to me by Daniel Murray Howerton, of Red Oak, Virginia, in an interview on Mr. Howerton's farm in Virginia on August 31, 1953. The Howerton farm now covers the land once occupied by the central portion of the Keileyville settlement. How much credence the oral legends of the region deserve is difficult to determine. They are mentioned here as a possible extenuation of the inflexible decision of Griffin.

54. Hannon to Griffin, Keileyville, November 26, 1879, Griffin Papers.

55. *ICBU Journal* (November 1879), p. 4.

tried to stay on. Father Habets did his best to encourage the little group, while his own illness, "a disease of the ear with a very long name," [56] was becoming increasingly burdensome. In a letter to Griffin, Hannon reported that the elderly priest was obliged to visit his physician so often and found traveling so difficult that he was able to be at Keileyville only for Sunday mass. The old pastor did what he could to lighten the financial burden of the settlers by refusing to allow a collection of 75¢ per month to be solicited for his support from each settler.[57] The picture of the dying colony presented in the quietly pathetic letters of Hannon and Father Habets is especially touching: the old priest, deaf, infirm, and living in a rented room, without even a residence of his own, hoping that something would turn up and making, in effect, his monthly contribution of 75¢ to each settler. It was the winter season, the best time of the year for provident farmers to move to a new farm if they intended to get in a crop in the spring.

That many of the Keileyville group did just this is evident from Griffin's tersely worded obituary notice on the colony, published in February 1880. In this statement he informed the public that the Philadelphia Colonization Board had dissolved and that its rights, title, and interest in the Keileyville lands had been returned to Samuel Barnes, in return for a sum of $2,000, which Barnes would pay when and if he could get it. This meant, of course, that the stockholders had lost their investment. The terrible finality of Griffin's closing paragraph must have sounded like a death knell for those still hoping to stay on in Keileyville:

> While this *Journal* will not devote its space, as heretofore, to the colony and its affairs, we state here that the place is, in our judgment, a good location as regards soil, climate, water and church facilities. Rev. A. Habets is the resident pastor, and he writes us that the people now there are cheerful of the present and future. We do not hesitate to recommend the *place*. But to work for it or be concerned in its management, we cannot. The settlement that has been made is satisfactory to us. For, as most of the stock had been taken

56. Hannon to Griffin, Keileyville, November 26, 1879, Griffin Papers.
57. Ibid.

through our efforts, we endeavored to secure its return to those who had given their money. Our demand, that the one dollar for "commission" should be taken off the present colonists being conceded, we are satisfied by the justification of our course that presents. We never expect to see Keiley-ville again. We wish it well. We gave it our best energies, and only regret that we cannot, in good faith, continue to do so. We shall not again refer to the place, further than to give news items relating to it.[58]

During the years of activity at Keileyville Father Butler was busily directing the work of the St. Louis ICBU Board of Colonization in its attempt to establish a similar colony on the grasslands of northern Kansas. In line with his own announcement at the Cleveland convention (1876) to the effect that colonization should henceforth be the responsibility of local councils, Butler, though still retaining the title of chairman of the national Board of Colonization, devoted most of his energies to organizing a joint-stock company on the local level in St. Louis, with the hope of perfecting a plan to put poor people on the farmlands of the West.[59]

Butler must have felt himself under some pressure at this time either to join Bishop Ireland's growing movement or to come forward with some feasible alternative of his own. His usual defense, in the face of this dilemma, was to assert that he would not take the responsibility for recommending any one place over another. "Not all persons would find the same locale equally congenial." This answer was far from convincing to Martin Griffin, who had assured himself long ago that the colonies in Minnesota had the best chance of success. They had good land, a most advantageous credit arrangement, a resident priest, a parish organized and a church built before the arrival of the settlers, a railroad through their lands, and a bishop who promised to be their patron. Griffin felt that the Irish had already passed up many good opportunities in America and that many of them were go-

58. *ICBU Journal* (February 1880), p. 5.
59. Ibid. (February 1877), p. 1.

ing down to defeat in the cities while their German Catholic confreres were enjoying the fruits of their common decision to pick out the best lands they could find and settle on these. In a pointed reference to Father Butler's tactics, Griffin observed that the urgent question arose from the Irish on all sides, "Where shall we go?" but that they took very little consolation from the Colonization Board's evasive assurance that it would provide them with accurate information on any land they selected. Griffin pleaded with Father Butler's board, citing the daily requests for direction coming to the *Journal* from immigrants wanting to go west. Griffin, of course, never hesitated to tell such inquirers to go to Minnesota; but neither did he relax in his campaign of prodding Father Butler to assume more responsibility in actively directing the immigrant flow.[60]

Possibly pressure from Griffin or the success of John Ireland's colonies finally impelled Father Butler to launch his colony in Kansas in 1877. A recent dissertation advances the opinion that when "many young men, impressed by the social injustice and economic insecurity [then] prevalent, turned to Butler seeking advice about settling on the land. . . . he determined to study at first hand what the scouts [of the St. Louis ICBU] had described so glowingly." [61] Whatever the reasons for his decision, Butler, after a personal inspection tour of the railroad lands available in Pottawatomie County, Kansas, decided to plant a colony in this region. His next problem was that of securing enough money to make the down payment. By this time he had convinced himself that Bishop Ireland's system of not buying the land from the railroad but of acting merely as a land agent was in some way illicit. He would have none of such "speculation." It was his intention to acquire complete title to large tracts of land, upon which he would make regular payments with money supplied by benevolent members of the ICBU in St. Louis.

On January 14, 1877, at St. Patrick's Hall in St. Louis, the St. Louis Colonization Board of the ICBU was organized. Father Butler was elected treasurer and it was agreed that this board

60. Ibid. (December 1876), p. 4.
61. Donohoe, p. 132.

would form its own local joint-stock company, and that 25,000 shares of stock would be issued, to be sold for $2 a share.[62] Within six months 11,000 shares had been sold: [63] but it was to be many long months before these stock pledges were redeemed with cash. Some pledges were never paid. There was also some difference of opinion on the site proposed for the new colony. A few members, impressed by the scouts' reports on the lands in Texas, held out for a site there; but in the end Butler's choice prevailed and Kansas was chosen. The land to be purchased was part of the original land grant to the Central Branch of the Union Pacific Railroad. The association agreed to pay $3.60 an acre for 12,000 acres; the railroad agreed to reserve 15,000 additional acres for a period of one year. The Colonization Board was given eleven years in which to pay for all the lands, and Father Butler felt "not the slightest fear of inability to pay the whole amount in less time—probably within two years." [64] Acting on this optimistic prediction he first announced that his thoroughly benevolent project would allow its settlers five years in which to pay for their lands. Later the period of grace was increased to eight years.[65]

The new Kansas colony was named St. Columbkille and placed under the patronage of that great Irish saint. The townsite was named Butler City. Given the generous credit terms allowed by the board in St. Louis, it was not difficult to find settlers for St. Columbkille's, but it quickly became evident that many of the stock pledges made at the January meeting were only paper promises. Some of the original subscribers notified Father Butler that since they had favored putting the colony in Texas, they could not go along with the project in Kansas,[66] although at the time he had purchased the lands Butler had reported that "the St. Louis Colonization Association of the I.C.B.U. *unanimously* voted in favor of a certain tract of land . . . in Pottawatomie County, Kansas." [67] Another excuse offered was that "many sub-

---

62. *ICBU Journal* (February 1877), p. 1.
63. Ibid. (July 1877), p. 1 (Hannon's annual report).
64. Ibid. (November 1877), p. 6.
65. Ibid. (December 1877), quoted in Donohoe, p. 134.
66. Donohoe, p. 135.
67. *ICBU Journal* (November 1877), p. 6 (italics mine).

scribers for stock failed to pay up their assessments on account of the hard times lately experienced." [68]

Deserted by many of his supporters, Father Butler began a series of ingenious money-raising projects to help meet his March 1878 payment of $5,000. He proposed at first that a raffle be staged, with town lots in Butler City as prizes. This project collapsed when those who favored Texas announced the withdrawal of their support.[69] Only with the help of several priests (who assembled $1,000) and of a Protestant friend (who advanced $2,000) [70] was Butler able to meet the deadline for his first big payment. Later in the same year and before the colony was six months old he had reason to regret his earlier advice to the national convention that local boards, not the national treasury, should subsidize the colonization movement. A recent writer has summarized Father Butler's dilemma at this time:

> As business problems multiplied and financial matters grew thornier, Father Butler lamented the lack of a general fund from which the local boards might draw sufficient cash to tide them over criticial periods. On one occasion when he was desperately in need of money, he called in person upon every society of the Union in St. Louis only to be repulsed. Disillusioned but still expectant, he next appealed to the societies of the Ancient Order of Hibernians only to meet a similar fate.[71]

It probably never occurred to the zealous Father Butler, when his colony began to totter, that the real fault lay not with the public

68. Ibid. (November 1878), quoted in Donohoe, p. 140.
69. Donohoe, p. 135.
70. *ICBU Journal* (August 1878), p. 5.
71. Butler to Griffin, St. Louis, May, 1878, Griffin Papers, quoted in Donohoe, p. 137. Evidence presented in this letter would seem to conflict with Sister Joan Marie's earlier statement (p. 134) dealing with the same matter: "There could be no better evidence of the soundness of the venture than a balanced financial statement which Father Butler recorded after the first two payments of $500 each had been settled. A third payment of $1,000 would follow; a fourth of $5,000, and then two years would elapse before further financial headaches would present themselves." Using the same material, I would conclude that Father Butler's ability to make two $500 payments would not warrant the statement that his position was sound—that on the contrary, his inability to meet the inevitable and larger payments at later dates proves precisely the opposite. His financial situation was from the beginning very precarious.

whom he accused of abandoning him but with the completely un-
sound financial basis upon which the venture had been undertaken. Rather than consider the internal weaknesses of his project,
after being turned down by the Hibernians in St. Louis, he even
went so far as to castigate his beloved Irish for what he termed
their lack of a practical sense and an excess of sentimentality: "You
will always be able to trace a resemblance of character between the
Irish and the French. Both are more likely to indulge in the sentimental than the practical. Our people would be more willing to
give five dollars to buy a fading green flag with tarnished sunburst,
than one dollar for an acre of land." [72] Within the ranks of all the
leaders of the Catholic colonization movement there was hardly a
man so sentimental, impractical, and mercurial as Father Butler;
yet he found it possible to upbraid his own people for the very
shortcomings so obvious in his own character.

The subsequent history of the Kansas colony proved Bishop
Ireland right on two scores: Butler's indebtedness was far too
great, and the source of his income was too insecure and unpre-
dictable. Even after these truths had been demonstrated, the St.
Louis priest refused to recognize that the near failure of his colony
was the fault of its organizers. The most ironical development of
all was that Father Butler, who regularly castigated Bishop Ireland
for dealing with the railroads, was finally forced, in order to save
his colony from disaster, to secure from the Central Branch of the
Union Pacific exactly the same kind of credit plan which Ireland
had arranged for his colonists seven years earlier with the St. Paul
and Pacific in Minnesota.[73]

Whatever hope Butler might have had for securing additional
funds for his colonies from the national ICBU was shattered when
the convention of 1881 in Indianapolis was disrupted by an open
breach between himself and Father John Fanning, the two leading
proponents of colonization within the national union. Fanning
proposed at this time to establish a new colony ("Fanningville")
in Franklin County, Nebraska. Many unpleasant questions, implying mismanagement, were asked from the convention floor about

72. *ICBU Journal* (August 1878), p. 1.
73. Ibid. (June 1882), p. 1.

funds previously voted for colonization work. Further discord
arose when Butler declared that he could not countenance Fanning's decision to solicit emigration from Ireland. Fanning cited
reports, still coming to America, about Irishmen literally dying in
the streets for want of food. In Butler's mind this was still not an
adequate reason for soliciting emigration. In the end the delegates
refused to back the proposed colony in Nebraska and Father
Butler returned to St. Louis without the funds he had expected.[74]

Just as the Keileyville colony had begun with sanguine predictions for its success but had ended by returning its lands to Samuel
Barnes and casting its dependents adrift on their own initiative,
the St. Louis sponsorship of Butler City was withdrawn in May
1882 when the parent Colonization Board announced that it was
no longer responsible for the settlement in Kansas. In the words of
Father Butler, "This wise action of our Board was the salvation of
the colony." [75] After the disastrous convention of 1881, the multi-
plication of splinter factions within the ICBU left no hope for the
St. Louis board in their plan to save the colony by seeking financial
aid from the national union. Even before this time, it had been
demonstrated that the colony could not survive on the funds that
could be collected in St. Louis. There was no alternative left save
that of seeking some kind of concession from the Union Pacific.

Butler was greatly relieved to learn that the railroad was perfectly willing to release him from his first contract. A new agreement was reached, calling for all unsold lands in the original tract
of 12,000 acres to revert to the ownership of the railroad. All the
settlers were called into Butler City, where their contracts with
the St. Louis ICBU Colonization Board were canceled and new
contracts were signed by all of them with the Union Pacific land
commissioner, one Mr. Gilmore. It was further stipulated that all
payments previously made by the settlers to the St. Louis board
would be credited toward their contracts with the railroad.[76] It
had taken Father Butler and his St. Louis Board seven years and
many disappointments to learn that in the end the plan originally
advocated by John Ireland was the best. The contracts signed by

74. Ibid. (October 1881), p. 6; (November 1881), p. 1; (February 1882), p. 4.
75. Ibid. (June 1882), p. 1.
76. Ibid.

Butler's colonists with the Union Pacific in 1882 were exactly the same kind as those signed by John Ireland's settlers with the St. Paul and Pacific in 1876.

Among other things, the new contract with the Union Pacific relieved Butler of the unpleasant task of forcing the tardy settlers to pay up their land bills. The railroad now became the collector, and although its credit period was liberal, the road expected regular payments from all settlers. This was not the purely benevolent plan originally intended. In fact, the purely benevolent plan had been converted to a purely businesslike plan. This hard fact was expressed more euphemistically by Father Butler: "I have learned a great lesson, which I now boldly confess to my brethren of the I.C.B.U. The work, as mapped out formerly at our conventions, for carrying on Catholic colonization *as a purely benevolent undertaking* is a great and fearful one. In fact, to be a *purely benevolent work* it has countless difficulties to overcome." [77] With a rhetorical dexterity that should forever amaze the readers of the *Journal*, Father Butler closed his obituary on the colony by rejoicing that his group had never become speculators or land agents for railroads! He assured all his readers that Butler City was a thriving center for a successful farming colony, that the settlement would henceforth be entirely on its own, and that disappointed investors in the syndicate would be rewarded with choice business lots in Butler City. His closing quote ("All's well that ends well") must have puzzled many a stockholder whose money would never return. The astonishing skill displayed by Father Butler on those many occasions when he calmly reported complete success after having been faced with a complete debacle should rank as a moral miracle. His most recent and favorable apologist has handled this paradox with great charity: "It is difficult, at times, to reconcile such perpetual oscillation between the poles of optimism and pessimism as is indicated in Butler's correspondence, unless it can be attributed to what one historian characterizes as a racial trait of the Irish, a mercurial temperament." [78]

In addition to its own lack of success, the Butler City colony contributed in another way to the weakening of the entire colo-

77. Ibid.
78. Donohoe, p. 139.

nization movement. Before undertaking the Kansas project, Butler repeatedly wrote that he did not believe Catholic leaders should recommend one colony site in preference to any other. Presumably this also meant that he did not feel they should attack or discredit any single site simply because it was not their site. Unfortunately his own pronouncements often violated this code. It will be recalled that he had once spoken favorably about the land, the climate, and the general prospects of Minnesota. Within one year, however, he not only withdrew this recommendation but embarked on a regular program of criticism, first against the weather in Minnesota, then against the railroads, then against Bishop Ireland, and finally against Bishop Spalding as well.

Butler's later pronouncements on the subject of colonization began to assume a new note—that of sharpshooting at the bishops behind the respective colony movements. As has already been pointed out, however, the patronage of a bishop was a *sine qua non* for any religious colony to succeed. The European press, especially the Irish journals, appreciated this basic fact and hence gave their loudest praise to John Ireland's colonies.[79] Colonies, if they exist at all, must exist in some definite, identifiable place. Yet behind Butler's criticism of the various colonizing bishops lurks the implied premise that by inviting colonists to their own territories they were somehow guilty of undue self-interest. After Butler had refused to join Bishops O'Connor, Ireland, and Spalding in their national colonizing effort at Chicago in 1879, he repeated his curious conviction that colonies could somehow be founded in a general location not part of any particular state: "There is a wide field for [colonization]. The earnest Bishops who are now working in the cause *confine their efforts within the limits of their own state or diocese*. It may be the climate of some of those northern regions will not suit some of our people. . . . *Minnesota and Nebraska are not the only States in the Union where Irishmen can and ought to colonize.*"[80]

It is quite possible that Butler's antagonism to Ireland's program arose from a clash of personalities. Ireland was not given to soft statements concerning men or actions he considered unwise. It is very likely that his direct criticism of Father Butler's

79. Liverpool *Catholic Times,* quoted in *NWC* (March 4, 1876), p. 4.
80. *ICBU Journal* (April 1880), p. 2 (italics are Butler's).

plan was taken by the latter as a personal insult. Butler's report
on their meeting in Chicago explicitly states that Ireland "ridi-
culed" the Kansas settlement plan. There is no evidence to indicate that either man made any effort to reconcile their obvious
differences of personality and opinion. For their failure to do so,
each of them was to pay dearly. Together they might have advanced their common cause; divided, they dissipated valuable energies which should have been coordinated. That the personal
factor played a large part, at least in explaining Butler's attitude
to Ireland, is often clear from the tone of his letters: "Before good
Bishop Ireland caught a glimpse of the frozen lakes of Minnesota
. . . the far-famed Irish writer, orator, and patriot Thomas D'Arcy
McGee, had been earnestly urging Irishmen in America to take
up the Virgin lands and begin agricultural life upon the fertile
fields of the West." [81]

Behind such criticism as this lay Butler's desire to prove that
somehow Ireland did not originate the idea of colonizing. Indeed,
as Chapter One endeavors to point out, Ireland was merely one
man working in an established tradition. It is immediately obvious
that Butler knew neither the fact nor the content of this tradition
when he tried to maintain that Bishop Ireland learned whatever
he knew about colonizing from Butler! [82]

The effect of such petty criticism within the ranks of the ICBU
can be readily imagined. Inevitably the fiber of union was weakened. Discerning readers today may compare statements with
documented facts and draw their own conclusions. At the time
when the controversy was raging it could not always have been
possible for the average reader to do so. Many prospective settlers
must have been genuinely puzzled by the conflicting advice given
them by Butler on the one hand, and Ireland and Griffin on the
other. An additional factor that did not render their task of deciding any easier was that Martin Griffin, though he repeatedly voiced
his lack of confidence in the plans of Father Butler, never once
spoke disrespectfully of the St. Louis priest. On the contrary, to

81. Ibid. (February 1881), p. 1. Father Butler is off a bit on his chronology in
this statement. John Ireland came to Minnesota in 1852 and had seen a good many
of its frozen lakes before D'Arcy McGee's colonization scheme was announced in
1855.
82. Ibid. (February 1881), p. 1.

the very end Griffin spoke with tender regard for his ardent zeal and priestly character.[83] Meanwhile, however, the once strong union was slowly disintegrating.

Commenting on the general history of the ICBU, the most recent chronicler of that federation remarks: "The impact of politics from within gradually transformed what at one time had been a formidable organization into one in which the objectives became vague and shifting, thereby hastening the ultimate collapse of the enterprise." [84] More particular study within the microcosm of the colonization committee supports this conclusion overwhelmingly. It was the fond hope of all those interested in the work of colonization that the union would prove to be the strong central force they needed to coordinate all their disparate efforts. Such prominent Catholics as General O'Neil in Nebraska and Bishops Ireland in St. Paul, O'Connor in Omaha, and Gross in Savannah all looked with pride and respect on the efforts of the union and wished it well in its colonizing projects. Men who knew the problems of planned settlements, however, were agreed that colonization by local subsidy was impossible. Thousands of members, organized over several states, were necessary to supply the funds needed to keep even a small colony in the field, but the Irish had never been able to organize such a unified society. In the light of this truth it is understandable that the Irish in America anticipated a "second spring" for their numbers when this union announced in 1876 that its membership had reached 30,000.[85] Unfortunately its very size at this time rendered it vulnerable to the latent forces of factionalism.

Long before the union took up the work of colonizing, Daniel O'Connell and D'Arcy McGee, his disciple, had advised all who would build Catholic colonies on the land that they must necessarily have the leadership and patronage of a bishop who would bind himself and his successors to promote their welfare. For those who would see, the Illinois Central and Northern Pacific railroads had brought the theory of colonization one step nearer perfection with their programs of land-grant subsidization. The countless

83. Ibid. (November 1881), p. 4.
84. Donohoe, p. 2.
85. Ibid., Appendix A, p. 211.

scientific studies of topsoil, rainfall, and growing seasons, prepared
by such experts as Wisconsin's Dr. I. A. Lapham and distributed
by territories and states throughout the nation for the benefit of
all prospective settlers,[86] were latter-day aids that should have
made the formula for colonization much less hazardous. Yet the
ICBU national and local boards saw fit to strike off on their own,
in unknown territory, neglecting entirely this respectable tradition
of theory. If the union had been in capable hands at the critical
time, the colonization project might have been saved in spite of
its initial neglect of these most obvious safeguards, but it was not
in such hands.

The year 1876 was the time of decision. In that year the union
reached its zenith, with a maximum membership of 30,000.[87] This
was also the year in which the delegates came to Cleveland instructed to vote for a common national plan of directed, unified
colonization. Interest had been aroused on a national scale by the
solid and steady progress which John Ireland had been reporting
from his colonies for nearly a year. It was Father Butler's responsibility to answer the challenge and direct the national effort then
being urged by the member groups. He chose to default on this
responsibility by passing it back to the local boards. From that day
his voice carried less and less weight in union circles. By the time
of the disastrous convention of 1881, membership had slipped to
16,464, slightly more than one-half the number registered five
years earlier. By then the roster of member societies, which once
had totaled 331, listed only 252 local councils.[88] Never again would
the lost ground be regained. At a crucial time which called for
leadership, cooperation, and a synthesis of effort, discord, weakness, and factional disputes reduced the strength of the union
to a level from which it was never to rise again.

Analysis of this decline is made more difficult by an extrinsic
factor of great importance. By the time the union decided to get
into colonization work, the era for benevolent unions was rapidly
passing away. The rise of labor unions, the improving economic
status of workers in many sections of the growing industrial econ-

86. Blegen, "The Competition of the Northwestern States for Immigrants," p. 13.
87. Donohoe, p. 211.
88. Ibid.

omy, the corresponding decline in the need for mutual insurance plans, the rapid "Americanization" of immigrants, especially the Irish, and the decline of that wave of virulent nativism which had once promoted immigrant unions [89] must all be considered as factors contributing to the natural difficulty of controlling the centrifugal forces usually generated in large groups of Irish. The effects of these disparate forces were evident in the declining membership of the ICBU even before the Keileyville and Butler City colonies were undertaken in 1877. Even if the colonization effort had been perfectly organized and disciplined from within, it is evident that it began after the ICBU had passed its zenith.

After the hectic sessions of the convention in 1881, the irascible but shrewd Martin Griffin summarized the life and death story of the colonization effort under ICBU auspices:

> We are of the belief, justified by our experience, that the "Local Board" plan is not the proper method for the I.C.B.U. to be an effective colonization agency. The Union idea is destroyed and localism given sway. Hence the power of the Union is not manifested, and the disjointed action of Local Boards results in detracting almost entirely from any merit the Union ought justly to be awarded. The establishment of colonies ought not to depend upon Local Boards. . . . The *Journal* simply believes that until the I.C.B.U.—as a National organization—establishes a colony and aids its foundation practically, no I.C.B.U. colonization work will go on. The I.C.B.U. lost a golden opportunity to be the great Catholic benefactor of this age. It cannot regain the position by system [sic] of Local Boards. . . . We believe further, that our Union cannot do this . . . until it has a Bishop to lead our colonization movement.[90]

The fall of the ICBU colonization committee, more than any other single factor, prevented Bishop Ireland's Minnesota colonization plan from reaching its complete fruition. On its own merits

89. See Arthur M. Schlesinger, *The Rise of the City, 1878–1898* (New York, 1927), pp. 289–90, for a general discussion of the shift which occurred after 1875, away from foreign national societies toward indigenous societies.
90. *ICBU Journal* (November 1881), p. 5.

and by reason of its own labor, his program went farther, established more successful colonies, and maintained solvency far better than any other plan ever advanced in the United States for settling Catholics on the land. The results of this program remain measurable and visible today. That the program stopped where and when it did resulted primarily from its inability to work out a successful large-scale credit plan for settling poor immigrants on western lands. If the ICBU had ever been able to secure the unified support of the mass of Irish-Americans, or if that union had not begun its active campaign against the Minnesota program, Bishop Ireland's colonies could have attained far greater success. The suspicion and hostility which were aroused against them were caused not by friction or imperfections within the colonies themselves but by such extrinsic factors as the disintegration of the one organization capable of securing the cooperation of the Irish Catholics. Such diverse forces as the opposition of eastern bishops, the lack of support from rich Catholics, the influence of Archbishop Hughes, the Irish dislike of farming, and the eastern suspicion of the West have all been suggested by competent authorities as reasons for the eventual failure of the colonization movement. Each of these factors played its part, as will be shown in the next chapter. Yet the radical cause for the eventual neutralization of this movement remains its inability to attract the interest or the money of the masses of Irish-Americans. For this failure the Irish Catholic Benevolent Union was primarily responsible.

CHAPTER TEN

The Close of Colonization

ON OCTOBER 20, 1880, Bishop John Ireland signed his last contract for railroad lands in Minnesota.[1] In the same year both the Chicago and North Western and the Milwaukee Railroads reached the Missouri River in Dakota Territory and opened that region for settlement.[2] In the preceding decade the population of Minnesota had increased by 77.6 per cent, the acreage of farm land by 107 per cent, improved farm land by 212 per cent, and the volume of wheat production by 83 per cent.[3] But by 1880 the tide of population had passed into Dakota, and southwestern Minnesota was mentioned less frequently in publicity from railroad offices. Posters prepared by the Chicago and North Western System advertised "30 million acres between the 44th and 48th degree of latitude, and between Minnesota and the Missouri River."[4] Summarizing John Sargent Pillsbury's administration as governor of Minnesota during this period (1876–81), Folwell remarked, "With the close of Governor Pillsbury's administration . . . the state of Minnesota . . . ended her period of adolescence."[5]

By an interesting coincidence Bishop Ireland's period of colonization in Minnesota corresponded to Pillsbury's regime as governor. And as the wave of land seekers passed over into Dakota Territory, the bishop had to decide whether or not to continue his colonization program on lands farther west. From time to time the Catholic Colonization Bureau in St. Paul had spoken of possible future settlements in Dakota.[6] In fact, William J. Onahan, writing

1. See above, p. 58.
2. Casey and Douglas, *Pioneer Railroad*, p. 164.
3. Folwell, *A History of Minnesota*, 3, 139–40.
4. Casey and Douglas, p. 182-H.
5. Folwell, 3, 143.
6. See Henthorne, *The Irish Catholic Colonization Association*, p. 81, for Bishop Ireland's proposal to the Irish Catholic Colonization Association regarding two new colonies in Dakota Territory, near Bismarck.

245

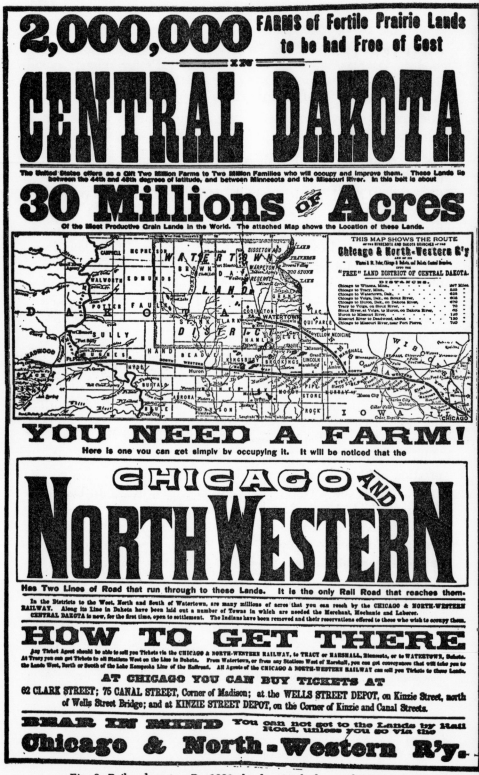

Fig. 9. Railroad poster. By 1880 the frontier had passed Minnesota.

from memory in 1917, spoke of the "numerous settlements and colonies formed [by Bishop Ireland] . . . throughout Minnesota and the Dakotas." [7] The truth is, however, that John Ireland never sponsored any Catholic colonies beyond the limits of western Minnesota. After 1880 he continued to direct the selling and settling of the many tracts in that state still under his control, but he signed no new contracts for additional lands after this date. In his own mind Ireland had set the year 1881 as the terminal date for his colonization program.[8] In the spring of that year he mentioned in a letter to John Sweetman his intention of giving up the colonization work at the end of the year, and expressed the hope that Sweetman would succeed him as the executive in charge of whatever colonization was still to be done in Minnesota.

It has been suggested that the failure of the Connemara settlers at Graceville during the preceding winter influenced Ireland's decision to terminate his active leadership in the colonization movement.[9] So reliable an authority as Ireland's own secretary has said that the bishop considered the Connemara affair "the greatest grief of his life." [10] The reverses suffered at Graceville, however, regrettable though they may have been to Bishop Ireland personally, were not of sufficient magnitude in themselves to destroy or even seriously weaken the larger colonization effort. The real reasons for Ireland's decision to close his colonization program were much less spectacular than some critics have supposed and were in no sense the result of intrinsic weakness within the program itself.

In the United States the Catholic Church has regularly followed the practice of laying down new diocesan boundaries along existing state lines. In the western territories the erection of new dioceses usually anticipated the establishment of new states. In

7. Onahan, "A Chapter on Catholic Colonization," p. 73.

8. John Ireland to John Sweetman, quoted by R. H. Froude in a letter to the editor of the London *Tablet* and reprinted in *NWC* (May 7, 1881), p. 4. See also John Ireland's letter to the Land Commissioner, St. Paul, Minneapolis, and Manitoba Railway, September 5, 1881, Great Northern Archives, Vault 602, Documents 17–12, item 42: "Under present circumstances I deem it best for all interests that my agency should cease and that the lands be put in the market subject to the immediate supervision of your office."

9. Maynard, *The Catholic Church and the American Idea*, pp. 122–3.

10. Moynihan, "Archbishop Ireland's Colonies," p. 222.

1850 the Diocese of St. Paul had been created eight years before Minnesota was admitted to the Union. Similarly, in 1879, on August 12, Rome erected the Vicariate Apostolic of Dakota and separated all the territory west of Minnesota and east of the Missouri River from the Diocese of St. Paul.[11] Just as the western railroads began the intensive advertising of Dakota lands and nine years before the two Dakota states entered the Union, the Reverend Martin Marty, O.S.B., was consecrated bishop of the new vicariate and installed in his see-city of Yankton, Dakota Territory, in February 1880.[12] After this date Catholics in Dakota Territory were no longer subject to the spiritual jurisdiction of the Bishop of St. Paul, and at the same time the colonization scheme originally proposed by John Ireland for Dakota became the responsibility of the newly consecrated Bishop Marty. In September of that year Marty began negotiations with the Northern Pacific Railroad for 50,000 acres of that road's lands in Dakota Territory.[13] But because he relied on the Irish Catholic Colonization Association for funds to underwrite his program, and since "Further purchases were not possible with the amount of capital at the disposal of the directors" [14] of that Association, it was necessary for the bishop to abandon his plans for colonization in Dakota.[15]

John Ireland had once explained that he invited Catholic settlers to Minnesota because only within that state could he, as bishop of the territory, assure them the ministrations of permanent pastors. And by the same token, once the Dakota Territory had its own bishop, Ireland was no longer in a position to sponsor new colonies in territory beyond his own jurisdiction. If he had wanted to continue his colonization projects after 1881, it would have been necessary for him to secure new lands within his own diocese. But this was no longer possible. The Northern Pacific still had some tracts of unclaimed timber land in Minnesota, but very little of it was suitable for farming. Moreover, the Vicariate of Northern

11. Reardon, *Diocese of St. Paul*, p. 186.
12. Ibid.
13. Pahorezki, *The Social and Political Activities of William James Onahan*, p. 99.
14. Henthorne, *The Irish Catholic Colonization Association*, p. 88.
15. Ibid., pp. 87–8; Boston *Pilot*, June 7, 1884.

Minnesota had been erected by Rome on February 12, 1875, at which time this northern portion of the state was removed from the jurisdiction of the Bishop of St. Paul and entrusted to the newly consecrated Bishop Rupert Seidenbusch, O.S.B.[16] Ireland could not extend his colonies into upper Minnesota for the same reason he could not extend them into Dakota—lack of spiritual jurisdiction. By 1880 he must also have been aware of the impending split of his own diocese and the creation of the new see of Winona in southern Minnesota. If Pillsbury's administration as governor may be called the era in which Minnesota came of age, it can also be said of John Ireland's episcopacy that it was the time when the Diocese of St. Paul attained its majority.

On July 31, 1884, Bishop Thomas L. Grace, who had been in ill health for some time, resigned as Bishop of St. Paul in favor of his Coadjutor, John Ireland.[17] Two years later, at the Provincial Synod in Milwaukee, the young Bishop of St. Paul joined the other bishops of the Province of Milwaukee in asking Rome to erect a new archdiocese west of Milwaukee to accommodate the recent growth of the Church in that region. On May 4, 1888, the Diocese of St. Paul was raised to the rank of an archdiocese and John Ireland was named its first archbishop.[18] The next year five new dioceses (Winona, Duluth, and St. Cloud in Minnesota and Sioux Falls and Jamestown in Dakota) were established and attached as suffragan sees to the new Archdiocese of St. Paul.[19] Shortly after the establishment of these new dioceses within the Province of St. Paul, the New York *Times* printed what it called "An Interesting Rumor" to the effect that "another Cardinal's hat was soon to be bestowed by Pope Leo upon an American prelate . . . John Ireland." [20] As if to lend credence to the unfounded rumor, the *Times* writer continued: "Churchmen who have watched the trend of events in the Catholic Church in this country, and who have observed the enormous growth of the Northwestern Diocese, believe that Archbishop Ireland may be appointed an associate in the

16. Reardon, pp. 185–6.
17. *NWC* (July 31, 1884), p. 4; Reardon, pp. 196–7.
18. Reardon, pp. 268–9.
19. Ibid., p. 271.
20. New York *Times*, January 6, 1890.

Cardinalate with Cardinal Gibbons." Newsmen were not alone in their belief that John Ireland's administration had brought unusual growth to the Church in Minnesota. Even Cardinal Gibbons felt that Ireland "had built up the Province of St. Paul as hardly any other man could have done." [21]

While such growth undoubtedly reflected credit on the colonization policies Ireland had introduced to increase the Catholic population in Minnesota, it also presaged additional episcopal administrative duties which left him less and less time for the work of colonization. As late as 1883 Ireland was still active in directing the settlement of new Belgian immigrants at Ghent, and as late as 1889 J. P. O'Connor was still closing out colony accounts with the St. Paul, Minneapolis, and Manitoba on that road's indemnity lands near Graceville; [22] but these were only tidying-up operations. The true end of Catholic colonization in Minnesota came in 1880 when Ireland decided to sign no more contracts for future settlement. In the years between 1876 and 1881 he had done his best to bring Catholic settlers to his diocese. The work had not been entirely successful, but it had built up a noticeable concentration of Catholics within the western and southwestern counties of Minnesota. It remained for the younger bishops in the newly established dioceses surrounding St. Paul to do as well with their territories. In the parent diocese "New problems were clamoring for solution and, as immigration had apparently reached its zenith [Ireland] felt that the objective had been attained and [that] he could devote his attention to more pressing concerns." [23] As late as 1895 he was still addressing immigration conventions, urging the states in the Northwest to organize permanent boards to furnish prospective settlers with exact information on the agricultural and mineral resources of that region, but he had long since withdrawn "from actual participation in the planning and directing" [24] of colonization. In answer to a question about colony taxes in Adrian, Father Knauf received the reply from J. P. O'Connor, "The

21. Moynihan, *The Life of Archbishop John Ireland*, p. 83. This quotation is Monsignor Moynihan's paraphrase of Gibbons' statement.
22. J. P. O'Connor to M. J. McDonnell, April 1 and 24, 1889; May 8, 1889, St. Paul Chancery Archives, Diocesan Letters, 1888–89, pp. 109–10, 145, 161–3.
23. Reardon, p. 245.
24. Ibid.

Archbishop is being kept so busy that I cannot get him to spare a moment. He tells me to write to you." [25]

Undoubtedly the death of Dillon O'Brien in 1882 also had some effect on Ireland's plans regarding colonization. After this date there did remain some parcels of unsold railroad land here and there in the western counties. But O'Brien was dead, Ireland was occupied with other duties, and John P. O'Connor, who had succeeded O'Brien, was intent on balancing the diocesan budget. The time for colonizing in Minnesota had passed. Although the Catholic Colonization Bureau continued to function throughout the decade following 1880, O'Connor's voluminous and meticulous correspondence during this period reveals that his efforts moved toward greater economy and efficiency and away from the more generous and imaginative visions which had motivated his predecessor. Such statements as "try to boom up the long resting Graceville Colony" [26] or "the Archbishop . . . trusts that the people will not disappoint him by being one day behind in their payments on the 1st of December," [27] appeared with increasing frequency in the new executive secretary's correspondence. And there is every reason to believe that in this new attitude O'Connor had the endorsement of the archbishop. Each year Ireland relied more heavily on the business acumen and tireless energy which O'Connor expended in the interest of diocesan finances.

During the period of greatest activity in the settlement of the American West by colonization, it was inevitable that the colorful John Ireland should receive wide newspaper publicity. The Archbishop of St. Paul was almost as well known to the American public in these years as Cardinal Gibbons, the ranking member of the American hierarchy. And thanks to the ringing colonization slogans popularized by Dillon O'Brien ("man made the city: God made the country"), the crusade for rural colonies became identified with the person of the Archbishop of St. Paul. Hence it is not surprising that in the intervening years conflicting evaluations of

25. J. P. O'Connor to Father Knauft (sic), December 31, 1888, Diocesan Letters, 1888–89, p. 50.

26. J. P. O'Connor to M. J. McDonnell, April 1, 1889, Diocesan Letters, 1888–89, p. 109.

27. Idem, April 24, 1889, Diocesan Letters, 1888–89, p. 145.

the colonization program have been spread abroad, stemming from the broader dispute concerning the historical significance of Ireland's own career.

The closing of the land frontier in Minnesota, the erection of new dioceses surrounding St. Paul, John Ireland's increasing preoccupation with other episcopal duties, the death of Dillon O'Brien, and the fact that Ireland had never really been able to make his colonies a haven for the poor—these were the true reasons which brought the work of the Catholic Colonization Bureau to an end after 1883. But other reasons have been suggested by various writers to explain the closing of this bureau or the general limitations of Ireland's colonization policy, and these opinions deserve to be considered here.

Any appraisal of Ireland's work as a colonizer must be based on the accomplishments of his own Catholic Colonization Bureau in the Diocese of St. Paul. In several respects this organization differed from the other national and local colonization projects of that day. Its most significant difference was that it did not rely on any joint-stock company or on public subscriptions for its finances. Ireland worked as hard as any of his contemporaries to encourage such companies, in the hope that funds thus obtained could at last make possible the large-scale subsidization of poor people on the land. But in his own diocesan bureau he never counted on any support from this source. Even while he was pleading the cause for the poor in the East in 1879 and 1880 he never relaxed the rules of his own Colonization Bureau or tried to make it a benevolent aid society for helping poor farmers. The men who were answering Dillon O'Brien's advertisements were in reality small businessmen with modest capital. And although John Ireland saw that his lands were filling up with a type of settler he had not solicited, he made no effective move to prohibit the admission of such persons. He must have realized early in his operations that since he could not get the settlers he wanted, he would be wise to accept those who could come. Hence the failure of the joint-stock companies, though it was undoubtedly the big reason why Bishops Ireland, O'Connor, and Marty, and Father Butler and William J. Onahan did not found more benevolent-aid colonies in the West, did not materially alter the course or affect the success of Ireland's Minnesota colonies because he never really counted on benevolent aid or public subscriptions to support these settlements.

The life-and-death story of the various joint-stock companies is thus not essential to any analysis of the Minnesota colonies; yet because of Bishop Ireland's energetic advocacy of such stock ventures, some attention should be given to the commonly accepted notion that these companies failed because they were not supported by rich Catholics. In summarizing the achievements of the Irish Catholic Colonization Association, the definitive study of that movement concludes: "That the movement failed to accomplish directly all that was hoped for it is attributable almost, if not entirely, to the holding back of men of wealth." [28] It cannot be denied that this association and many others like it would have welcomed large contributions from rich investors, but the fact is that the entire *modus operandi* of all these organizations aimed at selling stock in small lots to persons of moderate means. Ireland and Spalding did not make private visits to solicit large sums from leading American Catholics. They addressed mass audiences in populous urban centers. On more than one occasion Spalding and O'Connor publicly lamented the fact that rich Catholics had not come to the aid of their organization,[29] but it cannot seriously be maintained that the appeal had been directed primarily toward the rich. At the very start of the colonization movement, Patrick Ford, the capable editor of the *Irish World*, had advised the colonizers not to expect much support from the wealthy: "My advice to you is to carry out the plans you have sketched, do the best you can with the means you yourselves have at command, and then if you prove worthy of the support and encouragement which you now seek be assured it will not be wanting. Men of this class [the wealthy] possess the quality of caution in an eminent degree, and it will not permit them to engage in any enterprise that it [sic] is not of a purely business nature unless they can be assured of its success." [30] Acting on advice such as this and upon their own brief

28. Henthorne, p. 59.
29. Spalding, *The Religious Mission of the Irish People*, p. 195; James O'Connor, in the Dublin *Freeman's Journal*, June 14, 1885, quoted in Henthorne, p. 59.
30. Patrick Ford, in the *Irish World*, reprinted in *ICBU Journal* (September 1877), p. 7.

experience in soliciting money from the rich, the leaders in the association decided early in that organization's career to direct their appeal toward the middle and lower economic classes.[31] Hence if this organization ultimately fell short of its goal, the failure can only be ascribed to the apathy of the masses of Catholic people, not to the indifference of the rich.

In analyzing the same kind of failure in the ICBU, the historian of that organization has suggested two explanations: "either the colonization program was held in ill repute or else the vast majority of members lacked the material means to support it wholeheartedly." [32] The first of these alternatives can be dismissed immediately. Considerable evidence has already been produced to demonstrate that the colonization effort in all its phases suffered, rather, from too much public favor. Martin Griffin complained that everyone voted for the movement and no one supported it. Nor can it be seriously argued that the persons solicited for support could not afford to contribute to the program. Ireland and Spalding sought a relatively modest $100,000 for their association; O'Mulcahy sought only one-fourth of that sum for his Minnesota Company. Neither group attained its goal. And yet both goals taken together would have equaled only one-half the sum which poor Irishmen in the United States subscribed for the Land League in the same years. The fact is, the wealthy were never convinced that colonization was a sound investment, and persons of less means were never convinced that it was a more deserving charity than the resettlement of cottiers in Ireland.

If Father Thomas Ambrose Butler had not wrecked the popular subscription campaign of the ICBU, it is just possible that a nationwide colonization plan could have been put into operation to settle poor people on the land. Furthermore, if this proposed joint-stock plan had enlisted sufficient popular support, it is clear that John Ireland would have been ready to support the new movement and to use his local settlement plan as an archetype for future colonies. All this, however, is in the realm of speculation. As a matter of record, the national stock plan failed, and when it did John Ireland was no longer willing to sponsor a national pro-

31. Spalding, pp. 195–6.
32. Donohoe, *The Irish Catholic Benevolent Union,* p. 127.

gram. At the same time, merely by a coincidence of timing, Ireland's local settlement program was drawing to a close. The success of this diocesan program never hinged on the nationwide subscription campaign, although the extension of the Minnesota plan to other regions was entirely contingent on popular financial support. When this support was denied, Ireland abandoned any plans he had for nationwide colonization.

It has also been suggested that the various plans for Catholic colonies on western lands were proposed at an unpropitious time and that had they been advocated earlier, their success would have been assured. As recently as 1953 one writer advanced the opinion that the colonization work sponsored by Bishop Ireland in 1875 "did not get very far, because by then it was too late." [33] Of all the opinions proposed on the subject, this is the least defensible. The project of settling colonists on western land could never have been undertaken until after the railroads had entered the West. In western Minnesota this meant sometime after 1875. Ireland's project began that very year. Considerable evidence has already been presented to demonstrate that without the land, credit arrangements, and transportation facilities furnished by the western railroads colonization would have been impossible. The charge that the colonies were too early rests on the assumption that somehow successful colonies could have been planted in Minnesota before the railroads had reached that far. The most convincing refutation to this belief is offered by the history of the Catholic colonies in Nebraska which never obtained the advantages of rail service and hence never attained the stature planned by their sponsors.

It is equally certain that the Minnesota colonies could never have succeeded if their establishment had been attempted any later than it was. In each county where John Ireland contracted for railroad lands a land rush, in some instances only slightly less colorful than the famous race across Cherokee Strip, got under way immediately.[34] The publicity issued by Ireland's office may

33. Maynard, *The Catholic Church and The American Idea*, pp. 122–3.
34. Swift County *Advocate* (October 19, 1877), p. 1; (October 26, 1877), p. 4; (April 19, 1878), p. 1; Benson *Times* (May 8, 1876), p. 1; Worthington *Advance* (November 1, 1877), p. 3; NWC (April 5, 1879), p. 16.

in part have caused such land booms; but with or without his intervention the settlement of western Minnesota would have been
accomplished by 1880 simply because of the economic opportunities then available in that region. Whether Ireland foresaw all the
advantages that would accrue to his bureau by having exclusive
rights for railroad lands when the western boom got under way
cannot be known. It is abundantly clear, however, that when the
land craze did spread into Minnesota, Ireland had a definite advantage and was in a position to prevent much of the speculation
which had characterized settlement on other frontiers. On the
basis of such evidence it seems reasonable to state that the Minnesota colonization program could not have been achieved if it had
been undertaken at any date earlier or later than the period in
which it was attempted.

One of the most persistent legends surrounding the story of
colonization has been that the eastern bishops and priests who
feared the loss of their congregations sabotaged the colonization
program. In its usual form this charge either begins or ends by citing the perdurable influence of Archbishop John Hughes of New
York and his famous denunciation of colonization at the Broadway Tabernacle on March 26, 1857. In the years immediately following this event Hughes led an effective campaign against organized western settlement. But by the time John Ireland came
on the scene two decades later this hostility toward western settlement had disappeared. No bishops rose in 1876 to warn Catholics against the dangers of going west. In that day, as in this, the
eastern mind differed from the western mind; eastern pastors
often found it difficult to appreciate the mind of the West. This
radical lack of sympathy between eastern and western churchmen, however, is by no means sufficient grounds for saying that as
late as 1880 eastern clergymen set out to wreck the colonization
movement.

In defense of the older view, Carl Wittke, one of our most competent students of immigration, wrote in 1939: "Considerable
friction and rivalry developed between Western and Eastern bishops because of these colonization projects, for they involved a
fundamental conflict of interest between West and East. Clergy-

men in well-established Eastern parishes with large churches and schools—some of them still in debt—naturally opposed any movement which would deprive them of their membership. Archbishop Hughes of New York was always a vigorous opponent of colonization projects." [35]

But Hughes had been dead more than twelve years before the biggest colonization movement was ever proposed to American Catholics. Spalding admitted that Hughes' shadow had hung over earlier colonization projects. Spalding's own record, however, is one striking indication that Hughes' opinions no longer prevailed by 1876. Spalding, too, as a young priest in New York had opposed the western settlement of Catholics; but by the time he became a bishop in Peoria (1877) he had turned completely in favor of the colonization plan. Furthermore, Spalding and Ireland extended themselves to secure the explicit endorsement of the leading members of the American hierarchy when the colonization movement got under way. Cardinal McCloskey of New York and Archbishops Gibbons of Baltimore, Williams of Boston, and Feehan of Chicago, together with many bishops in smaller dioceses, gave public statements in support of the movement and in some instances bought stock certificates themselves.[36] Writing to Gibbons to thank him for his personal subscription of ten $100 shares in the Irish Catholic Colonization Association, John Ireland grandly remarked: "The one name of the Archbishop of Baltimore on our list did more than fifty discourses from little bishops in the West." [37] To state that these several bishops and archbishops allowed the various colonization efforts to solicit money within their dioceses does not, of course, establish that all of them were enthusiastic supporters of the movement. Possibly many of them retained personal doubts about the wisdom of the whole project. But the significant fact is that the tenor of the times had so changed since the days of Hughes that by 1875 no bishop felt secure in publicly opposing or denouncing the colonization movement. By then western solicitors were free to move among Catholics in the East and were no

35. Wittke, *We Who Built America*, p. 152.
36. *Catholic Review*, June 7, 1879, quoted in Henthorne, pp. 125–6. See also pp. 77–8, above.
37. Ireland to Gibbons, St. Paul, March 2, 1880, quoted in Ellis, *The Life of James Cardinal Gibbons, 1*, 194.

longer confronted by the public opposition of any member of the hierarchy.

In the time which elapsed between the Civil War and the opening of the trans-Mississippi West, eastern bishops were swamped by a tidal wave of immigrant Catholics coming into their dioceses. In such port cities as Boston, New York, Philadelphia, and Baltimore they were faced with the almost impossible task of providing sufficient priests and churches for the spiritual needs of these new arrivals.[38] Ecclesiastical as well as lay leaders were forced to reconsider their objections to western settlement. John Boyle O'Reilly, editor of the Boston *Pilot*, was won over completely to the new western movement after once having denounced it as an evil work. The revised attitude of James A. Mc-Master, together with his assurance that Hughes, had he lived, would have looked favorably on John Ireland's colonization plan, have already been cited.[39] Among the hierarchy this new view of colonization is best shown in the friendly invitation and cordial hospitality Archbishop Williams extended to Bishops Spalding and Ireland when they were seeking settlers and sponsors for the Irish Catholic Colonization Association. In Boston, Williams was faced with an Irish Catholic population far greater than his diocesan facilities could accommodate. It was natural that he would look on the western movement as a providential solution to some of his problems. Similarly, Archbishop Gibbons' personal subscription of $1,000 worth of stock in the new association can hardly be dismissed as a token gesture. Yet a recent writer on this topic has implied that Gibbons always retained a certain hostility to the westward movement of Catholics: "Gibbons' support of colonization was hardly consistent with his already expressed opposition to the westward movement from the South and was probably merely formal." [40] The reference here is to a sermon which Gibbons preached in 1871 when he was Vicar Apostolic of North Carolina, in which occurred the words, "Listen not to the Syren

38. John R. G. Hassard, *Life of John Hughes, Archbishop of New York* (New York, 1866), pp. 213–15.

39. See above, pp. 62–3.

40. Roohan, "American Catholics and the Social Question, 1865–1900," p. 219, n. 22.

voice which says: 'Go West, young man.' " [41] In citing such a statement, it is vitally important to consider its date and its place of origin. In 1871 in North Carolina, Gibbons was shepherd of a missionary diocese which consisted of 250 Catholics in all.[42] The westward departure of even one of these families would have been a noticeable loss to the struggling diocese. On the other hand, when Gibbons took over as the new Archbishop of Baltimore in 1877, his spiritual jurisdiction embraced almost 200,000 Catholics,[43] and each immigrant ship that docked in Baltimore brought additions to his flock. Hence it is hardly defensible to say that Gibbons' support of colonization after 1879 was inconsistent with his expressed opposition to the earlier movement. Times had changed, and Gibbons' opinion had changed also. In dealing with the opinions of the astute Archbishop of Baltimore it is no easy matter to know with certitude what his private opinion was on a given subject; he will long be known as one of the Church's great diplomats. But in the present context it seems far more reasonable to say that Gibbons' contribution of $1,000, his explicit endorsement of the Chicago convention of the Irish Catholic Colonization Association, and his acceptance of John Ireland's letter of appreciation should be taken at face value as indications that he looked with favor if not with enthusiasm on the colonization movement.

A more difficult question posed for any historian who would summarize the accomplishments of John Ireland's colonies is that of deciding whether they should be considered as a phase of *western* history or as an unsuccessful attempt to solve the problems raised in *eastern* cities by an industrial system which was suffering from growing pains. Originally Bishops Cretin and Loras had undertaken the work of colonization primarily as a means of attracting Catholic settlers to the open lands of their young dioceses in the Mississippi Valley; [44] but because this region was not ready for settlement in their day, the realization of their plans was delayed until John Ireland became Bishop of St. Paul. The

41. Ellis, *The Life of James Cardinal Gibbons*, 1, 167.
42. Ibid., p. 73.
43. Ibid., p. 167.
44. See above, pp. 33–4.

main idea of Bishop Spalding's treatise *The Religious Mission of the Irish People* is that colonization is primarily a religious apostolate by which Irish immigrants would bring Catholicism to unsettled portions of the American West. In a tribute to Bishop Loras, written in 1898, John Ireland said of the colonization plan originated by that prelate: "There was no surer way to lay wide and deep the foundation of the Catholic Church in the West." [45]

On the other hand, both Spalding and Ireland, by their often repeated statements on colonization as an answer to eastern labor problems have given subsequent historians reason to question whether western settlement was really their prime motive. In his recent treatise "American Catholics and the Social Question, 1865–1900" James E. Roohan maintains that western colonization is only significant if it is seen as an ameliorative proposal offered to relieve population pressure and labor unrest in the East. Given these premises, Roohan is quite correct in pronouncing the overall movement a failure:

> The historians of Catholic colonization have treated it largely as an episode in the western history of the United States [but] essentially it was an attempt to solve the problems created by the increasing congestion of eastern industrial cities, by the deepening abyss between rich and poor, and by the real or supposed threat of socialism that that cleavage offered. . . . And the few small colonies that finally were realized merely accentuated the utter failure of the movement to alleviate the problem it had undertaken. [46]

The difficulty with accepting this analysis completely is that it is not at all clear that the Bishops of Peoria, Dubuque, Omaha, St. Paul, and Sioux Falls were motivated "essentially" by a desire to solve the economic and social problems then pressing upon the dioceses of eastern bishops. Furthermore, if the colonization pro-

45. John Ireland, "Mathias Loras, First Bishop of Dubuque," p. 5. For additional evidence that Archbishop Ireland considered colonization as a means of building up the Catholic Church in the West, see his sermon "Fifty Years of Catholicity in the Northwest," delivered on July 2, 1901, in honor of the golden jubilee of the Diocese of St. Paul, reprinted in John Ireland, *The Church and Modern Society* (2 vols. St. Paul, 1905), 2, 266.

46. Roohan, "American Catholics," pp. 233–4.

gram was essentially an attempt to solve eastern labor, housing, and industrial problems, why did not the eastern bishops take the lead in the movement? The very authors who claim that colonization was a failure because it did not solve these eastern problems also maintain that the reluctance of the eastern bishops to support the movement brought about its early collapse.[47] If the general undertaking was made on behalf of eastern interests, it could reasonably be expected that the movement would have received its greatest support from the East. But this was clearly not the case. The leaders, the enthusiasm, and most of the money and settlers came from the West and Middle West.

From the point of view of the social historian writing about national events, it is certainly correct to say that the western colonization movement never attained sufficient momentum or enlisted a sufficient number of eastern dwellers to make any appreciable contribution toward the alleviation of economic and social tensions in the East. But it is hardly tenable to say that the sponsored movements for westward settlement were undertaken explicitly to alleviate eastern social unrest and that, since they did not accomplish this end, they deserve to be classed as failures.

It is impossible to determine with any accuracy the exact number of immigrants who came to Minnesota in the 1870's and 80's in response to the respective appeals of the state, the railroads, and Bishop Ireland's Colonization Bureau. It is clear, however, that by 1885 railroad propaganda was no longer publicizing southwestern Minnesota lands but advertising "Thirty Million Acres" of government land to be homesteaded in Central Dakota.[48] The frontier had passed beyond Minnesota. In one decade (1875–85), Minnesota's western triangle filled with settlers. Among these were some 4,000 Catholic families, settled on lands around the newly built towns of De Graff, Clontarf, Graceville, Minneota, Ghent, Avoca, Iona, Fulda, Currie, and Adrian. In each of these towns a resident Catholic priest and church, and in most of them a Catholic school, ministered to the spiritual needs of the

47. Ibid., pp. 219–21, 233–4; Wittke, *We Who Built America*, p. 152.
48. A reproduction of this handbill, supplied me by Frank J. Klein, land and tax commissioner for the Chicago and North Western, appears on p. 246. See also Casey and Douglas, *Pioneer Railroad*, p. 182.

settlers. A reasonable estimate of the acreage occupied by the Catholic farmers in these settlements would be about 400,000 acres, including all railroad, homestead, timber-culture, and pre-emption claims. In later years many of these settlers were to leave the land for the city, but the original settlements have remained to the present day vigorous Catholic centers and have provided at least six new parishes with the nucleus of a congregation, drawn from the original colonies.[49]

In the span of ten years (1875–85) western Minnesota was well settled. With or without John Ireland's intervention, this settlement would have occurred in response to the state and railroad advertising campaigns. As a result of his program, however, the character of that settlement was in part determined. For the nation as a whole, Catholics today make up slightly less than 20 per cent of the population, and since they are mostly urban dwellers, it follows that the large centers of Catholic concentration are the great cities of the North and East. Of the twenty-two states west of the Mississippi only seven have a Catholic representation equal to or higher than the national average. And if exception be made for Louisiana and New Mexico—states in which the present Catholic population stems not from the westward migration of immigrant Catholics, but from ancient French and Spanish settlements —no state west of the Mississippi River has so great a percentage of Catholics as Minnesota. Even California and Arizona, which owe their relatively high percentage to similar Spanish and Mexican origins, do not rank so high as Minnesota in this scale.

Among its immediate neighbors west of the Mississippi River, Minnesota's relative position in this scale is significant (Minnesota, 22.8 per cent; Iowa, 14 per cent; South Dakota, 17.1 per cent; North Dakota, 21.8 per cent).[50] In Lyon County, Minnesota, the

49. Danvers, Benson, Murdock, and St. Hegbert in Swift County; Barry and Beardsley in Big Stone County. See also the Benson *Times* (May 1, 1876), p. 4. Here Father John McDermot suggests that Bishop Ireland's program had already attracted more than 8,000 families. This extremely sanguine estimate is not verified by the research done for the present work. From evidence presented above, 4,000 families and 400,000 acres would seem to be a more reasonable estimate.

50. These figures are based on statistics given in the *Official Catholic Directory* (New York, 1955), in the United States census for 1950, and in letters sent to me by the chancellors of the Dioceses of St. Paul and Winona.

site of John Ireland's two best colonies (Ghent and Minneota), the Catholic population today is 32.3 per cent of the total.[51]

Once the colonies were established in western Minnesota, Bishop Ireland, with the financial assistance of James J. Hill, founded the St. Paul Seminary for the training of priests to staff the new parishes and western colonies of that diocese. The new seminary was begun in 1890. The work of construction and of assembling a faculty of diocesan priests was completed for the opening of the fall term in 1894. This was the second diocesan seminary established west of the Mississippi. Until 1939 it was the only one for all the dioceses in Minnesota, Iowa, Nebraska, South Dakota, North Dakota, Wyoming, Montana, Washington, and Oregon.

The experience of Bishops Loras and Cretin discussed above [52] proved that successful colonization among Catholics could not advance until an adequate number of priests could be provided to staff the colony parishes. In part John Ireland's success in colonization work stemmed from his earlier success in recruiting numerous priests from other states and from European countries. His ultimate intention, however, was to staff his parishes with American-born priests. To achieve this end, he found the financial assistance of James J. Hill an invaluable aid.

At some point this narration of Ireland's long-range plans passes beyond the mere story of his western colonies and becomes a chronicle of his diocesan projects. And yet the two stories are intimately connected at several points. Literally thousands of Catholics came to Minnesota after the colony lands were taken. It is, in fact, quite likely that a great portion of St. Paul's Catholic population (33 per cent of the total) has come to that city since 1900, largely because John Ireland gave that city and that diocese a head start in Catholic culture that has made it an attractive place for Catholics moving west. In great part, this effect was achieved through the publicity released by Dillon O'Brien and Ireland in the days of the Catholic colonies.

51. *NWC* (November 5, 1890), p. 1; Reardon, *Diocese of St. Paul*, p. 309.
52. See pp. 33–42.

Conclusion

THE LARGEST and most successful Catholic colonization program ever undertaken in the United States was that sponsored by Bishop John Ireland in Minnesota between 1876 and 1881. In subsequent years the specific virtues of this local western project have regularly been overlooked by historians who were interested only in describing the national scene. Most often Ireland's work as a colonizer has been lumped with that of the unsuccessful stock companies and pronounced a failure. The present study, it is hoped, has at least established the unfairness of this judgment and has demonstrated that Ireland's settlement program was unique and that it therefore merits separate consideration as a significant chapter in the history of the upper Mississippi Valley and as an illustration of that rare phenomenon in American history—successful colony settlement.

The besetting evil of most colonies throughout history has been the inflexibility of the plan on which they were established, usually with preconceived notions as to the type of settlers to be accepted, the economic basis to be adopted, and the social organization to be enforced. Such dogmatic bases have imparted to most colony settlements an internal rigidity and a degree of social isolation which separated them from the surrounding society. Religious colonies especially have been characterized by such singularity. Quite properly, histories of these settlements have most often been studies of the peculiar features of these "islands" in American society.

In contrast to this traditional pattern of exclusiveness in colonization programs, the Catholic colonies in Minnesota were organized according to an unusually flexible plan. They avoided both the fixity of a preconceived program of activity and the rigor of an imposed regime. Although they were designed primarily but not exclusively for people of Irish stock and Catholic faith, these were virtually the only a priori decisions made by their founders. The test for the type of settlers was a pragmatic one: Ireland wanted colonists who were qualified to succeed in a western agricultural enterprise. As to the financial basis, it was a very permissive one in which the colonizing agent held no permanent control but simply served to bring the colonist and the land owner (in this instance the railroad) into a productive relationship with each other (again the criterion was success). Socially, no regime was imposed and no exclusiveness was attempted—the only social policy was to provide churches under the guidance of well chosen priests— and the influence which the Church exercised was no different from that which it exercised over its members in other parts of the world. Social relations were worked out on a pragmatic basis. As new situations arose demanding changes in colony affairs, these settlements were able to adjust to the new status without the convulsions which occurred in earlier rigidly controlled communities. Also, the Minnesota colonies fitted into the society around them and did not become set-apart villages. The fact that they have been somewhat less distinctive than earlier similar foundations has possibly made them less appealing as a subject for writers who are in search of the unusual and the extreme. This same lack of singularity, however, makes them especially noteworthy in the history of western settlement in America. They represent a successful fusion of the group-settlement plan tried by so many utopian communities and the far more common pattern of westward migration by individual families.

In the pragmatic character of the Minnesota colony plan, in its voluntaristic or permissive conditions, in its emphasis upon success, and in the willingness to seek its objectives (the extension of Catholicism and the attainment of financial security) through competitive trials rather than through protection, there is something markedly American. Archbishop John Ireland is known in history as a prelate who did much to adjust Catholic beliefs to American attitudes, and the character of his colonial settlements furnishes a striking illustration of one way in which he succeeded.

Western conditions had forced many changes on the doctrinaire colonizing formulas originally proposed by such social planners as Daniel O'Connell, Henry Formby, and D'Arcy McGee, and in the end the kind of success achieved by Ireland's foundations in Minnesota was quite different from what he had set out to attain.

Even after his own paper, the *Northwestern Chronicle,* had diagnosed the great weakness in his campaign ("A most unhealthy dislike to farm life has grown up among us"),[53] his diocesan bureau continued to direct its appeals to men who would not come west. If, instead of this approach, Ireland and O'Brien had faced the facts of reality more squarely and had redirected their appeal toward the small farmers of neighboring middle-western states, there can be no doubt that they would have sold more railroad land and established larger colonies. As it was, most of the farmers who took up colony lands in Minnesota had heard about the project only indirectly and had never been overtly solicited to settle on colony lands. O'Brien's public lectures and Ireland's appeals were delivered in the great meeting halls of New York City, Boston, Philadelphia, and Baltimore. It is almost certain that these addresses would have recruited more settlers and highly probable that they would even have secured more financial backing if they had been delivered in the farming communities of Pennsylvania, Ohio, Indiana, and Illinois. The colonizers in general and Ireland and his group in particular were a long time in learning that depressed laborers in the East simply could not be transported in large numbers to the West, partly because there were no means to support the project but also because such laborers had no desire or talent for farming in the West. Those who did make the trip to colony lands in Minnesota or Kansas or Nebraska or Virginia were almost always unsuccessful: not knowing how to farm, they were unable to foresee the advantage they might have gained by continuing to work the soil. In Minnesota these were the settlers sponsored by O'Mulcahy in Swift County, by Onahan in Nobles County, by Sweetman in Murray County, and by John Ireland at Graceville; and among their numbers the rate of defection was far higher than among the other thousands of farming families who came to Minnesota almost unsolicited.

Although John Ireland filled many roles as churchman, social reformer, educator, and part-time international diplomat, his primary role was that of Bishop of St. Paul. In this capacity he worked energetically for the first five years of his episcopacy to build up Catholic numbers in a frontier diocese of the rural unsettled West.

53. *NWC* (August 11, 1877), p. 4.

And in this effort he was extraordinarily successful, if his achievements be compared with the fruits of any other similar colonizing program undertaken in this country before or since. In spite of his fondest hopes he never managed to bring enough people out of the tenements of the East to relieve noticeably the social tensions in that area. He did, nevertheless, bring enough Catholics into his diocese and establish there such a concentration of religious institutions that Minnesota became and has remained the center of Catholic culture for the entire Northwest.

Appendix

BISHOP JOHN IRELAND'S CONTRACT WITH THE
WINONA AND ST. PETER RAILROAD FOR
LANDS IN LYON COUNTY, MINNESOTA

THIS AGREEMENT made this Twenty first day of May in the year of Our Lord one thousand eight hundred and seventy nine (A.D. 1879) by and between the Winona and St. Peter Railroad Company, a corporation organized and existing under and by virtue of the laws of the State of Minnesota, party of the first part, and the Right Reverend John Ireland, of St. Paul, in the State of Minnesota, party of the second part, Witnesseth:

That the said party of the first part, for and in consideration of the covenants and agreements on the part of the said party of the second part, to be kept and performed as herein set forth and subject to the conditions herein contained, agrees to and with the said party of the second part;

First: To set apart and hold, subject to the terms and conditions of this agreement until the thirtieth (30th) day of June A.D. 1882, all its unsold lands, not heretofore reserved from sale, in Townships numbered One hundred and thirteen (113) of Ranges forty-two (42) and forty three (43) and in Township numbered One hundred and twelve (112) Ranges forty two (42) and forty three (43) and Sections twenty five (25) twenty seven (27) twenty nine (29) thirty one (31) thirty two (32) thirty three (33) thirty four (34) and thirty five (35) in Township, One hundred and fourteen (114) Range forty two (42) and Sections twenty five (25) twenty seven (27) twenty nine (29) thirty one (31) thirty three (33) and thirty five (35) in Township, One hundred and fourteen (114) Range, forty three (43), West of the fifth (5th) Principal Meridian; in the State of Minnesota, whereof a list is hereto attached and made a part of this agreement, on which list is specifically stated the prices per acre at which said lands have been and are now offered for sale by said party of the first part:

Second: That the said party of the first part will sell to the said party of the second part, or to whom he shall in writing direct, any of the said lands in the said list, at and for the prices so designated on said list, at any time prior to the expiration of the period above named, upon either of the following terms, at the option of said party of the second part, to wit:

1st For cash at the date of sale, at said listed prices, less a discount of twelve and one half per cent (12½%)

2nd At said list prices, receiving ten per cent (10%) of said purchase price in cash at the time of said sale, with interest in advance upon the remainder of said purchase price for one (1) year at the rate of six per cent (6%) per annum:

In one (1) year from said date of sale, one (1) years interest in advance upon the balance of said purchase price at the same rate:

In two (2) years from the date of said sale, ten per cent (10%) of said purchase price and interest in advance upon the balance thereof for one (1) year at six per cent (6%) per annum and at the expiration of each year thereafter until the whole of said purchase price is paid, twenty per cent (20%) thereof with interest in advance upon the balance, at six per cent (6%) per annum.

Third: That said party of the second part shall have the sole and exclusive right by himself or his agents thereto duly authorized in writing subject in all respects to the terms of this agreement, to make sale of said lands from and after the date of this agreement and until the said 30th day of June A.D. 1882, and for the prices in said list named, and upon the terms above set forth:

Fourth: That said party of the first part will assist said party of the second part in making sales of said lands by doing a reasonable amount of advertising at its discretion and by furnishing maps and price lists and such printed advertising matter as shall be from time to time issued by it, and that it will furnish passes over its lines of railway to said party of the second part and his agents, not exceeding two (2) in number to be designated by him; to transport land seekers recommended by the said party of the second part, and purchasers of any of said lands and their goods at the same rates allowed to other purchasers of lands of said party of the first part and will allow to such purchasers the same rebates for fare and freight paid as are allowed to other such purchasers.

Fifth: That said party of the first part will allow and pay to said party of the second part a commission of ten per cent (10%) of the purchase price of all lands set apart and held subject to the terms of this agreement and which are sold by said party of the second part after the date of this agreement and prior to the said 30th day of June A.D. 1882, one half (½) of such commission to be paid within sixty (60) days after the consummation of the sale and the other one half (½) thereof by payments of one per cent (1%) of the purchase price out of each instalment of principal paid by the purchaser of said land until such commission is wholly paid:

The amount of such commissions to be ascertained by an accounting and settlement by and between the parties hereto at the end of each quarter year, to wit: on the last days of March, June, September and December, until the full purchase price of all lands sold by said party of the second part, under and by virtue of the terms of this agreement shall be fully paid.

And whereas there are now unsold and belonging to said Railroad Company in the Town of Nordland (at the Station now known as Minneota on the line of the railway of said party of the first part) about two hundred and forty (240) town lots (exclusive of Warehouse lots) a list of which is hereto attached and made a part of this agreement; and the said party of the second part has undertaken to make sale of said lots; It is further agreed by and between the parties hereto that said party of the second part shall have the right, by himself, and his agents, to make sale of said lots, from and after the date of this agreement and until the said 30th day of June A.D. 1882, at and for the prices named in the said list, for one fifth (⅕) cash with a credit on the balance of the purchase price of one (1) year, with interest in advance at ten per cent (10%) per annum. In all cases the purchaser of such lots shall be bound to erect or cause to be erected on any lot or lots sold buildings of the value of not less than two hundred and fifty (250) dollars for each lot. No one person will be allowed to purchase more than two (2) lots and all regulations of the party of the first part relating to the sale of town lots now in force or that may be made from time to time shall be considered a part of this agreement.

The said party of the first part will allow and pay to the said party of the second part a commission of ten per cent (10%) of the purchase price of all lots, in said town, sold prior to the 30th day of June A.D. 1880 and if he, said party of the second part, shall sell the percentage of the lands herein agreed to be sold before the said 30th day of June A.D. 1880 then said party of the first part will pay to said party of the second part an additional twenty-three and one third per cent (23⅓%) of the purchase price of said town lots so sold before said last named date and will thenceforth allow and pay to said party of the second part one third (⅓) of the purchase price of all said lots sold before the 30th day of June A.D. 1882 or other sooner termination of this contract.

It is further agreed by the parties hereto that if the said party of the second part shall sell the percentage of land that he has undertaken and agreed to sell prior to the said 30th day of June A.D. 1882 and any of said town lots shall then remain unsold the party of the first part will convey to the said party of the second part one undivided one third ($\frac{1}{3}$) of all of said lots which on said 30th day of June A.D. 1882, shall remain unsold.

Said party of the second part hereby agrees to and with the said party of the first part that he will sell on or before June 30th A.D. 1880 ten per cent (10%) of the whole amount of the lands embraced in this agreement and fifteen per cent (15%) of the whole amount of said lands in each year thereafter during the said term of three (3) years, and that if he should fail to sell the percentage of the whole amount of land agreed as aforesaid to be sold during each of the periods, the said party of the first part may at its option, by written notice to the said party of the second part abrogate and cancel this agreement and any and every part thereof; such notice to be given by delivering the same to the said party of the second part or by leaving a copy thereof at his usual residence thirty (30) days before the time named in such notice at which this contract shall be abrogated and cancelled, and upon such notice being given or served as aforesaid, all rights, privileges and advantages accruing to the said party of the second part under and by virtue of this agreement shall thereupon cease and determine, subject to the right of the said party of the second part to receive commissions upon the sales of lands and town lots theretofore made by him according to the terms hereof.

It is further agreed by and between the parties hereto that all sales made under the provisions of this agreement shall be completed and concluded at the Land Office of the party of the first part at Marshall, Minnesota or at the Land Department of the party of the first part at Chicago, Illinois and that all payments for said lands shall be made to the regularly appointed and duly authorized Land Agent of the said party of the first part, or to its Land Commissioner, that all Contracts or agreements for the sale and conveyance of said lands shall be executed on behalf of said Company, by its Land Commissioner or other Officer in that behalf empowered by the Board of Directors thereof; that all receipts for money on account of the purchase price of said land shall be signed by its duly authorized Land Agent or Land Commissioner, and that no payment to any other person or persons than those last named, and no Contract or agreements executed otherwise than as aforesaid shall have any force or validity, or in any way be binding upon the said party of the first part.

Sources

1. *Diocesan and Parochial Archives*

THE PRIMARY SOURCES for this study are the chancery archives of
the Archdioceses of Omaha, St. Louis, and St. Paul, and the Dioceses
of Richmond (Virginia) and Winona (Minnesota), together with the
parochial registers and archives at Clontarf, De Graff, Graceville,
Ghent, Minneota, Currie, Avoca, and Fulda (all in Minnesota), Blaine
(in Kansas), and Danville (in Virginia).

The archives of the Archdiocese of Omaha are especially important
because of their large and extremely informative collection of letters
written by prospective colonists to Bishop James O'Connor and to William J. Onahan. There must have been a still larger body of such letters
addressed to Bishop Ireland concerning Minnesota lands, but I have
been unable to find them. Because the letters to Bishop O'Connor frequently ask for data on Nebraska *or* Minnesota lands, however, I have
used these Nebraska letters extensively in discussing the type of person
who went west. The Omaha archives also contain a large body of
letters to and from William J. Onahan, dealing with colonization
affairs. I had previously discovered that the official Onahan Papers,
housed in the archives of the University of Notre Dame, contained almost no letters dealing with colonization. The Omaha collection explains this fact and, taken together with those Onahan letters which
appear among the Adrian Colony Papers in the St. Paul Seminary
archives, more than compensate for the absence of such letters in the
official Onahan Papers at Notre Dame.

I had expected to find some of Bishop James O'Connor's contracts
with the Burlington and Missouri Railroad for portions of that road's
land grant in Greeley County, Nebraska, but no trace of such agreements appeared in the Omaha archives. Possibly these contracts could
be found among the Burlington Railroad Papers which have now been
entrusted to the Newberry Library, Chicago. I was invited by Stanley
Pargellis, librarian of this collection, to examine these papers for the
contracts, but since the Nebraska settlements were outside my focal
area, I declined the invitation.

The archives of the Archdiocese of St. Louis were consulted primarily for information on the life and character of Father Thomas

Ambrose Butler, who ended his years as a pastor in St. Louis. The official chancery record of Father Butler's assignments in the archdiocese helped in appraising the career of this active and zealous priest. In these archives also I obtained a copy of John Rothensteiner's *History of the Archdiocese of St. Louis* (St. Louis, 1928), in which the entry on Father Butler confirmed my estimate of his character. Complete files of the *Western Watchman,* which was the official diocesan paper during the years of Butler's colonization work in Kansas, are also part of the archdiocesan archives and are housed at present in the library of Kenrick Seminary, St. Louis. I consulted these files but found little material in them that was not also printed in the *Northwestern Chronicle* or the *ICBU Journal.*

The archives of the Archdiocese of St. Paul were disappointing in the extreme. The only body of material preserved in these archives and useful to the present study was the several bound volumes of diocesan letters which were kept by J. P. O'Connor after 1885. Not a single letter from or to Dillon O'Brien, the true director of the Catholic Colonization Bureau, was found. O'Connor's letters supply some useful information on the closing years of colonization and some enlightening facts about the sale of indemnity lands at Graceville, but they give absolutely no evidence concerning the important years of colonization activity (1876–81).

Somewhere a considerable body of additional manuscript material on Ireland's colonies may remain undiscovered, though for many years the story has circulated that Archbishop Ireland burned great portions of his private papers before he died. Considering the controversial nature of some of his undertakings, such a drastic step might have been defensible—at least for such items as his heated comments on nationalism in the Catholic Church—if it were not that Monsignor James H. Moynihan's recent *Life of Archbishop John Ireland* (New York, 1953), based as it is on the Ireland Papers, demonstrates conclusively that many of Ireland's most controversial writings have been preserved. Furthermore, most of Ireland's colonization activities were not controversial. He confidently prophesied, in fact, that for this work his name would be held in benediction by future generations. It is most unlikely that he would have deliberately destroyed materials which would one day help scholars describe his favorite project more accurately. Yet in his papers, in his diocesan archives, in John Sweetman's papers, and in the records of Dillon O'Brien's estate there are no traces of the voluminous correspondence which must have passed on the Minnesota colonies. The *ICBU Journal* once reported that Dillon

O'Brien was receiving 1,000 inquiries a month on colony affairs. Not a single letter from such correspondence was uncovered by my research.

The paucity of colonization materials in the official chancery archives in St. Paul is balanced at least in part by the collection of Adrian Colony Papers in the St. Paul Seminary archives. These are letters which passed between Father C. J. Knauf and William J. Onahan concerning the assisted emigrants sponsored at Adrian by the Irish Catholic Colonization Association. The settlers mentioned in these letters were not strictly members of Ireland's colonies, hence were not persons with whom Dillon O'Brien would have been in contact. However, in the absence of any letters between O'Brien and Ireland on the one hand and their settlers on the other, these Adrian Colony Papers assume an extraordinary value in the present study.

Nor is there any trace of colonization letters among the otherwise valuable and highly informative Archbishop Ireland Papers which are now part of the St. Paul Seminary archives. Among these papers, which Monsignor James H. Moynihan graciously put at my disposal, are a series of notes and a list of references to newspaper articles on the colonies. Presumably this list was made by Monsignor Humphrey Moynihan, in preparation for his article on Bishop Ireland's colonies in *Acta et Dicta*, 6 (1934), 212–31. In addition to such scattered items on the colonies, the Ireland Papers provide one extremely valuable source: the parish register, "Mission de Ghent," written in French by Father Jules Emile De Vos, the first pastor at Ghent. It contains extended accounts of the status of the parish, the trials of settlers, the establishment of a school, the costs of settlement, and several illuminating balance sheets on parochial finances. This small volume ranks with the various railroad land contracts (to be discussed later) as one of the most important fruits of my research.

The archives of the Diocese of Richmond (Virginia) provided the clue to the location of the lost colony of Keileyville. I knew from the *ICBU Journal* and from the Martin I. J. Griffin Papers at St. Charles Seminary in Philadelphia that a colony of this name had been started in the Richmond Diocese in 1878. But no such town exists today and my inquiries to the Richmond Chancery concerning such a parish brought the answer that no records of this foundation are extant; that the oldest priests now living in that diocese never heard of such a place; and that Monsignor Joseph F. Magri's history, *The Catholic Church in the City and Diocese of Richmond* (Richmond, 1906) does not mention this settlement. However, in the diocesan journal orig-

inally started by Bishop (later Cardinal) James Gibbons, I found an
entry by Gibbons' vicar general, Father Janssens, which gave the location and original name, Barnesville, of the colony site. Visiting the
present Barnesville, Virginia, I met a farmer, Mr. Daniel Murray
Howerton, who took me into the hills to the site of the old colony. The
grave markers in the parish cemetery supplied a few bits of information of family names and some idea of the duration of the colony. After
visiting the Catholic parishes in surrounding towns, I discovered that
in one of these, Danville, some of the Keileyville parish registers (Baptism, Confirmation, Matrimony) are still preserved. These records contain lists of the names of the settlers, and the entries for the administration of the various sacraments helped to fix precise dates for the
opening and closing of this ill-fated colony. On the strength of the information thus obtained I have based my profound disagreement with
the recent study by Sister Joan Marie Donohoe, S.N.D., *The Irish
Catholic Benevolent Union* (Washington, 1953), which pronounces
Keileyville "a successful colony."

The archives of the Diocese of Winona (Minnesota) were consulted
for the population statistics on Catholics now living in Murray and
Nobles counties. Originally these counties were the site of Ireland's
settlements at Avoca, Adrian, Fulda, Iona, and Currie. Since 1889,
however, these two counties have been part of the Winona Diocese. I
have also drawn on the Winona Chancery records for exact dates on
the opening of parochial schools in the towns in Murray and Nobles
counties.

The parish registers at Clontarf, De Graff, Graceville, Ghent, Minneota, Avoca, Currie, Fulda (in Minnesota), Blaine (in Kansas), and
Danville (in Virginia), provide a basis for studying the shift in population since the beginning of these settlements. The differences between parochial lists of 1876 and 1954 help to show the change in nationality that has come to some of these settlements. For example, the
parish lists at Ghent and Minneota reveal a gradual but definite
shift with each passing year after 1885, with Irish settlers leaving
regularly and their places being filled by the late-coming Belgian
immigrants. Family names are, of course, often unreliable indica-
tions of nationality; however, in most of these parishes the old-
fashioned custom of inscribing on a man's tombstone the town and
country of his birth presents an ancillary standard for judging national
origins. At St. Edward's cemetery in Minneota the names on grave
markers were often the only means of differentiating true English set-

tlers from those Irish settlers who came to America after a brief but unsuccessful stay in England.

At De Graff, Ghent, Minneota, Avoca, Currie, and Iona parish histories in booklet form or in typescript furnished helpful commentary on the reasons why some of the settlements (like Avoca) have declined while neighboring colonies on the same kind of land (like Fulda) have prospered. Lists of contributors and recorded payments on parish assessments have been used for the dual purpose of estimating the wealth of the settlers and judging the expenses of building churches, hiring teachers, and conducting schools in the colonies. Clippings in parish scrapbooks have provided several leads for uncovering useful articles in local newspapers. Among the parish papers at Minneota, the funeral eulogies preached for two deceased pastors amounted to a continuous account of parochial affairs over a period of two decades. Similarly, sermons preached on parochial anniversaries or in observance of civic events were found in almost every parish file, and in every instance supplied at least a helpful summary of parish history, in some instances providing long-sought answers to questions of past events.

2. Railroad Archives and Land Records

Only slightly less important than the diocesan and parochial archives are the land-office records of the Chicago and Northwestern Railway System (formerly Chicago and North Western, and so cited in the text and notes); the Chicago, Milwaukee, St. Paul, and Pacific; the Great Northern; and the Northern Pacific Railroads. Among these, the archives of the Chicago and Northwestern System were the most fruitful source for this study. The Corporation Minute Books for the Winona and St. Peter Railroad Company (now part of the Chicago and North Western) supply precise information on the manner in which Bishop Ireland's proposals were presented to the directors of that railroad in their board meetings. These entries also give the exact dates on which land contracts were signed between the bishop and the railroad. Once these dates are known, it is relatively easy to find the respective contracts, which are filed chronologically in the vaults of the land and tax commissioner. The contracts between Bishop Ireland and the Winona and St. Peter Railroad (six in all) and three similar contracts with English land agents are the most valuable single group of documents discovered in my research. To the best of my knowledge these primary documents have never been used before by any historian writing on the Minnesota colonization program. For all its verbosity, the legal jargon of the agreements supplies the historian with a wealth of information on the precise conditions by which congressional land grants passed through railroad ownership into private hands.

The Corporate History is a cumulative legal document which is kept by every railroad to record the sequence by which the various subsidiary companies were absorbed into the larger rail systems. It contains summaries of the various state and federal statutes which were enacted to facilitate the building of land-grant railroads, and also records the sequence of events during which the railroad acquired title to its right-of-way. In effect, it serves the historian as a kind of concise, proved abstract on railroad lands. It is especially useful in tracing the succession of owners who have held title to a given part of a congressional grant. For the section of the above work dealing with Bishop Ireland's attempts to bring more than one railroad into each of his colonies, the various corporate histories were particularly helpful sources.

The Annual Reports of the Land Commissioner to the directors and stockholders of the railroad give year-by-year accounts of Bishop Ireland's progress in selling railroad lands. These reports (for the W. and St. P. R.R.) are available as separate documents in the land and tax commissioner's office (C. and N.W. System) and are also incorporated in the Corporation Minute Book as part of each year's annual report. These reports have furnished some background for my own understanding of land sales in general but have not supplied much particular information for this study.

Considering the extremely small number of Bishop Ireland's letters extant in Catholic archives, the few letters addressed to the railroad land commissioner of the W. and St. P. R.R. and filed among the land contracts of the C. and N.W. System or incorporated in the minutes of board meetings and recorded in the Corporation Minute Book are a windfall to the historian.

The land records of the Industrial Department of the Chicago, Milwaukee, St. Paul, and Pacific Railroad Company contain no land contracts between the bishop and the railroad, since this line went through the West after Ireland had secured his sites from older companies. But the Milwaukee Road archives do contain copies of several deeds which indicate Bishop Ireland's transactions with that company in and around Fulda, Minnesota, where this line secured trackage rights, depot space, and a right of way from the bishop and on land which had formerly been granted to the older Sioux City and St. Paul Railroad. In the same archives there are a few helpful letters which passed between J. P. O'Connor and the president of the Milwaukee Road relative to Bishop Ireland's donations of land to that company.

The archives of the Land Office of the Great Northern Railroad yielded two extremely valuable contracts (one between Bishop Ireland and the St. Paul and Pacific for land in Swift County, dated June 28, 1879, and one with the St. Paul, Minneapolis, and Manitoba Railway Company for railroad lands in Big Stone and Traverse counties, dated July 17, 1880) and a good collection of letters to and from J. P. O'Connor concerning the indemnity lands at Graceville. In spite of such helpful material, however, the archives of this railroad were disappointing. I had hoped to find there the original copy of John Ireland's first railroad contract and had confidently assumed that I would find a wealth of correspondence between Ireland and James J. Hill relative to colonization. No such material was found. As yet the private papers of Mr. Hill have not been opened to scholars. I have asked permission of his heirs to examine his papers for material on the colonies, but this request has not been granted.

The Northern Pacific Railroad has done scholars a service by thoroughly organizing its archives. Unfortunately, this splendidly catalogued collection has little material important for a study of Bishop Ireland's colonies. He never acted as an agent for this line and therefore signed no contracts with it. However, the Northern Pacific's own emigration and colonization program was the prototype of Ireland's; hence its archives furnish a wealth of material for the background of colonization in Minnesota. Such writers as James B. Hedges, Harold Fern Peterson, and Howard Eston Egan have already studied the many pamphlets and emigrant letters, the voluminous reports from the road's foreign agents, the scrapbooks, and the official colonization department records in this collection. I have drawn liberally on the work of these scholars in composing the first and second chapters above.

3. Library and Historical Society Archives

The archives of the St. Paul Seminary contain a valuable collection, the Adrian Colony Papers, and extremely informative portions of William J. Onahan's letters on colonization. I have already mentioned the help which these collections gave me. The archives also contain the correspondence of Monsignor Anatole Oster, the French priest who

was the first pastor of the Clontarf colony. His letters supply the few
first-hand comments I could find on the original French settlers of the
Swift County colony. In the same archives I discovered copies of Dillon O'Brien's hard-to-find novels, *The Dalys of Dalystown, Frank
Blake,* and *Dead Broke.* In some respects O'Brien's role in the colonization work was even more important than Bishop Ireland's, yet there is
hardly anything of historical interest by or about O'Brien extant today.
Hence even these novels, written in his middle years, take on an added
significance for anyone who would try to know intimately this key figure in western colonization.

The splendid collection of biographies and histories in the American-
Irish Historical Society Library in New York City deserve to be better
known by scholars of immigration. The only item in this extensive collection which fitted into my research was a tiny volume on the life
of Dillon O'Brien, by his son, Thomas. I have since discovered that
portions of the same work are reprinted in the article on Dillon O'Brien
in *Acta Et Dicta, 6,* 1933. The value I placed on this single volume may
be judged by the frequency with which I have cited it as a source.

The John Sweetman Papers, now part of the Minnesota State Historical Society Manuscript Collection, contain an abundance of land
contracts signed by Sweetman and his colonists and also a few letters
which passed between the Irish-American Colonization Company and
its settlers. The business ledgers of this stock company, preserved entire in the collection, are a graphic proof that benevolent land schemes
were risky financial ventures. I have used these papers chiefly for the
few letters written to Sweetman by disappointed settlers and have
cited the succession of names inscribed on the land contracts as one
more way of checking on the exodus of the Irish from the colonies.
Much of the general material from the Sweetman Papers has already
been summarized in an article on the Currie settlement by Alice E.
Smith, "The Sweetman Irish Colony," *Minnesota History,* December
1928.

The Ignatius Donnelly Papers are also part of the collections of
the Minnesota State Historical Society. They contain an abundance
of material, almost all of it still unpublished, on the "Sage of Nininger,"
but I have drawn on them only to show that Donnelly's name was
solicited and used as a patron of the first St. Paul Emigrant Society.

The archives of the University of Notre Dame, thanks to their competent director, Father Thomas T. McAvoy, are a scholar's delight.
This extensive collection of letters, private papers, and writings of lead-

ing American Catholics is fully catalogued and completely indexed. Unfortunately, the William J. Onahan Papers which are part of the collection, have very little material concerning Onahan's colonization work, as mentioned above, though the portions of these papers I did read gave me considerable insight into the character of this shrewd Irish immigrant who became a leading figure in political circles in Chicago.

The Austin Ford Papers, also in the Notre Dame archives, supplied me with a few valuable letters from John Ireland to Ford when the latter was editor of the New York *Irish World*. These few letters reveal, more clearly than any other single documents, the political opinions of Bishop Ireland and were most helpful in my discussion of politics in the colonies. In one of the letters, Ireland confides to Ford that the second election of Grover Cleveland would almost certainly ruin the country.

The archives of the American Catholic Historical Society of Philadelphia, though still uncatalogued, have more primary material on Catholic immigrants in America than any other library. Research amid this mass of letters, papers, pamphlets, tracts, and books, collected largely by Martin I. J. Griffin, is exceptionally arduous but at the same time rewarding. Among the thousands of pamphlets assembled by Griffin I found copies of every one of Dillon O'Brien's brochures on the Minnesota colonies, copies of Sweetman's pamphlets on Currie, and countless railroad emigrant guides, as well as dozens of brochures on various other Catholic colonization schemes in states from Maine to Arkansas. Duplicate copies of a few of these pamphlets are among those in the Minnesota State Historical Society collections and also among the Coe Collection of Western Americana at Yale University; but the range and variety of colonization and immigrant literature at the Philadelphia archives is unmatched in this country.

In the same collection there are files (in many instances complete) for almost every Catholic newspaper published in the United States during the last three decades of the 19th century, including the *ICBU Journal* which Martin Griffin edited. Together with the *Northwestern Chronicle* (St. Paul) and the *Western Watchman* (St. Louis), this monthly newspaper is a primary source and a reliable historical guide of the rise and fall of Catholic colonization in America. Every phase of Catholic life is treated in its pages. Immigrant aid, colonization, schools, trusteeism, nationalism in the Church, teetotalism, benevolent-aid societies, and fraternal insurance are some of the items it discusses.

Martin Griffin's eloquent rhetoric offered in support of the Catholic movements he endorsed, and his vitriolic denunciations of those he disapproved, make fascinating reading. Since the files of this newspaper (which probably enjoyed greater circulation among the Irish in America than any of its contemporaries) are already in a bad state of repair, scholars are indebted to Sister Joan Marie Donohoe, S.N.D., for her recent history of the ICBU, recorded above, which is in great part a compendium of the views advanced by this organ on topics of its day.

The uncatalogued Martin I. J. Griffin Papers in the same collection are an encyclopedic source for historical information on almost all phases of American Catholicism between 1875 and 1900. Griffin was a prolific writer and tireless controversialist and was in almost daily correspondence with the leading Catholic clergymen and laymen of his day. Letters to and from him on the closing of the Keileyville settlement supplied vital material for Chapter 9, above. For having called my attention to these important but inaccessible letters, I am deeply grateful to Sister Joan Marie Donohoe, who must have spent many months acquiring her extensive knowledge of the masses of material housed in the Philadelphia society collections.

Among the voluminous Terence V. Powderly Papers now filed in the archives of the Catholic University of America there are probably some helpful letters and news items recounting the opposition of the Knights of Labor to the various programs for western colonization. However, since this collection is as yet uncatalogued, and because of the large mass of material in it, I was unable to find any data concerning the Knights and colonization.

In preparing the chapter on the social life in the colonies I have relied heavily on Father Thomas J. Jenkins' published account of his several trips from Kentucky to western Minnesota in the late 1870's and early 1880's (*Six Seasons on Our Prairies and Six Weeks in Our Rockies*, Louisville, 1884). This rare volume I first discovered in the archives of the Catholic University.

4. Printed Sources

It is always difficult and occasionally dangerous for an author to name his intellectual progenitors; yet an attempt must be made. As mentioned in the Preface, above, the explicit suggestion for this study came originally from the concluding chapter of Marcus Lee Hansen's

The Immigrant in American History (Cambridge, Mass., 1943); I would like to think it will find a place in the group of studies which has carried on the kind of intensive, sharply focused scrutiny of the American immigrant which was so brilliantly begun by Mr. Hansen and so quickly halted by his early death.

For assistance in delineating this scholarly tradition I have drawn on such representative studies as those by Sister Mary Evangela Henthorne, B.V.M., *The Irish Catholic Colonization Association of the United States* (Champaign, 1932) and Sister Mary Gilbert Kelly, O.P., *Catholic Immigrant Colonization Projects in the United States, 1815–1860* (New York, 1939). Both of these works were undertaken at the suggestion of Marcus Hansen and carried out under his direction. The first is the best published account of the colonies founded in Nebraska by Bishop James O'Connor. Sister Mary Gilbert's study of early Catholic colonies is a helpful but not exhaustive catalogue of Catholic settlements made in the United States before the Civil War. It is especially valuable for its definitive study of the Buffalo Convention of 1856.

My discussion of the contribution of the Irish immigrant to American life is based in great part on the work of Thomas N. Brown, whose penetrating essay "Nationalism and the Irish Peasant, 1800–1848," *Review of Politics*, 15 (1953), 403–45, takes the discussion of national traits out of the realm of intuition or prejudice and gives it a broad and firm foundation in the history and the literature of Ireland.

The several portions of this narrative touching on the vital role of the railroad in settling the West should reflect the direction I received from the works of James B. Hedges, "The Colonization Work of the Northern Pacific Railroad," *Mississippi Valley Historical Review*, 13 (1926), 311–42; Paul Wallace Gates, *The Illinois Central Railroad and Its Colonization Work* (Cambridge, Mass., 1934); and Harold Fern Peterson, "Railroads and the Settlement of Minnesota, 1860–1880," unpublished master's thesis, University of Minnesota, 1927. The pioneering work of Hedges is especially significant because of its thorough synthesis of the material on colonization to be found in the Northern Pacific archives and for its successful effort to tell the story of emigration from England and New England and of immigration to Minnesota. Paul Gates, in his work on the Illinois Central Railroad, proves the twofold thesis that large-scale colonization could never have been accomplished without the help of the western railroads and that the western roads needed the settlers quite as much as the newcomers needed the rail lines. Harold Peterson, in his treatise on settlement in

Minnesota, uses the general hypothesis advanced by Gates and documents it with specific evidence taken from the archives of the railroads in Minnesota.

Within the field of contemporary Catholic historical studies, Colman J. Barry's *The Catholic Church and German Americans* (Milwaukee, 1953) has been both a source and a guide. Father Barry's judicious handling and extensive documentation of the many-sided question of national multiplicity within the unity of the Catholic Church is a commendable contribution to all who would write Catholic history.

It is unfortunate that Dillon O'Brien never wrote a comprehensive account of Bishop Ireland's colonization work. Lacking such a primary source, we are fortunate to have Monsignor Humphrey Moynihan's sympathetic article "Archbishop Ireland's Colonies," *Acta Et Dicta*, 6 (1934), 212–31. This essay, which also appears as the second chapter in James H. Moynihan's *Life of Archbishop John Ireland* (New York, 1953), is the best short narrative available on the story of the Minnesota colonies.

The publication of James J. Reardon's new study, *The Catholic Church in the Diocese of St. Paul* (St. Paul, 1952) was providential for the present work. Monsignor Reardon's large volume has been a welcome thesaurus of information on the Catholic history of the upper Mississippi Valley. I have found the chronological summaries of parochial histories appended to the text particularly helpful.

Any writer in the field of history appreciates those rare and helpful essays in historiographical method which suggest to him new ways to organize effectively large masses of discrete material. For such direction I am grateful to Caroline F. Ware for her title essay in the collective work *The Cultural Approach to History* (New York, 1940), in which Miss Ware recommended as an organizational device the study of American history from the point of view of the various subordinate cultural units which make up the kaleidoscopic American scene. Using midwestern Catholic society as one such cultural unit, I have tried to pursue the method recommended by Miss Ware.

On one occasion I have ventured to disagree with a particular conclusion of James E. Roohan in his unpublished doctoral dissertation, "American Catholics and the Social Question, 1865–1900" (Yale, 1952), but this is an isolated instance. A close reading of my text will reveal the variety of ways in which I have drawn on Roohan's competent and stimulating research. I am, moreover, grateful to him for the many times while this work was in progress that I sought the benefit of his counsel and discerning judgment.

5. Newspaper Collections

In the portions of this study which describe social and economic conditions in the colony settlements I have drawn most of my material from the local newspapers of several western Minnesota communities. Chief among these are the Benson *Times,* the Swift County *Advocate,* the Worthington *Advance,* the Marshall *Messenger,* and the *Southwest Minnesotian.* Complete files for all these papers (with the exception of some issues of the Benson *Times*) are available in the newspaper collection of the Minnesota State Historical Society. Those issues of the Benson *Times* which are missing in the state society's collection are still available, but in the last stages of decomposition, in a basement room of the Swift County Courthouse at Benson, Minnesota.

The Boston *Pilot* is one of the oldest Catholic newspapers in this country. It has also been a traditionally influential paper, particularly among Irish Catholics. Its early disapproval of western colonization programs was a serious handicap to the colonizing bishops. I have drawn heavily on the *Pilot* for its extended accounts of colonization in the West under Bishop Loras in the 1840's and 50's. Complete files of this primary source on Catholic history in America can be found at St. John's Seminary, Brighton, Massachusetts (the originals), and in the archives of the Catholic University of America, Washington, D.C. (microfilm). I have consulted the originals at St. John's Seminary.

During the years of John Ireland's colonization work, the *Northwestern Chronicle* was the official diocesan paper in St. Paul. Complete files of this paper are preserved in the library of the St. Paul Seminary. In its pages Ireland published his official announcements and regular reports on the status of colony affairs. One could, in fact, write a very satisfactory account of the Catholic colonies in Minnesota, using only the material printed in this paper. I have drawn a greater quantity of information from the *Chronicle* than from any other single source. Countless times I was able to find in its pages conclusive evidence on questions of fact raised by other authors concerning the colonies in Minnesota.

Index

Authors and manuscript collections cited in the notes are indexed on first citation only.